Indiana Academic Standards

Standard 1—History

4.1.1　Identify and compare the major early cultures that existed in the region that became Indiana prior to contact with Europeans.

4.1.2　Identify and describe historic Native American Indian groups that lived in Indiana at the time of early European exploration including ways these groups adapted to and interacted with the physical environment.

4.1.3　Explain the importance of the Revolutionary War and other key events and people that influenced Indiana's development.

4.1.4　Summarize and explain the significance of key documents in Indiana's development from a United States territory to statehood.

4.1.5　Identify the causes of removal of Native American Indian groups in the state and their resettlement during the 1830s.

4.1.6　Explain how key individuals and events influenced the early growth of and changes in Indiana.

4.1.7　Explain the roles of various individuals, groups, and movements in the social conflicts leading to the Civil War.

4.1.8　Summarize the impact of Abraham Lincoln's presidency on Indiana and describe the participation of Indiana citizens in the Civil War.

4.1.9　Give examples of Indiana's increasing agricultural, industrial, political, and business development in the nineteenth century.

4.1.10　Describe the participation of Indiana citizens in World War I and World War II.

4.1.11　Identify and describe important events and movements that changed life in Indiana in the early twentieth century.

4.1.12　Describe the transformation of Indiana through immigration and through developments in agriculture, industry, and transportation.

4.1.13　Identify and describe important events and movements that changed life in Indiana from the mid-twentieth century to the present.

4.1.14　Research Indiana's modern growth emphasizing manufacturing, new technologies, transportation, and global connections.

4.1.15　Create and interpret timelines that show relationships among people, events, and movements in the history of Indiana.

4.1.16　Distinguish fact from opinion and fact from fiction in historical documents and other information resources and identify the central question each narrative addresses.

4.1.17　Using primary source, secondary source and online source materials, construct a brief narrative about an event in Indiana history.

4.1.18　Research and describe the contributions of important Indiana artists and writers to the state's cultural landscape. (Individuals, Society, and Culture)

Standard 2—Civics and Government

4.2.1　Explain the major purposes of Indiana's Constitution as stated in the Preamble.

4.2.2　Describe individual rights, such as freedom of speech and freedom of religion and the right to public education that people have under Indiana's Bill of Rights

4.2.3　Identify and explain the major responsibilities of the legislative, executive, and judicial branches of state government as written in the Indiana Constitution.

4.2.4　Identify major state offices, the duties and powers associated with them, and how they are chosen, such as by election or appointment.

4.2.5　Give examples of how citizens can participate in their state government and explain the right and responsibility of voting.

4.2.6　Define and provide examples of civic virtues in a democracy.

4.2.7　Use a variety of information resources to take a position or recommend a course of action on a public issue relating to Indiana's past or present.

Standard 3—Geography

4.3.1 Use latitude and longitude to identify physical and human features of Indiana.

4.3.2 Estimate distances between two places on a map, using a scale of miles, and use cardinal and intermediate directions when referring to relative location.

4.3.3 Locate Indiana on a map as one of the fifty United States. Identify and describe the location of the state capital, major cities, and rivers in Indiana; and place these on a blank map of the state.

4.3.4 Map and describe the physical regions of Indiana and identify major natural resources and crop regions.

4.3.5 Explain how glaciers shaped Indiana's landscape and environment.

4.3.6 Describe Indiana's landforms (lithosphere), water features (hydrosphere), and plants and animals (biosphere).

4.3.7 Explain the effect of the Earth/sun relationship on the climate of Indiana.

4.3.8 Identify the challenges in the physical landscape of Indiana to early settlers and to modern day economic development. (Individuals, Society, and Culture)

4.3.9 Explain the importance of major transportation routes, including rivers, in the exploration, settlement, and growth of Indiana and in the state's location as a crossroad of America.

4.3.10 Identify immigration patterns and describe the impact diverse ethnic and cultural groups have had on Indiana.

4.3.11 Create maps of Indiana at different times in history showing regions and major physical and cultural features; give examples of how people in Indiana have modified their environment over time.

4.3.12 Read and interpret thematic maps—such as transportation, population, and products produced—to acquire information about Indiana in the present and the past.

Standard 4—Economics

4.4.1 Give examples of the kinds of goods and services produced in Indiana in different historical periods.

4.4.2 Define productivity and provide examples of how productivity has changed in Indiana during the past 100 years.

4.4.3 Explain how both parties can benefit from trade and give examples of how people in Indiana engaged in trade in different time periods.

4.4.4 Explain that prices change as a result of changes in supply and demand for specific products.

4.4.5 Describe Indiana's emerging global connections.

4.4.6 List the functions of money and compare and contrast things that have been used as money in the past in Indiana, the United States, and the world.

4.4.7 Identify entrepreneurs who have influenced Indiana and the local community.

4.4.8 Define profit and describe how profit is an incentive for entrepreneurs.

4.4.9 Identify important goods and services provided by state and local governments by giving examples of how state and local tax revenues are used.

4.4.10 Explain how people save and develop a savings plan in order to make a future purchase.

INDIANA
Macmillan/McGraw-Hill TIMELINKS

Indiana in the Nation and the World

PROGRAM AUTHORS

James A. Banks
Kevin P. Colleary
Linda Greenow
Walter C. Parker
Emily M. Schell
Dinah Zike

CONTRIBUTORS

Raymond C. Jones
Irma M. Olmedo

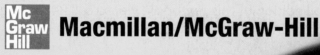

Mc
Graw
Hill **Macmillan/McGraw-Hill**

PROGRAM AUTHORS

James A. Banks, Ph.D.
Kerry and Linda Killinger
  Professor of Diversity Studies
  and Director, Center for
  Multicultural Education
University of Washington
Seattle, Washington

Kevin P. Colleary, Ed.D.
Curriculum and Teaching
  Department
Graduate School of Education
Fordham University
New York, New York

Linda Greenow, Ph.D.
Associate Professor and Chair
Department of Geography
State University of New York at
  New Paltz
New Paltz, New York

Walter C. Parker, Ph.D.
Professor of Social Studies
  Education, Adjunct Professor
  of Political Science
University of Washington
Seattle, Washington

Emily M. Schell, Ed.D.
Visiting Professor, Teacher
  Education
San Diego State University
San Diego, California

Dinah Zike
Educational Consultant
Dinah-Mite Activities, Inc.
San Antonio, Texas

CONTRIBUTORS

Raymond C. Jones, Ph.D.
Director of Secondary Social
  Studies Education
Wake Forest University
Winston-Salem, North Carolina

Irma M. Olmedo
Associate Professor
University of Illinois-Chicago
College of Education
Chicago, Illinois

HISTORIANS/SCHOLARS

Ned Blackhawk
Associate Professor of History
  and American Indian Studies
University of Wisconsin
Madison, Wisconsin

Larry Dale, Ph.D.
Director, Center for Economic
  Education
Arkansas State University
Jonesboro, Arkansas

Brooks Green, Ph.D.
Associate Professor of
  Geography
University of Central Arkansas
Conway, Arkansas

Thomas C. Holt, Ph.D.
Professor of History
University of Chicago
Chicago, Illinois

Rebecca L. Torstrick, Ph.D.
Associate Professor of
  Anthropology and Director,
  Women's Studies Program
Indiana University
South Bend, Indiana

 Students with print disabilities may be eligible to obtain an accessible, audio version of the pupil edition of this textbook. Please call Recording for the Blind & Dyslexic at 1-800-221-4792 for complete information.

The McGraw·Hill Companies

Mc Graw Hill Macmillan McGraw-Hill

Send all inquires to:
Macmillan/McGraw-Hill
8787 Orion Place
Columbus, OH 43240-4027

MHID 0-02-151253-1
ISBN 978-0-02-151253-9
Printed in the United States of America.
4 5 6 7 8 9 10 027/043 13 12 11 10 09

Indiana in the Nation and the World

CONTENTS

Unit 3 Creating a State 89

EXPLORE The Big Idea Why do people take risks?

EXPLORE **The Big Idea** How does change affect people's lives?

Unit 5 Indiana in Modern Times 175

 What causes a society to grow?

Unit 6   Indiana Today   223

EXPLORE The Big Idea — How do government and the economy affect people's lives?

Reference Section

Skills and Features

Skills and Features

Maps

INDIANA'S LAND AND PEOPLE

Wheat fields and other crops are important to Indiana.

Unit 1

Essential Question
How do people adapt to where they live?

FOLDABLES
Study Organizer

Main Idea and Details
Use a Five-Tab Book to take notes as you read Unit 1. Label each of the five tabs **Indiana's Geography, Indiana's Climate, Indiana's Resources, Indiana's Economy**, and **Indiana's People and Culture.**

LOG ON
For more about Unit 1, go to
www.macmillanmh.com

1

PEOPLE, PLACES, AND EVENTS

Infantrymen, War of 1812

The Amish

Wyandotte Caves

1812
The U.S. military mines saltpeter from caves, including Wyandotte Cave.

Shipshewana, Indiana

1839
The first Amish families settle in Indiana.

1800   1820   1840   1860

During the War of 1812, **Indiana infantrymen** used saltpeter found in **Wyandotte Cave** to make gunpowder.

Today you can visit the caves and see bats at the **Indiana Bat Hibernacula**.

In 1839 Amish communities began to grow in northern Indiana. In **Shipshewana,** the Amish still practice a simple lifestyle.

Today you can visit the **Menno-Hof Amish Center** and learn about the Amish.

Judge Elbert H. Gary

Carl Fisher

U.S. Steel Corporation

Indianapolis Motor Speedway

1901 | Elbert Gary builds the U.S. Steel Corporation and creates Gary, Indiana.

1911 | The very first Indianapolis 500 Race is held.

1880   1900   1920   1940

In 1901 **Elbert H. Gary** became the first chairman of **U.S. Steel Corporation.** The town of Gary, which was established on Lake Michigan, was named after him.

Today you can visit **Gary, Indiana,** and tour the steel mill.

Carl Fisher helped found the **Indianapolis Motor Speedway**. The first **Indianapolis 500** Mile Race was held there in 1911.

Today you can visit Speedway, Indiana, and tour the raceway and museum.

INDIANA'S GEOGRAPHY

VOCABULARY

geography p. 5

continent p. 5

landform p. 6

glacier p. 7

moraine p. 7

region p. 8

READING SKILL

Main Idea and Details
Copy the chart below.
As you read, fill it in with
details about Indiana's
geography.

Main Idea	Details

INDIANA ACADEMIC STANDARDS

4.3.1, 4.3.2, 4.3.3, 4.3.4,
4.3.5, 4.3.7, 4.3.12

Indiana's geography includes fertile, flat plains.

Visual Preview

How have people adapted to the geography of Indiana?

A Indiana has a "global address" on Earth and is located in the United States.

B Indiana's landforms include lakes, sand dunes, caves, and rivers.

C Many landforms were created by glaciers.

D Indiana has three regions.

INDIANA'S LOCATION ON EARTH

Look out your classroom window. Can you see hills or plains? Do you cross a river or stream on your way to school? Is there a lake nearby? These parts of the land may not appear to change in your lifetime. However, in the lifetime of Earth, they have changed a lot.

Geography is the study of Earth and the way that people live on it. Describing a place by its location on Earth is also part of geography. Indiana can be described by its location and by its geography, too.

Indiana has a "global address," which describes its location on Earth. Indiana is part of the United States, which in turn is a part of North America. North America is a **continent**. A continent is one of Earth's seven great bodies of land. They include Africa, Antarctica, Asia, Australia, Europe, North America and South America. Most continents contain several different countries.

To find Indiana on a map, you must first locate North America. Within the continent of North America, find the country of the United States. Finally, look in the middle section of the United States to locate Indiana.

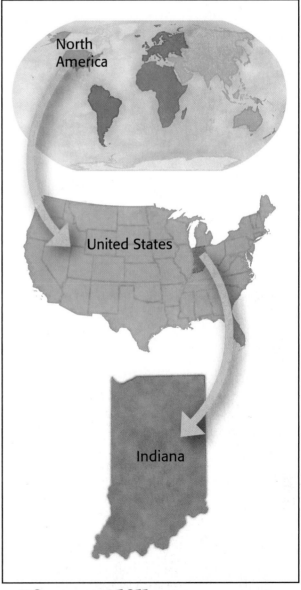

North America

United States

Indiana

QUICK CHECK

Main Idea and Details Describe Indiana's location on Earth.

Diagram Skill

On a piece of paper, extend the diagram to include your city or town.

B INDIANA'S LANDFORMS

Landforms are part of geography, too. A landform is a natural feature of Earth's surface. Landforms change over time. Lakes, such as Lake Michigan, are one common kind of landform. Sand dunes are another kind of landform. Sand dunes are hills of sand that have been shaped by wind. They can be found throughout Indiana, but mostly in the northwestern part of the state.

Another type of landform in Indiana is caves. In our state, caves form in areas that have soft rock. Water has worn away the soft rock, creating holes and paths underground. Some famous Indiana caves are Wyandotte Cave and Marengo Cave.

QUICK CHECK

Main Idea and Details **What are some landforms that can be found in Indiana?**

INDIANA'S LANDFORMS

- Lake Michigan
- Indiana Dunes National Lakeshore
- St. Joseph River
- MICHIGAN
- Kankakee River
- Tippecanoe River
- Lake Wawasee
- Maumee River
- Eel River
- St. Marys River
- Wabash River
- Salamonie River
- Mississinewa River
- ILLINOIS
- OHIO
- Whitewater River
- Indianapolis ★
- Eel River
- White River
- Hoosier National Forest
- Monroe Lake
- George Rogers Clark National Historical Park
- East Fork White River
- Wabash River
- Marengo Cave
- Ohio River
- Hoosier National Forest
- Wyandotte Caves
- KENTUCKY

Legend:
- ☐ Hills
- ☐ Plains
- ☐ Plateaus
- ★ State capital
- National park/ forest
- ● State park

Scale: 0 — 25 — 50 miles
0 — 25 — 50 kilometers

Map Skill

LOCATION **What landforms lie along the Kentucky border?**

GLACIERS FORMED THE LAND

About 20,000 years ago, most of the northern United States was covered by giant sheets of ice called **glaciers**. These glaciers moved slowly across the land. This time in history is called the Ice Age. During the Ice Age, a big part of what is now Indiana was covered with glaciers.

Glaciers shaped many of the landforms of Indiana. Deep basins, or bowl-shaped holes, were carved out in some areas as glaciers moved rocks and dirt away. After many thousands of years, the Ice Age ended. The glaciers melted, and water filled the large holes. This is how Lake Michigan and the other Great Lakes were formed. As glaciers moved south, they also helped shape the land in upper Indiana.

Another landform created by glaciers is called a **moraine**. A moraine is a line of low hills formed by rocks that were pushed up by glaciers. There are also many till plains in Indiana. Till is made up of layers of rocks, gravel, clay, and soil left behind by melted glaciers. These till areas have rich soil that makes it easy for farmers to grow crops.

Glaciers did not cover all of Indiana. The southern part of the state was untouched as the glaciers melted. There are many hills, rivers, forests, and valleys in this area of the state.

Quick Check
Main Idea and Details **What landforms did glaciers form in Indiana?**

Sand dunes at Indiana Dunes National Lakeshore, Lake Michigan

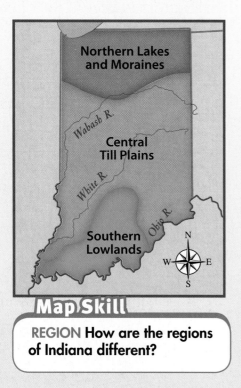

Map Skill

REGION How are the regions of Indiana different?

Indiana can be divided into three distinct **regions**. A region is an area with common features. Our state is divided into these three geographic regions based on the landforms and climates found in each one.

Regions can also be defined by human features, such as the history or the language of the people who live there. Many times, a region's features help explain the history of the people who settled there. For example, in the 1800s, the southernmost region of Indiana attracted many people from central Europe. This was because there were job opportunities in the coal mines that were similar to the jobs they had held in their home countries.

Northern Lakes and Moraines
This region covers the northern third of Indiana. Lake Michigan and many moraines and rivers were formed by glaciers. The steel industry is important in this region.

Central Till Plains
This region received its name from the large, flat, till plains that cover it. The rich soil here makes it easy for farmers to grow crops. Other landforms in this area include rivers, valleys, and gently rolling hills.

Indiana's Three Regions

In the northern part of the state, near Lake Michigan, is the Northern Lakes and Moraines region. Besides gently rolling hills and moraines, there is an abundance of natural resources in the region. The steel industry is important here, and many people work in manufacturing jobs.

In the center of the state lies the flat farmland of the Central Till Plains region. Here the soil is very rich, which makes it perfect for growing a variety of crops. This area also has several large rivers flowing through it, providing even more nutrients to the rich soil.

In the south, at the bottom of Indiana, are the Southern Lowlands. This region has many forests and rivers. The area is also rich with minerals. People here may work in the forests or the many coal mines. Untouched by glaciers, this region has many interesting landforms, including underground rivers and caves.

QUICK CHECK

Main Idea and Details **How does a region's landforms affect the jobs its people hold?**

Southern Lowlands
The glaciers that helped form the two northern regions never reached southern Indiana. The glaciers melted, leaving the hills untouched. When the glaciers melted, water wore away the soft rocks and minerals, forming caves and rocky riverbeds.

Check Understanding

1. **VOCABULARY** Write a sentence for each of the following vocabulary words.
   continent   landform   moraine

2. **READING SKILL Main Idea and Details** Use the Main Idea and Details Chart from page 4 to summarize Indiana's geography.

Main Idea	Details

3. **Write About It** Write a paragraph about how the people in your region have adapted to its landforms.

Map and Globe Skills

Understand Latitude and Longitude

VOCABULARY

global grid

latitude

longitude

degrees

equator

parallels

meridian

prime meridian

Each place on Earth has a "global address" based on its location. To describe the address of a place, geographers use a **global grid**, which is made up of lines that can be seen on a map or globe. These lines are called **latitude** and **longitude**. Lines of latitude run east and west, and lines of longitude run north and south. Latitude and longitude are measured in units called **degrees**. The symbol for degrees is °. The **equator** is an imaginary line that lies halfway between the North Pole and the South Pole, at 0° latitude. The latitude of each place on Earth is measured by its distance from the equator.

Learn It

● Lines of latitude are also called **parallels**. Lines of latitude north of the equator are labeled N. Lines of latitude south of the equator are labeled S.

● A **meridian** is another name for a line of longitude. The **prime meridian** is the starting place for measuring distance from east to west. Lines of longitude east of the prime meridian are labeled E. Lines of longitude west of the prime meridian are labeled W.

● To describe a location on a map, give the latitude first and the longitude second.

Lines of Latitude

Lines of Longitude

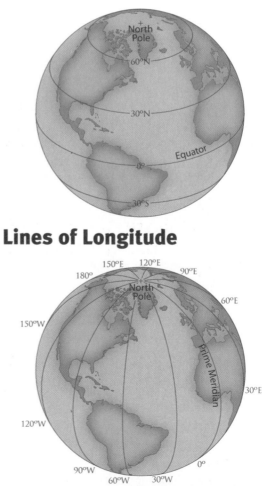

MAP A The World

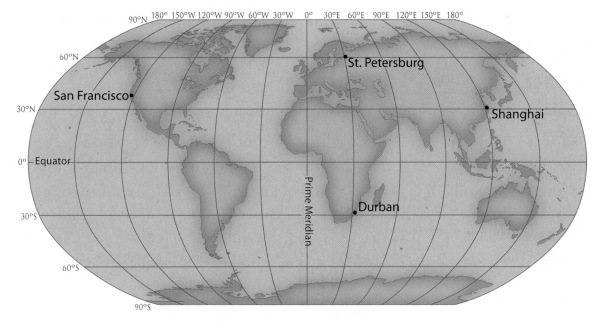

Try It

- Look at Map A. The lines of latitude and longitude shown here crisscross to form a global grid. This grid can be used to locate any place on Earth.

- Look at Map A. Locate Durban, South Africa. You can find it east of the prime meridian. The address for Durban is 30° S, 30° E.

Apply It

- Look at Map B. Estimate the latitude and longitude of Terre Haute.

MAP B

INDIANA'S CLIMATE

VOCABULARY
climate p. 13

temperature p. 13

lake effect p. 14

precipitation p. 16

tornado p. 17

READING SKILL
Main Idea and Details
Copy the chart below. As you read, fill it in with details about Indiana's climate.

Main Idea	Details

INDIANA ACADEMIC STANDARDS

4.3.2, 4.3.3, 4.3.4, 4.3.7, 4.3.12

Rainstorm coming in over Lake Michigan

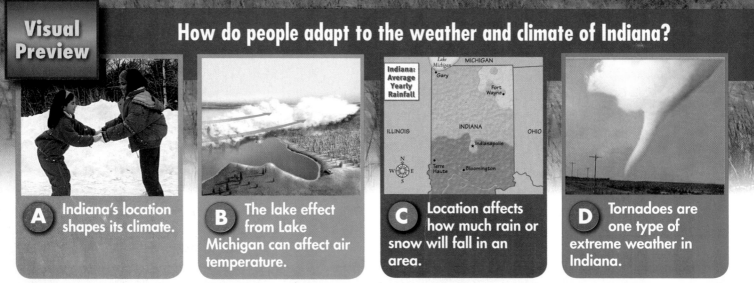

Visual Preview

How do people adapt to the weather and climate of Indiana?

A Indiana's location shapes its climate.

B The lake effect from Lake Michigan can affect air temperature.

C Location affects how much rain or snow will fall in an area.

D Tornadoes are one type of extreme weather in Indiana.

Ⓐ INDIANA'S WEATHER

Weather is the condition of the air at a certain time in a certain place. Wind, rain, and snow are all parts of weather. What is the weather like today in Indiana where you live?

Different places on Earth have different kinds of weather. The pattern of weather in a certain place over many years is called the **climate**. Weather and climate vary from place to place, even in different areas of the same state.

The distance between Indiana and the equator has a big effect on our state's climate. The equator is an imaginary line that lies halfway between the North Pole and the South Pole. How far any place on Earth is from the equator affects that place's **temperature**. Temperature measures how hot or cold things are. Areas around the equator are the hottest places on Earth. As you move north or south from the equator, the temperature becomes cooler.

Indiana's climate is similar to that of the other states in the Midwest. States in this region have four distinct seasons—spring, summer, winter, and fall. Winters in Indiana are not as cold as they are in states farther north, but they are colder than winters in most southern states.

EVENTS

As the Earth revolves around the sun, it rotates on a tilted axis. The tilt of the Earth as it revolves causes our seasons. In some areas on Earth, this tilt causes four seasons with different weather patterns. The weather in Indiana changes from season to season.

Winter in Indiana

Weather and climate can vary in different areas of the same state, too. For example, the air temperature in Terre Haute is usually warmer than the air temperature in South Bend. This is because Terre Haute is in the southern part of Indiana, while South Bend is farther north. In the winter, the northern part of the state will usually get more snowfall than the southern part. What do you know about temperature changes in Indiana over the course of the year?

QUICK CHECK

Main Idea and Details **How does Indiana's location affect its climate?**

LANDFORMS AND THE LAKE EFFECT

Landforms, such as the Great Lakes, also affect the weather of an area. Large bodies of water, for example, can cause the **lake effect**. The lake effect is a change in the weather when large bodies of water are near land. The effect happens when cold Arctic air moves over the warmer water of a lake. When the cold air passes over the warmer lake, the air is heated and clouds form. If the temperature is above freezing, rain results.

In the winter, when temperatures are low, the lake effect produces snow. Sometimes snowstorms near Lake Michigan can bring over a foot of snow in just a few hours! Gary and other northern Indiana cities see more snow than southern cities like Evansville.

QUICK CHECK

Main Idea and Details **Why does the lake effect happen?**

Lake Effect

WINTER ❶ Wind blows from west to east across Lake Michigan. ❷ The winds pick up moisture from the lake and form clouds. ❸ Air over the land is usually cooler than air over the lake. When the clouds move over the cooler land, the moisture in the clouds cools, and snow falls.

SUMMER The land is warmer than the water in Lake Michigan. Winds blowing over the lake bring cooler air. This prevents the land temperature from getting too hot.

Diagram Skill

What happens to moisture that is picked up over Lake Michigan?

❸

C RAIN AND SNOW

As you can see, location can affect how much precipitation an area will get. **Precipitation** is the amount of rain, snow, sleet, or hail that falls in an area. The type of precipitation depends on the air temperature.

You have already read how cities by Lake Michigan get more snow in the winter because precipitation forms over the lake. How much precipitation is there in the area where you live? Do you receive more rain than snow?

DataGraphic

Indiana: Average Annual Precipitation

The map shows the average yearly precipitation in Indiana. The bar graph shows the rainfall in several Indiana cities. Use the map and the graph to answer the questions below.

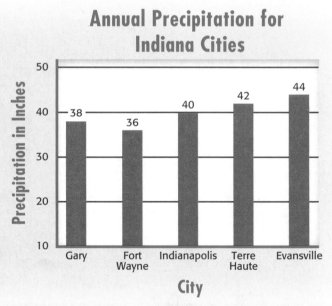

Think About It

1. How does precipitation in northern and southern Indiana compare?
2. Which city has the highest amount of precipitation?
3. Why does Gary get more rain than Fort Wayne?

Sometimes the weather in Indiana can be pleasant, but it can also be extreme, with strong winds and heavy amounts of precipitation. Thunderstorms or heavy snowstorms, called blizzards, can form when winds are strong.

Most winds in Indiana come from the southwest. When these winds meet cooler air, **tornadoes** can form. A tornado is dangerous wind that forms a funnel shape and moves over the ground very quickly.

Indiana is in an area of the country known as "Tornado Alley." It includes states from North Dakota to Texas and Colorado to Indiana and Ohio. In Indiana, between the years 1950 and 2000, over 1,000 tornadoes caused more than one billion dollars of damage.

QUICK CHECK

Main Idea and Details **What are some ways that weather can affect people?**

Indiana can experience extreme storms such as tornadoes.

Check Understanding

1. **VOCABULARY** Draw a picture for each of the vocabulary words listed. Make sure to label the pictures.

   lake effect   precipitation   tornado

2. **READING SKILL Main Idea and Details** Use your Main Idea and Details Chart from page 12 to write about Indiana's climate.

Main Idea	Details

3. **Write About It** Write a travel brochure about the region of Indiana where you live. Describe the climate and tell how people adapt.

INDIANA'S RESOURCES

Lesson 3

VOCABULARY

resource p. 19

environment p. 19

renewable resource p. 19

mineral p. 21

limestone p. 21

nonrenewable resource p. 21

READING SKILL

Main Idea and Details

Copy the chart below. As you read, fill it in with details about Indiana's resources.

Main Idea	Details

INDIANA ACADEMIC STANDARDS

4.3.3, 4.3.4, 4.3.5, 4.3.6, 4.3.8, 4.3.11, 4.3.12

Fossil beds at the Falls of the Ohio State Park in Jeffersonville, Indiana

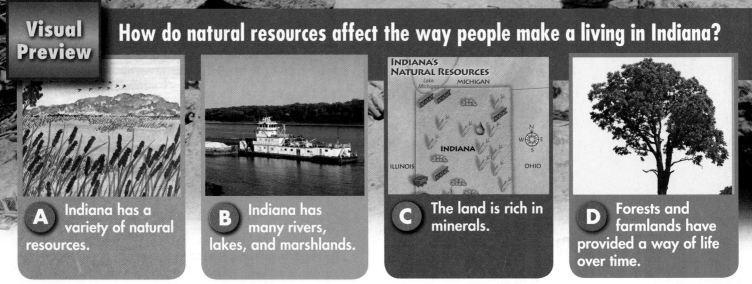

Visual Preview

How do natural resources affect the way people make a living in Indiana?

A Indiana has a variety of natural resources.

B Indiana has many rivers, lakes, and marshlands.

C The land is rich in minerals.

INDIANA'S NATURAL RESOURCES

Lake Michigan · MICHIGAN

ILLINOIS · INDIANA · OHIO

D Forests and farmlands have provided a way of life over time.

18

A MANY NATURAL RESOURCES

*Indiana has a variety of natural **resources**. A resource is something that can be used to help us survive. Natural resources are found in the **environment**, or the surroundings in which we live on Earth.*

Natural resources include forests, water and waterways, and the rich soil used for farming. Resources found underground, such as coal, can be used for fuel. Stone, shale, and other materials found underground can be used in buildings or manufacturing. Many different kinds of natural resources can be found in Indiana.

Some of our natural resources are **renewable resources**. Renewable resources can be replaced. Rain, for example, replaces water drawn from rivers. Trees are another renewable resource. People can plant new trees to replace ones that have been cut.

Waterways, forests, and other natural resources are usually spread throughout regions. Indiana's regions share many of the same natural resources. Since these resources are important to Indiana's economy and environment, the state works to protect the resources in each region.

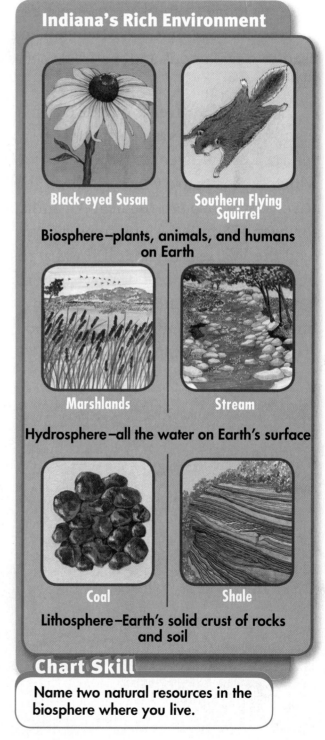

Indiana's Rich Environment

Black-eyed Susan   **Southern Flying Squirrel**

Biosphere–plants, animals, and humans on Earth

Marshlands   **Stream**

Hydrosphere–all the water on Earth's surface

Coal   **Shale**

Lithosphere–Earth's solid crust of rocks and soil

QUICK CHECK

Main Idea and Details **What is one way that renewable resources can be replaced?**

Chart Skill

Name two natural resources in the biosphere where you live.

B RIVERS AND WATERWAYS

Water is an important natural resource. People use water resources in many ways, including for drinking, cooking, and cleaning. Farmers use water from streams and rivers to water their crops. People also use waterways, such as rivers and lakes, to move from place to place. Ports, such as the ones on Lake Michigan, are used to move goods and materials across the country.

The Wabash River is one of Indiana's main waterways. Native Americans referred to the river as *Wah-Bah Shik-Ki,* which means "pure white." The Wabash River flows through the heart of Indiana for over 475 miles. Many small rivers feed the Wabash River as it flows across our state. The Wabash forms the border between Indiana and Illinois. It is an important waterway for shipping goods around the Midwest region.

PLACES

Jasper-Pulaski Wildlife Area is located in northwestern Indiana. Every fall, thousands of sandhill cranes migrate south, stopping by the wetlands and neighboring farmlands to rest.

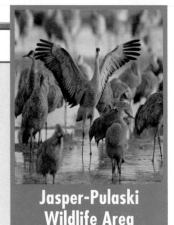

Jasper-Pulaski Wildlife Area

In the southern part of Indiana, the grand Ohio River curves across the state for more than 300 miles. There are several cypress swamps, forests, rock formations, and caves that share its banks. The Ohio River forms Indiana's southern border.

QUICK CHECK

Main Idea and Details **The Wabash River forms a border between Indiana and what state?**

▼ Towboat and barge on the Ohio River

C A LAND OF MINERALS

The natural resources found in different regions of Indiana affect the ways people use the land to make a living. The kinds of minerals found in each region depend on that region's landforms. A **mineral** is a natural substance found on Earth that does not come from plants or animals. In Indiana, coal, natural gas, and petroleum, or oil, are all natural resources that are used as fuels.

Indiana is one of the top states in producing metals. Steel and aluminum are important to several manufacturing industries in Indiana. Our state also contains large amounts of **limestone**, a soft rock that is crushed and then used to make roadways and buildings. Sand, gravel, and clay are other natural resources that come from rock or stone.

Minerals are **nonrenewable resources**. That means that there is a limited supply of them. When they have been used up, they will be gone forever. Indiana and other states are always working to find new sources of fuel and better ways to use existing resources.

INDIANA'S NATURAL RESOURCES

Lake Michigan • MICHIGAN

INDIANA

ILLINOIS

OHIO

N W E S

KENTUCKY

Legend:
- Corn (Biofuel)
- Stone
- Forests
- Steel (Iron Ore)
- Coal
- Oil

Map Skill

LOCATION **In what region of Indiana is most of the state's corn grown?**

QUICK CHECK

Main Idea and Details **How do people use natural resources to make a living?**

▶ A factory worker checks the strength of steel used in manufactured automobiles.

Over 100 years ago, forests covered most of Indiana. They were a valuable resource for Native Americans and early settlers. Both groups used wood for fuel and shelter. Later, many forests were cut down to make roads and to clear the land for farming.

◄ Walnut tree in freshly mowed hay field

The fertile soil left by glaciers in the Northern Lakes and Moraines and the Central Till Plains is perfect for growing vegetables and other crops. Fertile means that the soil is full of the minerals that plants need to grow. This rich soil is a natural resource that lets farmers produce healthy crops.

QUICK CHECK

Main Idea and Details **Name two ways that forests were used by early peoples in Indiana.**

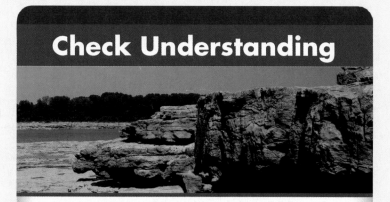

Check Understanding

1. **VOCABULARY** Write a sentence for each of the following vocabulary words.
   environment **mineral** **limestone**

2. **READING SKILL Main Idea and Details** Use your Main Idea and Details chart from page 18 to highlight the natural resources in Indiana.

Main Idea	Details

3. **Write About It** Write a paragraph about renewable resources and what your community can do to preserve the environment where you live.

EXPLORE The Big Idea

A Girl of the Limberlost

By GENE STRATTON-PORTER

▲ Gene Stratton-Porter wrote *A Girl of the Limberlost*, a book about the marshlands around her home in Geneva, Indiana.

Chart and Graph Skills

Read Circle Graphs

VOCABULARY

graph

circle graph

A **graph** is a drawing that helps you compare information by showing the relationship between things. Bar graphs, line graphs, and circle graphs are different types of graphs. These types of graphs can show the same information in different ways.

The graph shown here is a **circle graph**. Circle graphs show how parts of something fit into the whole. Because each part looks like a slice of pie, a circle graph is sometimes called a pie graph or a pie chart. Each slice of the graph represents a percentage. All of the slices added together equal 100%.

Learn It

- The title of a graph tells you what it shows. The graph on the right shows the types of trees in Indiana.

- The legend, or key, tells you what each slice represents.

- The size of the slice represents an item's part of the whole. The larger the slice, the higher the percentage.

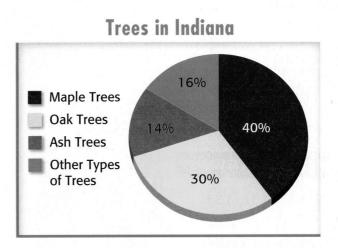

Trees in Indiana

- ■ Maple Trees
- ▢ Oak Trees
- ▨ Ash Trees
- ▨ Other Types of Trees

Try It

- Look at the circle graph. What percentage of Indiana's trees are maple?

- What percentage of Indiana's trees are oak?

- What tree type makes up only 14 percent of the trees in Indiana?

Apply It

- In groups, research the types of trees, plants, or vegetation that are found in your area. For example, find the amount and types of flowering plants that grow in a state park close to you. Create a circle graph showing the information, and share your results with the class.

VOCABULARY

economy p. 25

manufacturing p. 25

agriculture p. 25

productivity p. 26

biotechnology p. 28

pharmaceutical p. 28

READING SKILL

Main Idea and Details
Copy the chart below. As you read, fill it in with details about Indiana's economy.

Main Idea	Details

INDIANA ACADEMIC STANDARDS

4.1.12, 4.3.4, 4.3.8; 4.3.11, 4.3.12, 4.4.1, 4.4.2

INDIANA'S ECONOMY

Farmers harvest a field of corn, Indiana's most important crop.

Visual Preview

How do people in Indiana use natural resources to make a living?

A Agriculture and other industries are important to Indiana's economy.

B Indiana is one of the country's top corn producers.

C Manufacturing is big business in Indiana. Pharmaceutical production started with Eli Lilly.

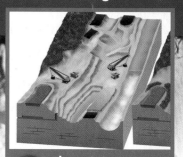

D The mining industry in Indiana produces limestone and coal.

A MAKING A LIVING IN INDIANA

Indiana employs many people in a variety of jobs. You may know someone who is a farmer or who works in an automobile factory. What job do you think you would you like to have?

The way a place uses and produces natural resources, goods, and services is its **economy**. The work that people do affects the economy of our state. There are many industries and types of work in Indiana.

Indiana is one of our country's leaders in manufacturing. **Manufacturing** is when people use machinery to make other goods. The manufacturing industry grew during and after World Wars I and II, when ammunition and other military products were produced.

Agriculture is also very important in Indiana. **Agriculture** is the business of growing crops and raising animals. Early in our country's history, the fertile soil of our state attracted many settlers, and agriculture grew.

Other industries are also important to Indiana's economy. Indiana's natural resources have helped make mining an important industry. For example, in the 1800s, many people immigrated to Indiana from other countries to work in the coal mines.

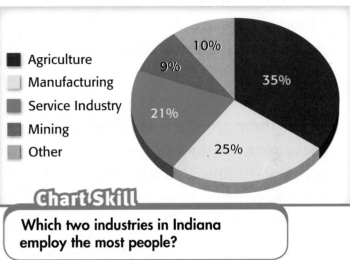

Indiana's Workforce

- Agriculture
- Manufacturing
- Service Industry
- Mining
- Other

35%
25%
21%
9%
10%

Chart Skill

Which two industries in Indiana employ the most people?

Limestone from our state was mined and used to build many famous buildings, including Indiana's state capitol and the Empire State Building in New York City.

The service industry also provides jobs for many people in Indiana. In the service industry, workers do not make things, but instead provide services. Teachers, salespeople, and police officers are examples of people who work in the service industry.

QUICK CHECK

Main Idea and Details **How does using natural resources help the economy?**

AGRICULTURE AND THE CORN BELT

As we have read, agriculture is a very important part of the Indiana economy. Indiana's fertile soil is suitable for raising many different types of crops. Some of the most important crops in Indiana are corn, soybeans, and wheat. Farmers also raise cattle, hogs, chickens, and turkeys for food. There are about 60,000 farms in Indiana, covering more than 15 million acres of land.

New tools and methods help farmers increase their productivity. **Productivity** is the amount of goods or services made in a period of time. Farmers use state-of-the-art tractors and other machinery to plant and harvest crops.

Agricultural research has also improved productivity. For example, scientists have developed ways to help farmers raise crops that resist diseases and pests. Scientists have also discovered how to create fuel from corn and soybeans.

Improved education in agriculture has provided farmers with the skills needed to produce healthier crops and to work more efficiently. Today, farmers are able to grow more crops per acre of land than they could in years past.

QUICK CHECK

Main Idea and Details **What are some ways that farmers have improved their productivity?**

Many Indiana farmers harvest wheat and store hay for food for livestock.

Our state's most important farm product is corn. Indiana is located in the Corn Belt of the United States. This area produces more corn than anywhere else in the world. Look at the map on this page to see the area included in the Corn Belt.

Indiana is the biggest producer of popcorn in the country. In the 1950s, Orville Redenbacher started one of the largest popcorn companies in the United States in Valparaiso. Other products made from corn include cereals, corn syrup and sweeteners, and dry pet food. In fact, there are more than 3,500 uses for corn products.

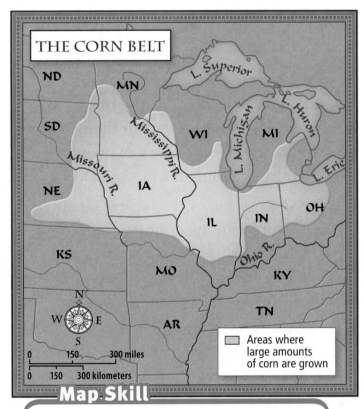

THE CORN BELT

Areas where large amounts of corn are grown

Map Skill

REGION What two regions of Indiana are in the Corn Belt?

QUICK CHECK

Main Idea and Details How does Indiana's location in the Corn Belt help the state's economy?

© MANUFACTURING AND TECHNOLOGY

With so many farms in Indiana, you might think that most people in our state are farmers. That was true in the past, but not today. Now, about one of every four jobs is in the manufacturing industry.

Our state is one of the largest steel manufacturers in the country. Steel from Indiana is used to make trucks, car parts, and other products. The U.S. Steel Corporation in Gary is the largest steel mill in the United States. It was founded by Elbert Gary in 1901. During its first year, the mill made 67 percent of all the steel produced in the United States.

Technology and Medicine

Technology has grown in Indiana in recent years in response to the manufacturing industry. Companies in Kokomo and Fort Wayne use computer technology to make microchips used in cars, motorcycles, and fighter planes.

Biotechnology is a kind of technology that has also grown in recent years. Biotechnology is the science of using natural materials like plants and improving them to make products. The **pharmaceutical** industry is using biotechnology to grow plants that may cure some illnesses. Pharmaceuticals are medicines sold in drugstores.

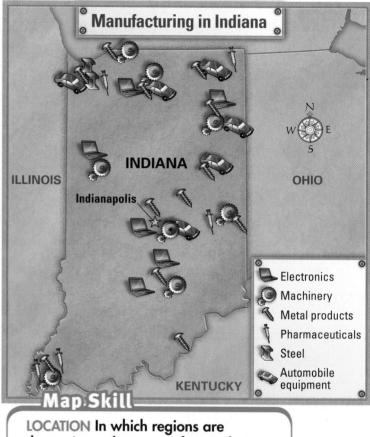

Manufacturing in Indiana

ILLINOIS

INDIANA

Indianapolis

OHIO

KENTUCKY

- Electronics
- Machinery
- Metal products
- Pharmaceuticals
- Steel
- Automobile equipment

Map Skill

LOCATION **In which regions are electronic products manufactured?**

PEOPLE

Colonel Eli Lilly started his pharmaceutical company in 1876. Colonel Lilly was a pharmacist who had served as a Union officer in the Civil War. He founded a laboratory in Indianapolis and started Eli Lilly and Company. His new idea to coat pills with gelatin helped make the company successful.

Colonel Eli Lilly

QUICK CHECK

Main Idea and Details **How can new technologies increase productivity?**

ⓓ MINING UNDERGROUND RESOURCES

Strip Mining

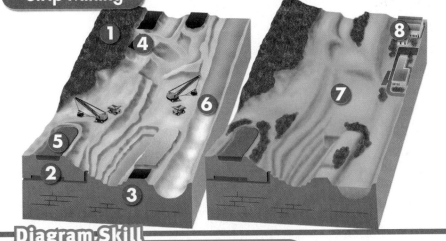

1. untouched forest
2. abandoned mine
3. coal seam
4. coal
5. dirty pond
6. mined area being filled in
7. filled-in mine area
8. new buildings

Diagram Skill

After the mine area is filled in, what can be done to reuse the land?

Mining underground resources is also important to Indiana's economy. One of Indiana's major underground resources is coal. Coal miners use huge machines to strip away the ground covering the coal. This process is called strip mining.

Limestone is another natural resource that is found underground. Limestone is mined in central and southern Indiana from deep pits called quarries.

Strip mining and limestone quarry sites damage the environment because they leave the ground bare. Many companies are turning strip mines into nature centers and old quarries into research centers for biotechnology.

QUICK CHECK

Main Idea and Details How has mining natural resources helped the economy of Indiana?

Check Understanding

1. **VOCABULARY** Create a poster about jobs in Indiana. Label the poster with the following vocabulary words: **agriculture manufacturing biotechnology**

2. **READING SKILL Main Idea and Details** Use your Main Idea and Details Chart from page 24 to write about why Indiana is a good place for agriculture.

Main Idea	Details

3. **Write About It** Write a paragraph about the pharmaceutical industry in Indiana.

Indiana's People and Culture

VOCABULARY

culture p. 31

ethnic group p. 31

heritage p. 31

immigrant p. 32

urban p. 33

Great Migration p. 33

READING SKILL

Main Idea and Details
Copy the chart below. As you read, fill it in with details about Indiana's people and culture.

Main Idea	Details

INDIANA ACADEMIC STANDARDS

4.1.14, 4.1.17, 4.2.6, 4.2.7, 4.3.9, 4.3.10, 4.3.11

Fans await the NFL kick-off party at Monument Circle in Indianapolis before the Colts' season opener football game.

Visual Preview

How have the people of Indiana adapted over time?

A Indiana is home to people from many different cultures.

B Immigrants from Ireland and other countries in Europe came to Indiana for a better life.

C Indiana celebrates its many cultures with festivals and sporting events.

D Many famous people in the arts, music, and sports have come from Indiana.

Ⓐ MANY WAYS OF LIFE

Many people from Indiana can trace their roots to Germany, England, Scotland, Switzerland, or Ireland. Some people have families that came from Africa. Where does your family come from?

More than 6 million people live and work in Indiana. Our state is home to people from many different **cultures**. Culture is the way of life shared by a group of people, including their language, beliefs, music, food, and holiday traditions.

The citizens of Indiana also belong to different **ethnic groups**. Ethnic groups are groups of people whose ancestors are from the same country or area. People of the same ethnic group share a common **heritage**. Heritage is the history that a group of people share. As citizens of Indiana, we share a heritage as Hoosiers.

The people of Indiana have been nicknamed Hoosiers since the early 1830s. There are several stories on how we became known as Hoosiers. One story tells of a canal boss named Samuel Hoosier who liked to hire men from Indiana. These men were known as Hoosiers. Another story states that the word *hoosier* comes from England and means a woodsman or person from the hills.

QUICK CHECK

Main Idea and Details **What makes up a culture?**

Indiana's Cultural Groups

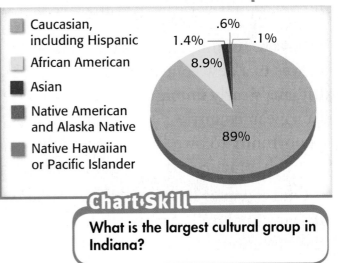

	Caucasian, including Hispanic
	African American
	Asian
	Native American and Alaska Native
	Native Hawaiian or Pacific Islander

89% 8.9% 1.4% .6% .1%

Chart Skill

What is the largest cultural group in Indiana?

Many of Indiana's early immigrants came from European countries.

THE PEOPLE OF INDIANA

Native Americans were the first people to live in Indiana. They grew corn, squash, and beans in the fertile land along the Ohio River. The first Europeans in the area were French explorers and fur traders. Settlers also came from other states and colonies to plant crops in Indiana's rich soil.

Many **immigrants** came to Indiana to find a better life and to gain religious freedom. An immigrant is a person who moves to a new country to live. Most of Indiana's early immigrants came from European countries. They came for an opportunity to own land, to find jobs, or to freely practice their religious beliefs.

One group of immigrants that came to Indiana in search of freedom to practice their religious beliefs was the Amish. The Amish are members of a religious group that believes in living a simple life. They left their homelands in Germany and other European countries because they wanted to practice their religion freely. The Amish formed their first settlement in Indiana in the 1830s. Their beliefs influence their behavior and lifestyle. For example, they follow rules that limit their use of electricity and other modern technology. Most Amish communities are in rural areas.

Some European groups settled in Indiana to escape hunger and to find jobs building roads, railways, and canals. Irish immigrants came in large numbers in the mid-1800s for these reasons. Other Europeans came to work in Indiana's many coal mines.

In the early to mid-1900s, African Americans from the South started coming to Indiana to look for jobs. Many found employment in the steel and automobile industries in **urban** centers of the state. An urban area is a city and its surroundings. This time in history when many African Americans moved north to find jobs is known as the **Great Migration**.

Today, immigrants still come to Indiana from all over the world. Many people came from Latin America looking for jobs after World War II. Recent immigrants have settled in our state from India, Bulgaria, Mexico, and the Democratic Republic of the Congo. All these people bring with them their culture and celebrate their heritage.

QUICK CHECK

Main Idea and Details Give details about the Great Migration.

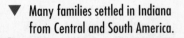
▼ Many families settled in Indiana from Central and South America.

Primary Sources

"Mother came from North Carolina to Indiana by ox team when she was one year old. That was the year that the stars fell. They were camping under a big oak tree that night when the stars began to fall....Some of them said that if those big balls of fire drop on us we'll all be gone. They huddled close together under the tree."

From *American Life Histories: Manuscripts from the Federal Writers' Project*, written by Hattie Zellars, September 1938

Write About It Interview a family member, neighbor, or teacher to find out how their families came to Indiana. Write a paragraph to share with the class.

INDIANA CELEBRATIONS AND TRADITIONS

Hoosiers recognize their heritage in a number of ways. The people of Indiana hold many different festivals and events that celebrate our cultures.

One of the many celebrations is the International Festival in Indianapolis. The festival takes place every November and celebrates the heritage of all the different people who have settled in Indiana.

Other celebrations honor the many ethnic groups of our state. The annual Festival of Fun in Oldenburg pays tribute to the German heritage of the city. The Scottish Festival in Columbus includes highland games, dances, and traditional music. The city of Berne remembers its Swiss roots with several days of music, parades, and fireworks.

▼ Swiss Days Court in Berne

▼ Many people from Scotland celebrate their heritage at the Scottish Festival in Columbus, Indiana.

One of our state's most famous sports events is the Indianapolis 500. The "Indy 500" is a 500-mile automobile race. It is held every year on Memorial Day weekend at the Indianapolis Motor Speedway. Carl Fisher started building the speedway in 1909. The first Indianapolis 500 took place in 1911. Today, more than 250,000 racing fans attend the Indy 500 each year.

Our state is known for other sporting events as well. Indiana's professional football team is the Indianapolis Colts. The University of Notre Dame has won the national college football championship eight times.

Many sports fans enjoy the numerous basketball games played in our state. Indianapolis is home to two professional basketball teams, the Indiana Pacers and the Indiana Fever. At Indiana University, former college coach Bobby Knight led the Hoosiers basketball team to 11 Big Ten championships.

Other forms of recreation include visiting the Circus Capital of the World and Circus City Festival in Peru. The Children's Museum of Indianapolis is a fun place to learn about a variety of things. There is a three-story climbing wall made of limestone, a planetarium with slide shows about the Indiana night sky, and puppet plays from around the world.

QUICK CHECK

Main Idea and Details **Name two sporting events that are famous in Indiana.**

Citizenship
Being Informed

When a girl from Indiana named Tanya heard that some cities celebrated a festival called Juneteenth every June 19th, she decided to do some research. She knew that if she was going to petition her city to start a Juneteenth celebration, she needed to be informed enough to have her opinion count. Tanya found out that many African Americans celebrate June 19th as the day that the end of slavery was announced in Texas. Muncie, Indianapolis, and Lafayette are just a few of the cities that celebrate Juneteenth. Tanya decided to attend a city hall meeting to see if her town could celebrate Juneteenth, too.

D FAMOUS PEOPLE IN THE ARTS, MUSIC, AND SPORTS

Throughout history, Indiana has been home to many great writers, musicians, artists, and athletes. Many famous television and movie entertainers are from our state as well.

Several Indiana writers have become famous for their work. Some of these well known writers include Theodore Dreiser, Booth Tarkington, and James Whitcomb Riley. Kurt Vonnegut was a famous author who wrote novels about his experiences in World War II.

Hoosier songwriters have written many popular songs. Musicians from Indiana include Cole Porter and Hoagy Carmichael. Several new rap and hip-hop musicians are recording songs in Indianapolis and Fort Wayne. There are numerous recording companies and studios in these cities.

In addition to writers and musicians, famous artists came from Indiana. Artist Janet Scrudder made scultures. Dancer Twyla Tharp created many dances.

Kurt Vonnegut

Kurt Vonnegut wrote many novels about his life experiences and observations.

Jane Pauley

Jane Pauley hails from Indiana and was a famous television news anchorwoman.

Hoagy Charmichael

Hoagy Charmichael was a famous songwriter and composer.

Indiana is also home to many famous athletes. Wilma Rudolph is one of our state's Olympic champions. She overcame a serious childhood illness, and in 1960, won three gold metals in track and field. Other famous athletes from Indiana include basketball players Oscar Robertson and Larry Bird.

Many Hoosiers have made a positive impact in literature, music, the arts, and sports. These people, along with other citizens of our state, have helped to create and celebrate the culture of Indiana.

QUICK CHECK

Main Idea and Details **Name some famous Hoosiers who have contributed to the arts.**

Check Understanding

1. **VOCABULARY** Write a letter inviting someone to visit Indiana. Include the following vocabulary words.

   culture   **heritage**   **urban**

2. **READING SKILL Main Idea and Details** Use your chart from page 30 to write about the different ethnic groups of Indiana. Create a time line to show when each group came.

Main Idea	Details

 3. **Write About It** Write a paragraph about cultural celebrations in Indiana and how you celebrate your heritage.

Wilma Rudolph

Wilma Rudolph won three Olympic medals in Track and Field.

Larry Bird

Larry Bird played college basketball in Indiana and went on to play professionally for the Boston Celtics. He is pictured here charging past the Atlanta Hawks's Tree Rollins.

Vocabulary Review

Number a sheet of paper from 1 to 4. Beside each number, write the word from the list below that best completes the sentence.

glacier   limestone

culture   climate

1. A very large sheet of moving ice is known as a _____.

2. A pattern of weather in a certain place is called the _____.

3. _____ is the way of life of a people.

4. Coal and _____ are natural resources that benefit the economy of Indiana.

Comprehension and Critical Thinking

5. Why is agriculture important to Indiana's economy?

6. **Reading Skill** Name and give details about the three regions of Indiana.

7. **Reading Skill** What was the main reason that many Amish left Europe?

8. **Critical Thinking** Why do you think most mines and quarries in Indiana are located in the southern part of the state?

Skill

Understand Latitude and Longitude

Create a blank map of Indiana. Use the map on the right to help you. Place these addresses on your map, using their latitude and longitude. Label the cities.

9. 40° N, 86° W

10. 38° N, 88° W

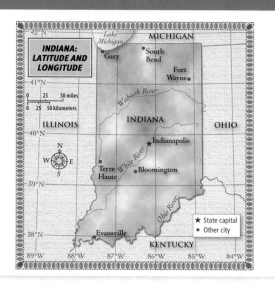

INDIANA: LATITUDE AND LONGITUDE

Indiana Statewide Test Practice

Read the passage below. Then choose the best answer or write a short response to each of the following questions.

> Indiana can be very cold in the winter. Blizzards, or winter storms with strong, cold winds and snow, can form in states in the Midwest. Cold winters in areas by the Great Lakes are partly due to a weather condition called the lake effect.
>
> Lake effect snow occurs when cold, dry air from Canada meets warmer, damp air over the Great Lakes. Moisture in the air cools over the lake water and becomes snow. Lake Michigan coastal cities, such as Michigan City and Gary, usually receive larger amounts of snowfall than southern Indiana cities like Evansville and Terre Haute.

1 **The main idea of this passage is that _____.**

   Ⓐ the weather in Canada causes mild winters in Indiana
   Ⓑ Indiana experiences lake effect snow
   Ⓒ the Midwest gets little snow
   Ⓓ the Great Lakes have no effect on Indiana's climate

2 **What is one reason Michigan City receives more snow than Terre Haute?**

   Ⓐ Michigan City experiences lake effect snow.
   Ⓑ The warm air from Canada brings more snow.
   Ⓒ Terre Haute gets warm air from the Great Lakes.
   Ⓓ Terre Haute is farther north than Michigan City.

3 **Suppose that you live in Evansville and are thinking of moving to Gary. How might the weather in Gary affect your decision?**

   Write your answer on a separate piece of paper.

The Big Idea Activities

How do people adapt to where they live?

Write About the Big Idea

FOLDABLES™
Study Organizer

Descriptive Essay

In Unit 1, you read about Indiana's location, geography, economy, resources, and people. Review the notes in your completed Foldable, and then write an essay describing one region in Indiana. In your essay, discuss the geography, climate, and economy of the region. Your essay should talk about the Big Idea question, *How do people adapt to where they live?*

Indiana's Geography

Indiana's Climate

Indiana's Resources

Indiana's Economy

Indiana's People and Culture

Create a Collage

Create a collage of your family's heritage. Make sure to show different parts of your family's culture. Here's how to make your collage:

1. Research your family's history and heritage.

2. Come up with ideas about what you want to show in your collage. Be sure to show images and symbols that celebrate your heritage.

3. Look through magazines for photos that show your ideas. Draw pictures or symbols of things important to you and your family. Collect family photographs that you have permission to use.

4. Arrange your photos and drawings on construction paper.

Present the collage to your class. As a class, display each collage on a bulletin board or heritage wall.

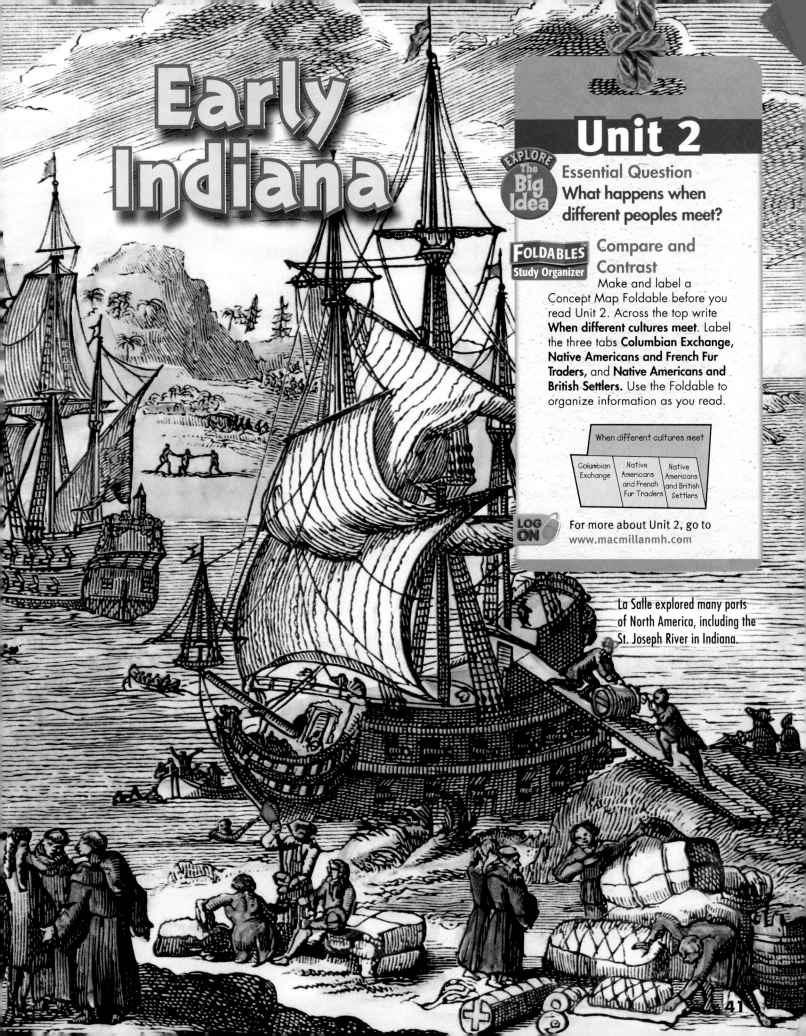

Early Indiana

EXPLORE The Big Idea

Essential Question
What happens when different peoples meet?

FOLDABLES Study Organizer

Compare and Contrast
Make and label a Concept Map Foldable before you read Unit 2. Across the top write **When different cultures meet**. Label the three tabs **Columbian Exchange, Native Americans and French Fur Traders,** and **Native Americans and British Settlers.** Use the Foldable to organize information as you read.

When different cultures meet

| Columbian Exchange | Native Americans and French Fur Traders | Native Americans and British Settlers |

LOG ON
For more about Unit 2, go to
www.macmillanmh.com

La Salle explored many parts of North America, including the St. Joseph River in Indiana.

41

PEOPLE, PLACES, AND EVENTS

Mississippian People

René-Robert Cavelier, Sieur de La Salle

Angel Mounds State Historic Site

South Bend

1100
The Mississippian people establish a large community in Indiana.

1679
La Salle explores the St. Joseph River.

1100

1600

From 1100 to 1450 the **Mississippian people** lived in a town that is now the **Angel Mounds State Historic Site**.

Today you can visit the site that is one of the best preserved historic sites in the United States.

While **La Salle** was exploring the St. Joseph River, he found a bend in the river he called the "south bend."

Today South Bend is the economic and cultural center of a region known as Michiana.

For more about People, Places, and Events, visit
www.macmillanmh.com

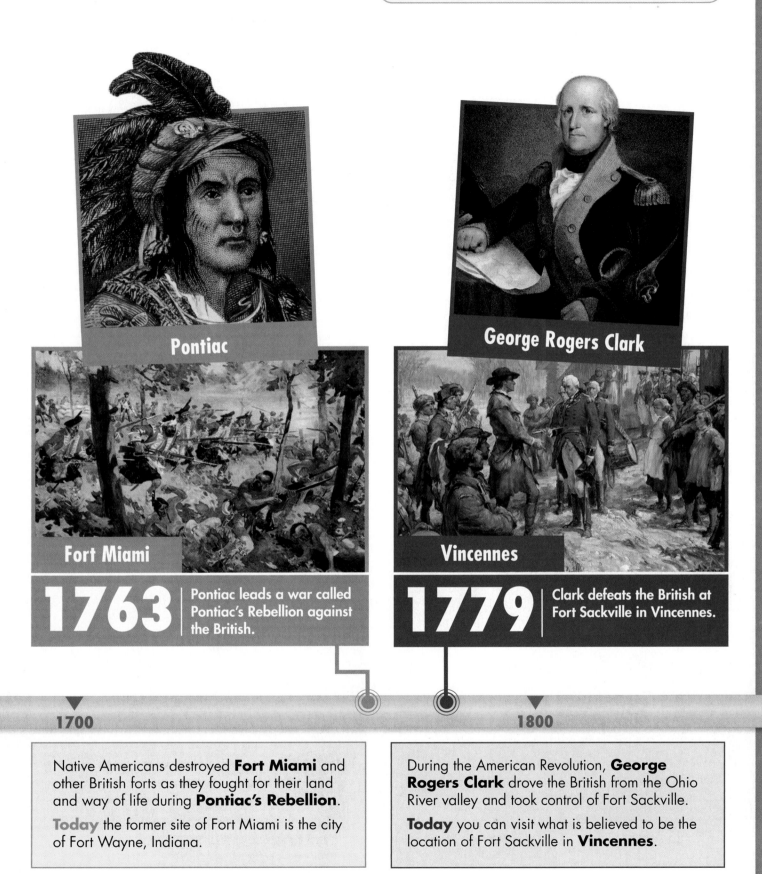

Pontiac

George Rogers Clark

Fort Miami

Vincennes

1763
Pontiac leads a war called Pontiac's Rebellion against the British.

1779
Clark defeats the British at Fort Sackville in Vincennes.

1700

1800

Native Americans destroyed **Fort Miami** and other British forts as they fought for their land and way of life during **Pontiac's Rebellion**.

Today the former site of Fort Miami is the city of Fort Wayne, Indiana.

During the American Revolution, **George Rogers Clark** drove the British from the Ohio River valley and took control of Fort Sackville.

Today you can visit what is believed to be the location of Fort Sackville in **Vincennes**.

The Earliest People

Lesson 1

VOCABULARY

migrate p. 45

hunter-gatherer p. 45

archaeology p. 46

artifact p. 46

trade p. 47

READING SKILL

Compare and Contrast
Copy the chart below. As you read, use it to compare and contrast farmers and hunter-gatherers.

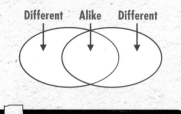

Different   Alike   Different

INDIANA ACADEMIC STANDARDS

4.1.1, 4.3.5, 4.3.8, 4.3.10, 4.4.3

Hunter-gatherers were the first people in North America.

Visual Preview

How did early groups live and work together?

A The first people moved from place to place hunting and gathering food.

B Traders had contact with other groups and shared information.

Ⓐ MIGRATION THEORIES

How did the first people get to North America? They walked for thousands of miles from Asia. Others may have come in small boats from Europe. They came to Indiana about 15,000 years ago.

In Unit 1 you read how glaciers grew and shrank during the last Ice Age. Sometimes so much water was frozen into glaciers that ocean levels dropped. In some places, this drop in water levels created land bridges, or land connecting two larger land areas. During the last Ice Age, a land bridge called Beringia joined Asia with North America.

Many scientists believe that people from Asia used Beringia to **migrate**, or move, to North America. Others believe that people migrated to North America by boat. They may have sailed along the Pacific North Coast or along the glaciers between northern Europe and the northeastern part of North America.

Not everyone agrees with the scientists. Many Native Americans believe that they never migrated to this land. They believe they have always lived in North America. Early people

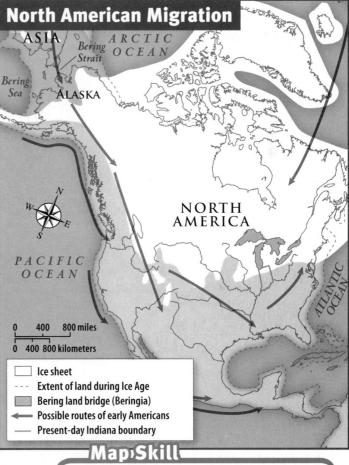

North American Migration

ASIA
Bering Strait
Bering Sea
ALASKA
ARCTIC OCEAN
NORTH AMERICA
PACIFIC OCEAN
ATLANTIC OCEAN

0   400   800 miles
0   400 800 kilometers

☐ Ice sheet
- - - Extent of land during Ice Age
▨ Bering land bridge (Beringia)
← Possible routes of early Americans
— Present-day Indiana boundary

Map Skill

LOCATION **Which present-day state was part of Beringia?**

hunted animals and collected fruits, nuts, and other foods. They lived as **hunter-gatherers**.

QUICK CHECK

Compare **How were the lives of the earliest people similar to the lives of people today?**

B EARLY FARMING

The first people, Paleo-Indians, depended on hunting for food. They traveled in search of animals such as mammoths, bison (a kind of buffalo), and later on, deer and elk. About 1,500 years ago, most Native Americans who lived in what is now Indiana stopped moving from place to place. They learned to farm, and each group chose an area in which to raise crops. They cut down and burned trees to clear fields. Then they grew corn, squash, beans, pumpkins, and tobacco. They also fished in nearby rivers. Because people stayed in one place to farm, villages developed.

▲ Native Americans used tools like these to hunt and fish.

Early Tools

Early people carved stone tools and weapons such as axes, knives, and spearheads. They fished with hooks made from animal bones. They used baskets and animal skins to hold and carry things. Later, they learned to make clay pots and bowls. Over time, their tools and weapons improved.

Studying the Past

The study of people who lived long ago is called **archaeology**. Archaeologists are scientists who study the people who lived long ago. Archaeologists often dig up the remains of ancient villages and burial sites. They may find tools, pottery, or works of art. The remains of objects made or used by people in the past, such as arrowheads, are called **artifacts**. Artifacts give us clues about life in the past.

EVENT

Agriculture, or farming, first happened in Southwest Asia about 11,000 years ago. It forever changed the lives of humans. When farmers were able to produce food beyond the needs of their own families, other family members were free to work on projects in areas other than food production. Farmers also improved their lives by exchanging their extra goods for things they did not produce.

Agriculture

By studying artifacts, archaeologists can learn a lot about how early people lived in present-day Indiana. Artifacts tell us that early people learned to **trade** about 10,000 years ago. Trade means to buy or sell goods, or to exchange goods with other people to get things you want but do not have. Groups with different cultures learned from each other through trade. They likely shared information about farming and how they lived.

QUICK CHECK

Contrast How are farmers different from hunter-gatherers?

▼ This painting shows how Paleo-Indian hunters lived.

Check Understanding

1. Write a paragraph about early people using the terms below.

   migrate   **trade**
   hunter-gatherer

2. **READING SKILL Compare and Contrast** Use your chart from page 44 to write about hunter-gatherers and farmers.

3. **Write About It** Write an essay about what early people may have learned from other groups.

MOUND BUILDERS

Lesson 2

VOCABULARY

mound p. 49

civilization p. 49

religion p. 50

historian p. 52

READING SKILL

Compare and Contrast
Copy the chart below. As you read, use it to compare and contrast the Adena and Mississippian peoples.

Different — Alike — Different

INDIANA ACADEMIC STANDARDS

4.1.1, 4.3.8, 4.4.3

The Great Serpent Mound in Ohio is a snake-shaped mound that winds back and forth for 1,330 feet.

Visual Preview

How did early civilizations grow and fall?

A Agriculture and trade brought wealth to some early civilizations.

B The Hopewell and Mississippian people grew wealthy from trade.

C Wars and disease may have led to the fall of the Mound Builders.

Ⓐ MOUND-BUILDING CULTURES

*Beginning about 2,200 years ago, people living along the Ohio River worked together to build **mounds**. A mound is a hill or ridge of earth. The people who built them are known as Mound Builders.*

Mound-building people formed some of North America's earliest **civilizations**. A civilization is a group of people who have highly developed trade, agriculture, government, art, and science.

These early civilizations built mounds for many reasons. They often buried the dead there. People also came to mounds to worship or hold religious ceremonies.

▲ Adena carving of a man

The Adena People

The Adena people lived in the area of present-day Indiana about 2,800 years ago. Archaeologists believe that these Native Americans probably lived together in groups. Some of their settlements may have had as many as 12 houses.

The Adena learned to shape and decorate pottery that they hardened with fire. They held special ceremonies when people died. They buried their dead in log tombs covered with mounds of earth.

Hunter-Gatherers and Farmers

The Adena people were mostly hunter-gatherers, but they did some farming of pumpkins and sunflowers. Hunters used spears that had small triangle-shaped stone points called arrowheads.

Today, you can see Adena mounds, including the largest earthwork, the "Great Mound," at Mounds State Park, near Anderson, Indiana.

QUICK CHECK

Compare How were the Adena similar to Paleo-Indians?

The Hopewell were another group of Mound Builders. "The Hopewell were doing things a little bit bigger and grander than the Adena people," says archaeologist Bradley Lepper. They built bigger mounds, created finer artwork, and had stronger leaders. The Hopewell hunted, farmed, and traded with other groups. They got silver from Canada and turtle shells from the Gulf of Mexico.

Hopewell Ceremonies

Like most Native Americans, the Hopewell had their own **religion**. Religion is the way people worship. The Hopewell believed their religious leaders could cure some sicknesses using plants. They also believed certain ceremonies, or formal acts, would help hunters.

Some mounds had religious meaning for the Hopewell. They used them as burial sites for community leaders. Other mounds were used as trading posts where they displayed goods.

Village Life

The Hopewell people often built their villages near rivers where there was plenty of water. Families lived in domed homes called wigwams. Wigwams were made of wood and animal skins. A hole in the roof let out smoke from the fire pits.

In the fall, villagers left home to hunt and to gather nuts, roots, and other food needed to last through the winter. Food often ran low in the early spring, so people left home again to find more food.

The Mississippian People

After the Hopewell people, the Mississippian people settled in the Ohio River valley for some 700 years, until about 1600. These Native Americans settled in larger communities. Some of their towns covered hundreds of acres. Hundreds or even thousands of people may have lived there.

The Mississippian people tended large farms and hunted deer, turkey, and other animals. They used stone tools and made bowls and jars from clay.

Angel Mounds

Like the Adena and Hopewell people, the Mississippian people also built mounds. One of the most famous of these mounds was located at a place today known as Angel Mounds. This settlement was built on the northern bank of the Ohio River. It was the largest settlement of the time, with as many as 1,000 to 3,000 people living there. Other people traveled there to attend meetings and to trade goods. Angel Mounds contained about 200 houses. In the fields around the town, farmers grew corn, beans, and squash. For about 300 years the site of Angel Mounds was a successful Native American community.

Today, you can visit Angel Mounds State Historic Site, near Evansville, and walk to the top of a 40-foot mound.

QUICK CHECK

Compare and Contrast **How were Hopewell and Mississippian people alike and different?**

This drawing shows what the Angel Mounds might have looked like.

ⓒ FALL OF THE MOUND BUILDERS

Look at the chart of Mound Builder culture below. The Adena and Hopewell civilizations began during the period of time known as "before Christ." This is abbreviated in the chart as B.C. The letters A.D. stand for the Latin term *anno Domini,* which tells how many years have passed since the birth of Jesus Christ.

Historians, or people who study the past, are not sure what became of the mound-building civilizations. Some think the Adena were defeated by the Hopewell people, who also lived in the Ohio River valley. Other historians think the Adena may have used up all of their natural resources or died from disease.

MOUND BUILDER CULTURE

Adena
800 B.C.–A.D. 200
The Adena were mostly hunter-gatherers, but they did not move from place to place. Skilled Adena artists used tools like flint drills that, when twisted, were able to cut through wood, bone, and stone. The Adena buried stone tools and other items with their dead. They believed these items would help the dead on their journey to the next world.

Hopewell
200 B.C.–A.D. 400
The Hopewell civilization was larger and better organized than the Adena. They had developed a stricter class structure. Agriculture and trade were important to the Hopewell. The Hopewell spread beyond their cultural roots, into the east and the rest of the Midwest.

Mississippian
A.D. 100–A.D. 1600
The Mississippian culture reached its peak between the 1100s and 1300s. They lived in the Midwest, the East, and the Southeast. Surrounding their mounds were merchants, hunters, farmers, laborers, and artisans selling goods. By setting up trade networks, they may have traded with people as far away as Central America.

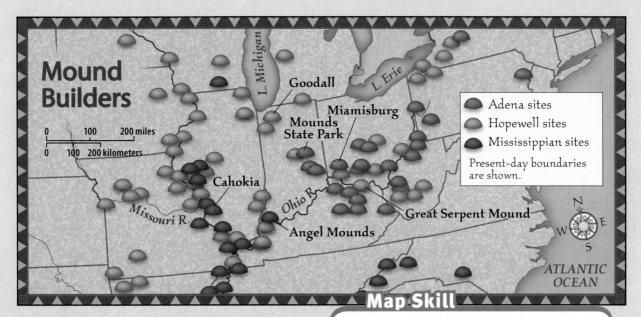

Mound Builders

0   100   200 miles
0   100   200 kilometers

L. Michigan

L. Erie

Goodall

Miamisburg

Mounds State Park

Cahokia

Missouri R.

Ohio R.

Angel Mounds

Great Serpent Mound

● Adena sites
● Hopewell sites
● Mississippian sites
Present-day boundaries are shown.

N
W   E
S

ATLANTIC OCEAN

Map Skill

LOCATION **Which group built mounds in northern Indiana?**

About 1,600 years ago, North America's climate suddenly became much cooler. Some historians think this cold spell may have made it hard for the Hopewell to hunt. No one knows why, but the Hopewell civilization began to weaken at this time and was completely gone around 100 years later.

Historians think that climate change, wars, and disease led to the fall of the Mississippian civilization. Archaeologists have found that in the Mississippian city of Cahokia, people were using land in a way that caused flooding. They cut forests upstream and floated the logs downstream. Removing large areas of trees caused mud slides and flooding. The flooding caused diseases and conflicts among groups that led to wars.

Quick Check

Cause and Effect **How did climate change affect the Hopewell and Mississippian civilizations?**

Check Understanding

1. Write a paragraph about Mound Builders. Use the vocabulary words below.

   mound   **historian**
   civilization

2. **READING SKILL Compare and Contrast** Use your chart from page 48 to write about Adena and Mississippian civilizations.

   Different   Alike   Different

3. **Write About It** Write an essay about why historians think mound-building civilizations disappeared.

VOCABULARY

alliance p. 55

dugout p. 57

lacrosse p. 60

READING SKILL

Compare and Contrast
Copy the chart below. As you read, use it to compare and contrast the Delaware and Shawnee people.

Different   Alike   Different

INDIANA ACADEMIC STANDARDS

4.1.2, 4.3.8, 4.3.10, 4.4.3

Native Americans After 1700

This drawing shows how the Shawnee people lived.

Visual Preview

How did Native Americans and Europeans interact?

A Some Native American groups formed alliances with European groups.

B The Delaware traded with the British and Dutch.

C The Shawnee often traded furs for tools and clothes at European trading posts.

D The Potawatomi traded maize with the French.

A NEW GROUPS ARRIVE

What happened to the Mississippian people after their decline? Some historians believe the remaining Mississippian people in Indiana became the Miami people. The Miami were driven out of Indiana in the 1660s by the powerful Iroquois of New York.

By the mid-1600s, the French, Dutch, and English were paying the Iroquois good money for furs, especially beaver. To hunt for more furs, the Iroquois forced their way into the Ohio River valley to expand their hunting grounds.

During the 1680s, the Miami moved back from Illinois to western Indiana. During the 1700s, they were joined by new arrivals including the Delaware, Potawatomi, Shawnee, Wyandotte, and others. Many of them settled in Indiana after being forced out of their homes in other parts of North America by other Native American groups or by Europeans.

The Delaware were pushed west from the New Jersey area by European settlers. The Shawnee were forced out of Pennsylvania into Indiana. Other groups migrated to Indiana because of wars with other Native American groups.

Some Native Americans developed **alliances** with different European groups. An alliance is an agreement between two or more groups to work together in doing something. For example, the Wyandotte were allied with the French because they had developed a friendship through trade. Their alliance stayed strong even during times of war.

QUICK CHECK

Compare How were the migrations of Native American groups into Indiana similar?

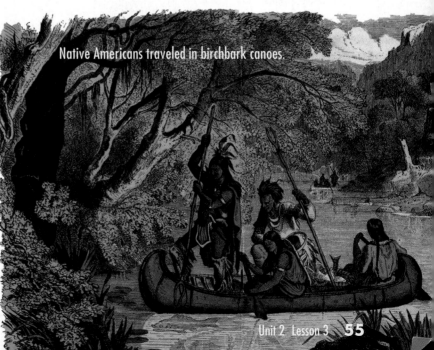

Native Americans traveled in birchbark canoes.

NATIVE AMERICAN SHELTERS

Native Americans in Indiana lived in a variety of shelters. Some were permanent houses where they lived all year long. Others were temporary shelters that groups used as they moved around to hunt. By 1750, large numbers of the Miami people were living in northern Indiana, near what is now the cities of Fort Wayne and Lafayette.

The Wikiami

The houses in Miami villages were permanent structures covered with bark or earth-covered mats. The Miami called these houses *wikiami*. Each village also had a large house that was used for meetings and ceremonies. Miami leaders led the meetings to find solutions to village problems.

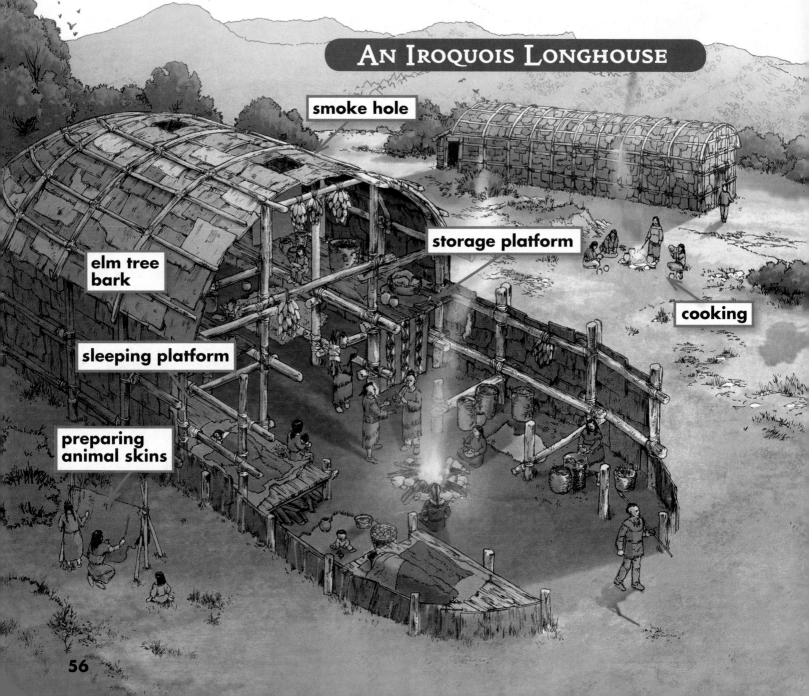

AN IROQUOIS LONGHOUSE

smoke hole

elm tree bark

storage platform

cooking

sleeping platform

preparing animal skins

The Longhouse and Wigwam

The Delaware, also known as the Lenape, came to the Indiana area from the East in the 1770s. The Delaware lived in rectangular longhouses or round wigwams. Both were made of long, bent wooden poles tied together near the top. The poles were covered with bark from elm trees. An opening in the roof let the smoke from a cooking fire escape.

Look at the diagram of a longhouse on page 56. A normal longhouse might be about 50 feet long. Larger longhouses stretched several hundred feet and housed up to 20 families.

Wigwams were round, single-family homes. They were easier to heat than longhouses. Even groups that lived in longhouses most of the year often switched to wigwams in the winter.

In order to trade furs with the British and Dutch, the Delaware traveled to their hunting grounds in **dugout** canoes, which they made by hollowing out logs. On long trips, the Delaware used portable wigwams that could be rolled up and carried.

QUICK CHECK

Contrast **How were wigwams different from longhouses?**

gathering berries

collecting firewood

Diagram Skill

What jobs do you see people doing? How do these jobs affect the way they lived?

Indiana's Native Americans lived off the land in different ways, depending on the season. In early spring, men cleared fields and planted crops like maize (corn), beans, and squash. These three crops were so important to their survival that many Native American groups called them the Three Sisters.

Primary Sources

> Always give a word or sign of salute when meeting or passing a friend, or even a stranger if in a lonely place. Show respect to all people, but [bow] to none. When you rise in the morning, give thanks for the light, for your life, for your strength. Give thanks for your food and for the joy of living.

Passage from a speech by Tecumseh, early 1800s

Write About It What do you think Tecumseh meant when he said "the joy of living"?

In summer, women and children worked in the fields growing crops, while the men fished and hunted vast herds of bison. In the fall, families would go into the woods to collect nuts and roots to store for the long winter months. Then, as now, fall was deer-hunting season. Hunters waited patiently for deer to visit natural salt deposits called licks.

The Long Winter Months

During winter, Native Americans hunted thick-furred animals such as bear and beaver. These furs could be taken to trading posts run by Europeans and traded for tools and clothes. In late winter, Native Americans made maple syrup. Sometimes this syrup was all they had to eat before the fishing and planting began again in the spring.

Showing Respect

All through the year, Native American groups showed respect for nature and to members of their group. Read on this page the words of Shawnee leader Tecumseh, who reminded his people to show respect to others.

Harvest Festivals

Native Americans celebrated important events and religious occasions with big ceremonies and festivals. For all groups, fall harvest time was one of the biggest yearly events and a time to give thanks.

Several groups, like the Shawnee and the Wyandotte, celebrated the "Green Corn Dance." This festival was held during the full moon when the first maize crop was ready to harvest. It lasted up to 14 days.

The Delaware called their fall harvest festival the *Gamwing*, or Big House Rite.

The Gamwing was an ancient tradition. Like the Green Corn Dance festival, it included dancing, feasts, and storytelling.

QUICK CHECK

Compare **How were the Green Corn Festival and the Gamwing similar?**

DataGraphic
Native American Cultures

Native Americans in what is now Indiana came from different parts of North America. Many shared similar customs and beliefs. Look at the chart and map below to learn more about these Native American groups.

Indiana Native American Cultures

	Delaware	Miami	Potawatomi	Shawnee	Wyandotte
Shelter	Longhouse and Wigwam	Wikiami	Longhouse and Wigwam	Longhouse and Wigwam	Longhouse
Ceremonies	Gamwing	Peace Pipe	Green Corn Dance and Sacred Food Ceremony	Fall Bread Dance and Green Corn Dance	Strawberry Feast and Green Corn Dance
European Alliance	Dutch and British	None	French	French and British	French
Original Home	New Jersey, Pennsylvania, and Delaware	Indiana and Illinois	Northern Michigan	Pennsylvania and South Carolina	Canada

Migration Routes of Native Americans, 1700s

Think About Native Americans

1. Which group migrated to Indiana from the south?

2. Which groups celebrated the Green Corn Dance?

D LACROSSE AND THE POTAWATOMI

In the 1600s, the Iroquois drove the Potawatomi out of northern Michigan to northern Wisconsin. By the 1760s, the Potawatomi had left Wisconsin for the hunting grounds of northern Indiana. At that time, Potawatomi had horses they had bought from Europeans. Horses helped the Potawatomi hunt the herds of bison that roamed northern Indiana. They also traded maize with other Native American groups and the French.

Early French explorers saw Native Americans playing a ball game in which players used a curved wooden stick to throw a ball at a goal. The goal was usually a large rock or tree. The French word for a curved stick was "crosse." The game became known as "**lacrosse**." Lacrosse sticks were several feet long with a pocket made of leather strips.

The ball was made of animal hide stuffed with hair or carved from a piece of wood. There were as many as 1,000 players on each side, usually men. Games sometimes lasted for several days. Goals were often placed several miles apart.

This drawing shows how Native Americans played lacrosse.

The Potawatomi were good lacrosse players. However, lacrosse was much more than just a game to Native Americans. It was also a religious ceremony they believed would help them in various ways. The Potawatomi played lacrosse to heal the sick or settle disputes. Lacrosse is still a popular sport today, though it is no longer a religious ceremony as it was with the Potawatomi.

QUICK CHECK

Cause and Effect Why did the Potawatomi migrate to northern Indiana?

Check Understanding

1. Write a paragraph about Native American culture. Use the vocabulary words below.
   alliance   **dugout**   **lacrosse**

2. **READING SKILL Compare and Contrast** Use your chart from page 54 to write about the Delaware and Shawnee people.

 3. **Write About It** Write a paragraph about how Native Americans and Europeans cooperated.

Chart and Graph Skills

Read Cutaway Diagrams

VOCABULARY

cutaway diagram

In the last lesson, you read about how some Native Americans lived in longhouses. In order to look at this type of house more carefully, you can use a **cutaway diagram**. A cutaway diagram shows the inside and outside of an object at the same time. It can show the "hidden parts" of an object by peeling away the outer layers. Cutaway diagrams also allow you to see how all the parts of an object are connected.

The inside of a longhouse

Learn It

- Identify the title of a cutaway diagram. The title will tell you what you will be looking at.

- Read the labels to understand the cutaway diagram. Labels are used in cutaway diagrams to identify some of the inner and outer parts of the subject.

- Look at an actual picture of the subject being represented in a cutaway diagram. For example, the photograph to the left shows what a longhouse looks like without the cutaway.

Use the cutaway diagram below to answer these questions.

- Which labels show you the outside of the longhouse?
- Which labels show you the inside of the longhouse?

- What does the cutaway diagram of the longhouse tell you that the photograph on page 62 does not tell you?
- What are some other things that could be shown in a cutaway diagram?

AN IROQUOIS LONGHOUSE

smoke hole

storage platform

elm tree bark

cooking

sleeping platform

preparing animal skins

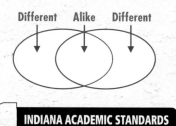
Europeans in the Americas

The arrival of Columbus and his ships in the Caribbean changed the world forever.

Visual Preview

How did Europeans affect the lives of Native Americans?

A Columbus and the Taíno exchanged gifts to show respect.

B European diseases killed millions of Native Americans.

64

A COLUMBUS'S VOYAGE

In 1492 Christopher Columbus sailed across the Atlantic Ocean from Europe to the Americas. His journey changed the lives of both Europeans and Native Americans forever. Other explorers soon followed Columbus. They sought land, riches, and adventure.

Christopher Columbus, an Italian sea captain, believed that he could find the Indies in Asia by sailing west across the Atlantic Ocean. In August 1492, he set sail from Spain with three ships—the *Niña*, the *Pinta*, and the *Santa María*.

Columbus's Mistake

After about two months at sea, a sailor shouted "*Tierra! Tierra!*" ("Land! Land!"). Columbus was sure he had reached the Indies in Asia. He called the people who lived there "Indians." Columbus was not in the Indies. Instead, he had reached the Bahama Islands.

Columbus Meets the Taíno

One of the Native American groups Columbus met were the Taíno. The Taíno greeted Columbus and his crew warmly. They gave gifts to the visitors as a way of showing respect and friendship. Columbus gave the Taíno gifts in return. These included beads, brass bells, and, as Columbus said, "many other things of small value, in which they took so much pleasure and became so much our friends that it was a marvel."

QUICK CHECK

Compare What did the Taíno and Columbus both do when they first met?

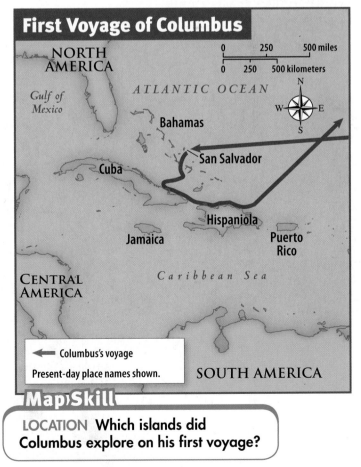

First Voyage of Columbus

NORTH AMERICA

Gulf of Mexico

ATLANTIC OCEAN

0   250   500 miles
0   250   500 kilometers

N
W   E
S

Bahamas

San Salvador

Cuba

Hispaniola

Jamaica

Puerto Rico

CENTRAL AMERICA

Caribbean Sea

← Columbus's voyage
Present-day place names shown.

SOUTH AMERICA

Map Skill

LOCATION Which islands did Columbus explore on his first voyage?

Columbus set out to **explore** the Caribbean islands. To explore is to travel to unfamiliar places in order to learn about them. One of Columbus's goals was to set up **colonies**. A colony is a country or region that is ruled by another country.

The Columbian Exchange

Europeans came to the Americas with new crops such as wheat and sugarcane. They also brought horses that would eventually change the way many Native Americans lived. Horses made hunting much easier for Native Americans.

Not everything about the arrival of Europeans was good for Native Americans, though. Europeans unknowingly brought diseases such as measles with them. Native Americans had never come into contact with these diseases, and they could not fight the illnesses. As a result, millions of Native Americans died.

When Columbus returned to Spain, he took gold, parrots, and plants from the Americas with him. In time, crops from the Western Hemisphere, such as corn, potatoes, and peanuts, were brought to countries in Europe, Africa, and Asia. This movement of foods, animals, and diseases is all part of what is called the **Columbian Exchange**.

La Salle

Almost 180 years after Columbus's first voyage, explorer René-Robert Cavelier, Sieur de La Salle, arrived in North America. The king of France had asked him to find a route to Asia through North America and claim it for France. This shortcut to Asia, which no one was sure existed, was called the Northwest Passage.

In 1666 La Salle moved to New France, France's colony in Canada, where he became a successful fur trader. Native Americans told him about large rivers in the land to the southwest. La Salle was very excited. He thought that these rivers might be the Northwest Passage.

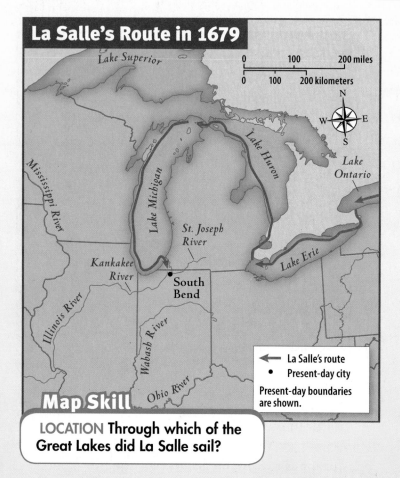

La Salle's Route in 1679

Lake Superior

0   100   200 miles
0   100   200 kilometers

Lake Huron

Lake Ontario

Lake Michigan

Mississippi River

St. Joseph River

Kankakee River

South Bend

Lake Erie

Illinois River

Wabash River

Ohio River

← La Salle's route
• Present-day city
Present-day boundaries are shown.

Map Skill

LOCATION **Through which of the Great Lakes did La Salle sail?**

La Salle was the first European to explore the
St. Joseph and Kankakee Rivers in Indiana.

In 1679, while searching for the
Northwest Passage, La Salle paddled
his canoe down the St. Joseph River. A
Mohegan named White Beaver guided
La Salle. Together they found a bend in
the river. They called it the "south bend"
of the St. Joseph River. Later the city of
South Bend was established at that spot.

Next, La Salle and his men carried their
canoes overland to the Kankakee River.
This part of their trip took them through
parts of northern Indiana.

Native Americans helped La Salle make
his journey successful. They taught him
several Native American languages and
how to survive the harsh winter.

QUICK CHECK

Compare **How were Columbus and La Salle
alike?**

Check Understanding

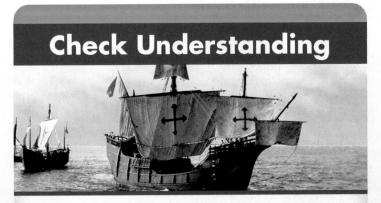

1. Write a paragraph about exploring the
Americas. Use the vocabulary words below.
explore **Columbian Exchange**
colony

2. **READING SKILL Compare
and Contrast** Use your chart
from page 64 to write about
Columbus and La Salle.

 3. **Write About It** Write about
the effects Europeans had on Native
Americans.

Map and Globe Skills

Use Elevation Maps

elevation

sea level

In the last lesson, you read about how La Salle explored the St. Joseph and Kankakee Rivers. Have you ever wondered what determines the direction of a river? The answer has to do with elevation. Every river begins at a higher elevation than where it ends. You can use an elevation map to find out in which direction a river flows. **Elevation** is the height of the land above sea level. **Sea level** is the level at the surface of the sea. The elevation at sea level is zero feet.

Learn It

- Look at the map on page 69. Read the map title. The title of the map is "Indiana: Elevation."

- Elevation maps use colors to show the height, or elevation, of land. Different colors mean different heights.

- The map key tells you what each color on the map means. For example, all the yellow areas are between 600 and 800 feet above sea level.

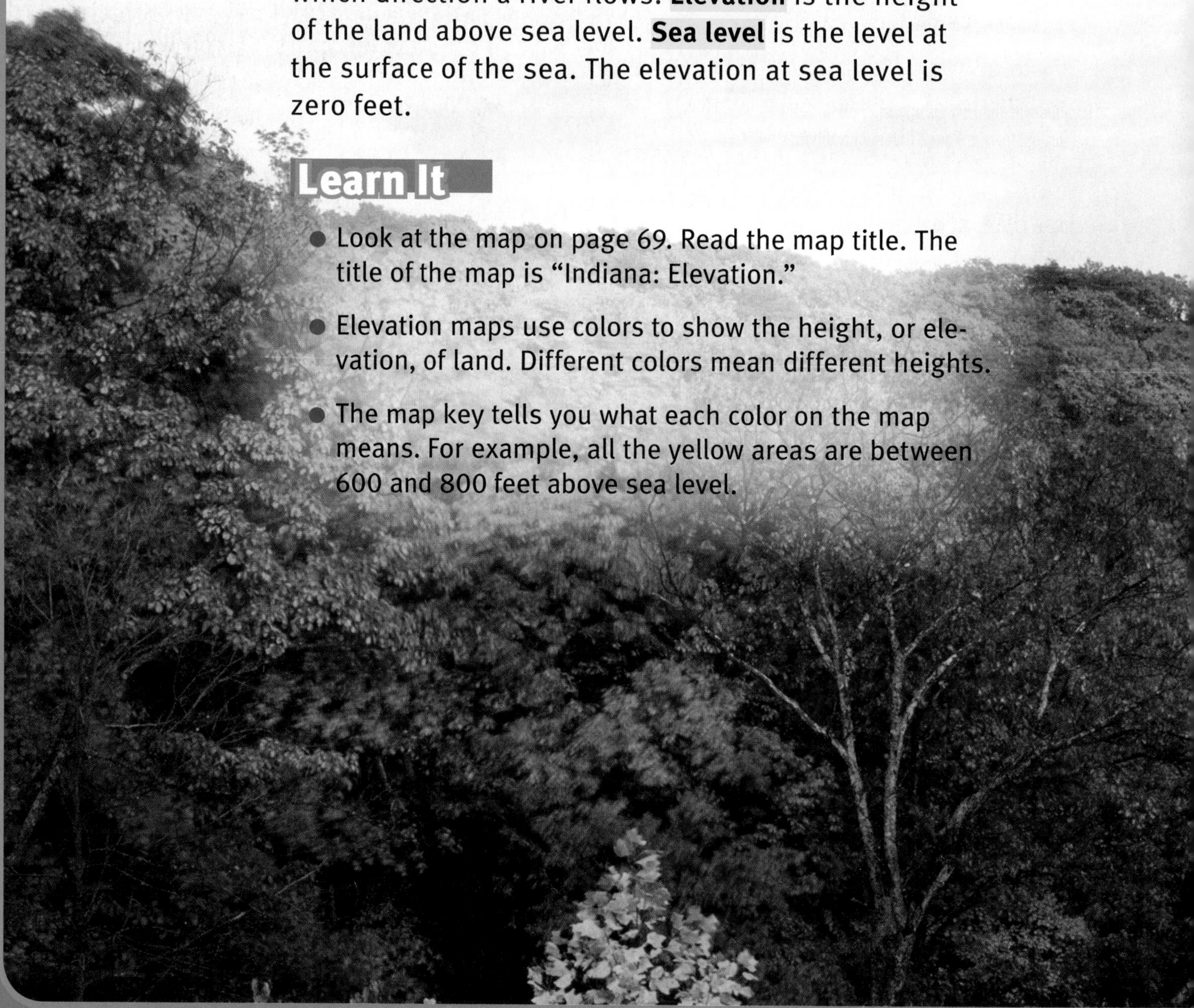

Try It

Use the map below to answer these questions.

- Which region of Indiana has the lowest elevation?

- How would you describe the elevation in South Bend, Indiana?

- In which direction does the White River flow?

Apply It

- How can an elevation map help you learn about a place?

- What else can an elevation map tell you about plants, resources, and people of an area?

Brattle Knob, Indiana

Indiana: Elevation

Feet	Meters
1200	370
1000	310
800	250
600	190
400	120
0	0

☆ State capital
● Other city
▲ Highest point
▼ Lowest point

THE FUR TRADE

Lesson 5

VOCABULARY

voyageur p. 71

coureur de bois p. 71

missionary p. 72

READING SKILL

Compare and Contrast
Copy the chart below. As you read, use it to compare and contrast the French and Native Americans.

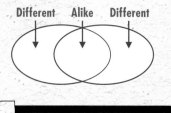

Different   Alike   Different

INDIANA ACADEMIC STANDARDS

4.1.2, 4.3.8, 4.3.10; 4.4.1, 4.4.3, 4.4.4

Native American fur traders

Visual Preview

How did the fur trade affect the French and Native Americans?

A Native Americans worked with the French in the fur trade.

B Native Americans and the French lived with and learned from each other.

A LA SALLE AND THE FUR TRADE

The French came to the Midwest searching for a water route to the Pacific Ocean. Instead they found furs. One explorer explained how the fur trade began: "Several [Native Americans] . . . came to see us, and brought fine Furs to [trade] for our Axes."

In 1681 La Salle met with leaders of the Miami and other Native American groups. La Salle promised the Miami that French soldiers would protect them from enemy Native American groups. He also spoke to them about trading with the French.

French Fur Traders

In the early 1700s, many French fur traders came to the lands La Salle had explored. Fur was used to make hats and coats in Europe. The fur of animals such as raccoon, fox, and beaver was valuable and could bring a good price in Europe.

Fur traders learned that Native Americans would exchange furs for certain goods. These goods included hunting knives, guns, hoes, blankets, and glass beads. The Native Americans also traded for mirrors, combs, and salt. Soon there was a growing fur-trading business in New France. Hunters and French trappers called **voyageurs** brought their skins to Quebec, the first trading post in New France.

▲ René Robert Cavelier, Sieur de La Salle

Coureurs de Bois

With a growing fur trade in North America, the French government wanted to make money from the fur trade too. A new law forced trappers to buy a special license to hunt in New France. Illegal trappers, or those who did not have a license, tried to stay out of the way of French soldiers and officials. They were called "runners of the woods," or **coureurs de bois**.

QUICK CHECK

Contrast **How were voyageurs and coureurs de bois different?**

NEW FRANCE GROWS

The French were the first Europeans to live in what is now Indiana. Many of them hoped to get rich in the fur trade. Contact between the French and Native Americans changed both groups.

A New Way of Life

French traders often lived with Native Americans and learned about their way of life. Some married Native Americans and raised families.

Native Americans also learned about the French way of life. Some learned this through **missionaries**. A missionary is someone who teaches others about his or her religion. French missionaries taught Native Americans about Christianity. Some Native Americans became Christians, but most continued to follow their own religion.

Still, Native American life had changed. Native Americans had always hunted with bows and arrows to meet their needs for food and clothing. Now they hunted with guns and killed animals to get furs to trade with the French.

trading post

blacksmith

blockhouse

stockade

garden

French Forts

In the early 1700s, the French built forts to protect themselves from unfriendly Native Americans and other Europeans, such as the British.

Fort Ouiatenon was built on the Wabash River in 1717. The French named it for the Wea Native Americans who lived in the area. Fort Ouiatenon was located near where the town of Lafayette is today.

The French also built a fort called Fort Miami near the Native American village of Kekionga in 1715. Fort Miami was built between the Wabash and Maumee rivers. Today, Fort Wayne stands where Fort Miami once stood.

Each fort had a large fence, called a stockade, to keep out enemies. Inside the stockade was a blockhouse. A blockhouse was a large, high, square building made of logs. A blockhouse was the best place from which to defend, or protect, a fort. If enemies attacked, soldiers could shoot through small holes in the walls. The walls protected the soldiers.

As the fur trade grew, the traders began to think of the forts as their real homes. The forts became like small towns once the traders' families were able to live with them. Children living in the forts helped their parents plant crops and bundle furs.

QUICK CHECK

Contrast How were the lives of Native Americans different after the fur trade began?

Citizenship
Cooperation and Compromise

When Native Americans and the French decided to work together trading furs, they were using cooperation. People cooperate when they work together to make rules or laws or to solve a problem. People compromise when they give up part of something they want. By getting along and working together, people can solve problems in a way that will satisfy the most people.

Write About It Write a paragraph about a time you gave up something you wanted to solve a problem or settle a disagreement.

Check Understanding

1. Write a paragraph about French fur traders. Use the vocabulary words below.
   voyageur   coureur de bois

2. **READING SKILL Compare and Contrast** Use your chart from page 70 to write about the French and Native Americans.

3. **Write About It** Write a essay about how Native Americans and the French worked together to expand the fur trade.

THE FRENCH AND INDIAN WAR

Lesson 6

VOCABULARY

Treaty of Paris of 1763 p. 75

Pontiac's Rebellion p. 76

Proclamation of 1763 p. 77

READING SKILL

Compare and Contrast
Copy the chart below. As you read, use it to compare and contrast the French and Indian War and Pontiac's Rebellion.

Different   Alike   Different

INDIANA ACADEMIC STANDARDS

4.1.3, 4.2.7, 4.3.10

French officers meet with leaders of the Wyandotte.

Visual Preview

Why did the British fight for lands west of the Appalachian Mountains?

A France and Britain both claimed land west of the Appalachian Mountains.

B Pontiac led Native Americans in a rebellion against British settlers.

74

A BATTLE OVER LAND

In 1754 France and Great Britain fought over land in North America. George Washington, who would become our nation's first President, led the first battle against the French army. This battle marked the beginning of the French and Indian War.

By 1750, England, now known as Great Britain, had 13 colonies in North America. They were located along the Atlantic Ocean. The British also wanted the French-controlled lands that surrounded the 13 colonies. The war that resulted was called the French and Indian War, because Native Americans and the French joined together to fight the British.

France and Britain both claimed land in what is now Pennsylvania, near the Ohio River. The French built a fort called Fort Duquesne near what is now Pittsburgh.

The British wanted to force the French out of Pennsylvania. In 1754 they sent a young soldier named George Washington to Fort Duquesne. Washington's men defeated a small force of French soldiers near the fort, but they did not capture the fort at that time. Britain finally captured the fort in 1758.

During the war, British troops captured Fort Miami and Fort Ouiatenon in what is now Indiana. The British also won many other battles against the French during the war.

The war ended when both sides signed the **Treaty of Paris of 1763**. A treaty is an agreement between two or more countries or groups of people. In this treaty, France gave up control of its land to Britain. Soon, Native Americans would fight for this land.

QUICK CHECK

Compare **How were the British and the French alike?**

A young George Washington at ▶ Fort Duquesne

After the French and Indian War, more British settlers moved to lands west of the Appalachian Mountains. Land in the west cost much less than land east of the Appalachians. Many Native Americans saw these new settlers as a threat to their way of life. The settlers often took over Native American hunting grounds and used the land to set up farms.

Native Americans Unite

Pontiac, an Ottawa chief, knew that there were many groups of Native Americans losing land to the British. These groups included the Ottawa, the Miami, and the Potawatomi. He asked these groups to:

drive off your land those . . . who will do you nothing but harm.

Pontiac's Rebellion

Pontiac's Rebellion began in 1763 to drive the British from lands west of the Appalachian Mountains. A rebellion is an armed fight against a government. Native Americans in the region were trying to protect their way of life from British western expansion. Pontiac and his men took over

Fort Miami, Fort Ouiatenon, and other forts. They captured and burned British settlements. Eight forts were destroyed, and hundreds of colonists were killed or captured.

One of the most well-known stories about the war took place when British officers gave Native Americans blankets that had been exposed to a deadly disease called smallpox. However, many historians now believe the smallpox outbreak among Native Americans was most likely caused by warriors returning from attacks on white settlements.

Still, ruthless and bloody attacks were waged on both sides. Pontiac asked for help from his French allies, but they never sent help. In the end, Pontiac was unable to drive the British from the region. However, the brutal nature of the war forced the British to look for a way to bring peace to the region.

PLACE

In 1717 the French built **Fort Ouiatenon** to protect the Ohio River valley from the British. Its location in the Wabash River Valley also made it an ideal center for the fur trade. At its peak, over 2,000 people lived in Fort Ouiatenon. Today, a reconstruction of the fort's blockhouse is open to tourists.

Fort Ouiatenon

This painting shows how settlers west of the Appalachians lived in the late 1700s.

The Proclamation of 1763

Great Britain realized that protecting the colonists from conflict with Native Americans would be costly. Britain issued the **Proclamation of 1763** to end the conflict. A proclamation is an official announcement to the public. The Proclamation of 1763 reserved lands west of the Appalachians for Native Americans. Colonists were furious at being closed off from western lands. Many were already living in Kentucky or had claimed land there. Also, colonists were beginning to dislike being told what to do by the British government. Some began to talk about independence.

QUICK CHECK

Contrast **How were the Treaty of Paris of 1763 and the Proclamation of 1763 different?**

Check Understanding

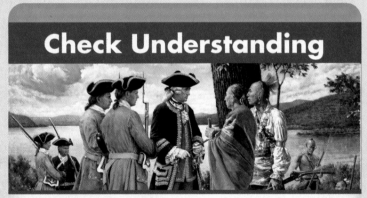

1. Write a paragraph about Pontiac's Rebellion using the terms below.

   Pontiac's Rebellion
   Proclamation of 1763

2. **READING SKILL Compare and Contrast** Use your chart from page 74 to write about the French and Indian War and Pontiac's Rebellion.

   Different Alike Different

3. **Write About It** Write about the importance of allies to a nation.

Lesson 7

VOCABULARY

treason p. 79

tax p. 79

frontier p. 82

constitution p. 85

amendment p. 85

Bill of Rights p. 85

READING SKILL

Compare and Contrast
Copy the chart below. As you read, use it to compare and contrast the British and Americans during the Revolutionary War.

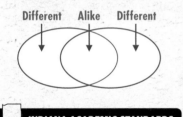

Different   Alike   Different

INDIANA ACADEMIC STANDARDS

4.1.3, 4.2.2, 4.2.5, 4.2.6, 4.3.8

Indiana and the Revolutionary War

The British surrender to George Rogers Clark at Fort Sackville

Visual Preview

Why did the colonists fight for independence from Great Britain?

A The colonists were angry over taxes and other forms of British control.

B The Continental Congress voted to become independent from Britain.

C British troops and Native Americans attacked American settlements in the West.

D France and Spain joined the Americans to defeat the British.

A THE CALL FOR INDEPENDENCE

*In 1776 colonists declared their independence from British rule. The leaders of the American Revolution took a great risk when they voted for independence. They could have been arrested for **treason**, or not being loyal to one's country.*

Great Britain had spent a large amount of money fighting the French and Indian War. The British government felt that it had spent much of this money to protect the colonists in North America. British leaders wanted the colonists to help repay some of this money.

New Taxes Anger the Colonists

To raise money, the British put **taxes** on some goods colonists bought. A tax is money that people must pay to their government.

These taxes angered the colonists. They told the British, "No taxation without representation!" These words meant that the colonists would pay taxes only if they could be part of the government of Britain and help make decisions.

The Boston Tea Party

When the British passed a tax on tea, the colonists decided to protest against this tax. One night, a group of men snuck on board three British ships in Boston Harbor and dumped a load of expensive tea overboard.

The colonists were also still angry over the Proclamation of 1763. It said that colonists could not move to lands west of the Appalachian Mountains. The colonists' anger over the new taxes and the Proclamation of 1763 helped lead to the American Revolution.

QUICK CHECK

Contrast Why did the colonists and the British disagree over taxes?

▲ Colonists disguised as Native Americans dumped British tea into Boston Harbor.

B THE BREAK WITH BRITAIN

Primary Source

What would they have? Is life so dear, or peace so sweet, as to be purchased at the price of chains and slavery? Forbid it, Almighty God! I know not what course others may take; but as for me, give me liberty or give me death!

Excerpt from "Give me liberty or give me death" speech —by Patrick Henry, March 1775

Write About It Suppose you were a colonist in 1775. Write a journal entry explaining why freedom is important.

In 1774 leaders of the colonies gathered in Philadelphia, Pennsylvania. This meeting was known as the Continental Congress. The congress talked about how it should deal with the colonies' problems with Great Britain.

More and more people began to speak out against British rule. Read on this page the words of Patrick Henry, a speaker and statesman from Virginia who supported individual freedom and states' rights in the early years of United States history.

The Declaration of Independence

By 1776 the Continental Congress had agreed that the colonies should become independent from British rule. Thomas Jefferson led a group of men who wrote a document explaining the decision. This document is known as the Declaration of Independence. It begins: "We hold these truths to be self-evident, that all men are created equal." Women did not hold the same rights as men at this time.

▼ The signing of the Declaration of Independence

The War Begins

The British army was one of the best in the world. Its soldiers were well trained. They had more weapons and money than the colonists. Most colonists in the American army were farmers, not soldiers. However, they fought hard to defend their homes and win freedom from British rule.

The war went on for six years. At first, the British won many battles. At times it seemed that the colonists' revolution would fail. One important turning point for the colonists was the Battle of Saratoga in New York. Their victory proved to France that the Americans could defeat the British. Early in 1778, France joined the war against Britain. They sent soldiers, ships, and money to help the colonists.

QUICK CHECK

Contrast **How were the British and American armies different?**

THE REVOLUTION IN THE WEST

Most of the battles of the American Revolution took place in the 13 colonies. However, some were fought west of the Appalachian Mountains. One important battle occurred in the area that is now Indiana.

Henry Hamilton

Henry Hamilton led the British army in the west. He knew that Native Americans could help him defeat the Americans.

Hamilton gave the Miami, Potawatomi, and other Native American groups food and weapons. He told them that the Americans would steal their land.

In 1777 Native Americans raided American settlements in the west. People called this the "bloody year" because many Americans and Native Americans died.

George Rogers Clark

George Rogers Clark was a young man living on the frontier in Virginia. A **frontier** is the land at the edge of a settled area.

Clark wanted to stop the Native Americans and the British from attacking Americans. He gathered about 175 men to serve in his army.

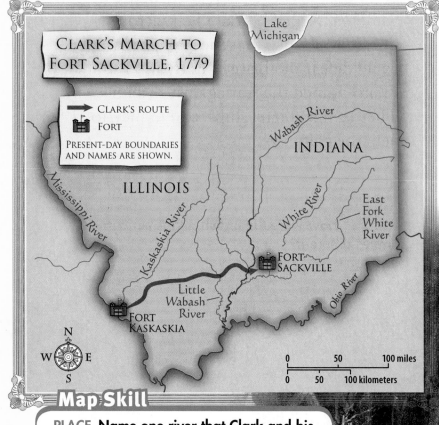

CLARK'S MARCH TO FORT SACKVILLE, 1779

→ CLARK'S ROUTE

🏰 FORT

PRESENT-DAY BOUNDARIES AND NAMES ARE SHOWN.

Lake Michigan

Mississippi River

ILLINOIS

Kaskaskia River

Wabash River

INDIANA

White River

East Fork White River

FORT SACKVILLE

Little Wabash River

FORT KASKASKIA

Ohio River

N W E S

0   50   100 miles
0   50   100 kilometers

Map Skill

PLACE **Name one river that Clark and his troops crossed to reach Fort Sackville.**

Clark knew that the British still had troops in Vincennes at a fort called Fort Sackville. Henry Hamilton was in charge of the fort. Clark thought he could capture the fort in a surprise attack.

In the winter of 1779, Clark and his men set off from an American fort at Kaskaskia in what is today the state of Illinois. They headed east toward Fort Sackville.

A Long March

The journey toward Fort Sackville took 18 days and was difficult. The snow had melted and flooded the land. Cold rain fell, and there was little to eat. The men marched through water that was often up to their waists, and they slept on bare ground. They were very tired, and many were sick. But George Rogers Clark was a great leader. He kept the men's spirits up by telling stories. Look at the map on page 82 to locate the route that Clark and his men took to Fort Sackville.

Reaching Fort Sackville

When Clark reached the fort at Vincennes, he and his men crept to the top of a hill near the fort. The small army of men marched back and forth waving all of their flags. The British at the fort saw the flags and thought they were being attacked by a much larger American army.

Henry Hamilton and his soldiers were caught by surprise. Hamilton had thought that no army would attack during the cold winter.

Clark's men fired on the fort at night. Their aim was so good that the British were afraid to stand up and return fire. Henry Hamilton and his army soon surrendered. Clark and his men had taken Fort Sackville.

QUICK CHECK

Contrast **How were the French and Indian War and the Revolutionary War in the west different?**

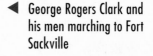

◄ George Rogers Clark and his men marching to Fort Sackville

In 1779 Spain joined the war on the American side. Spain had gained control of the territory west of the Mississippi River after the French and Indian War. A territory is an area of land that is controlled by a nation. Spain opened up the port of New Orleans to American ships and stopped trading with Britain. Spain also sent money to the Americans.

The Battle of Yorktown

In 1781 General Charles Cornwallis led 7,000 British soldiers to Yorktown, a village on a peninsula in Virginia. Cornwallis hoped his army could rest until supply ships reached his tired soldiers.

However, France sent its navy to block Chesapeake Bay and prevent British supply ships from reaching Cornwallis.

Cornwallis faced other problems in addition to the blockade. One of his servants, James Armistead, was a spy for the Americans. To confuse Cornwallis, Armistead told the general that the Americans planned to attack British headquarters in New York City. Cornwallis thought he was safe in Yorktown. Meanwhile, General George Washington and a large French army surrounded Cornwallis.

French and American troops battled the British army for three weeks at Yorktown. On October 19, 1781, the British surrendered, or gave up. The Americans had won the war.

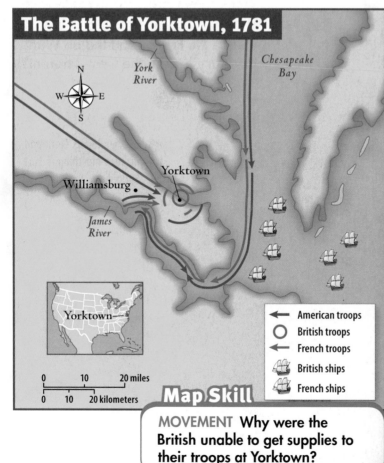

The Battle of Yorktown, 1781

York River
Chesapeake Bay
Yorktown
Williamsburg
James River

Yorktown

0   10   20 miles
0   10   20 kilometers

← American troops
○ British troops
← French troops
🚢 British ships
🚢 French ships

Map Skill

MOVEMENT Why were the British unable to get supplies to their troops at Yorktown?

▼ The British surrender at Yorktown

A New National Government

After the war, American leaders had to form a new national government. In 1787 they created the United States **Constitution**. A constitution is a plan of government. The U.S. Constitution was written so that it could be added to or changed as times change. For example, when the Constitution was written, women did not have the right to vote. That changed in 1920 when an **amendment**, or addition, was added that gave women the right to vote.

The first ten amendments to the Constitution are called the **Bill of Rights**. These laws promise basic rights to citizens such as freedom of speech.

PEOPLE

Known as the Father of Our Country, **George Washington** was a central figure in the founding of the United States. He led our nation to victory over the British in the Revolutionary War. He also served as president of the Second Continental Congress, which created our nation's constitution. In 1789 Washington was elected the first President of the United States. He served two four-year terms.

George Washington

QUICK CHECK

Compare **During the American Revolution, how were Spain and France alike?**

Check Understanding

1. Write a paragraph about the United States Constitution using the terms below.
   constitution   Bill of Rights amendment

2. **READING SKILL Compare and Contrast** Use your chart from page 78 to write about the Revolutionary War.

3. **Write About It** Write an essay about why countries fight for independence.

Vocabulary

Copy the sentences below. Use the list of vocabulary words to fill in the blanks.

artifact   colony

explore   missionary

1. An object that was made or used by people who lived in the past is called an _____.

2. A _____ is a person who teaches his or her religion to others who have different beliefs.

3. A place that is ruled by another country is called a _____.

4. To _____ is to travel to unfamiliar places in order to learn about them.

Comprehension and Critical Thinking

5. Why did France establish a colony in North America?

6. Why did Native American groups migrate to Indiana in the 1700s?

7. **Critical Thinking** Why did Spain and France help Americans during the Revolutionary War?

8. **Reading Skill** What did Columbus and La Salle both hope to find when they sailed to the Americas?

Skill

Use Elevation Maps

Write a complete sentence to answer each question.

9. Which region of Indiana has the highest elevation?

10. Why does the Tippecanoe River flow south?

Indiana: Elevation

Feet	Meters
1200	370
1000	310
800	250
600	190
400	120
0	0

☆ State capital
● Other city
△ Highest point
▽ Lowest point

Indiana Statewide Test Practice

Read the passage below. Then choose the best answer or write a short response to each of the following questions.

> René-Robert Cavelier, Sieur de La Salle traveled the world at a time when most people stayed close to home. At the age of 23, he left France for Canada, where he became a rich fur trader.
>
> La Salle was not satisfied with wealth. What he really wanted was to find a water route to Asia. In the 1670s, he set out to explore the Mississippi River. He faced many hardships along his journey. One of his ships sank, and a fort he had built was destroyed. None of this stopped La Salle. He kept going until he reached the end of the Mississippi River. La Salle did not find a passage to Asia. He did, however, claim all the land around the Mississippi River for France.

1 Why did La Salle explore the Mississippi River?

Ⓐ to become a rich fur trader

Ⓑ to claim land for France

Ⓒ to reach the end of the river

Ⓓ to try to find a passage to Asia

2 Which word best describes La Salle?

Ⓐ angry

Ⓑ lonely

Ⓒ strong

Ⓓ weak

3 What hardships did La Salle face while he explored the Mississippi River?

Write your answer on a separate piece of paper.

The Big Idea Activities

What happens when different peoples meet?

Write About the Big Idea

Expository Essay

Use the Unit 2 Foldable to help you write an expository essay that answers the Big Idea question, *What happens when different peoples meet?* Use the notes you wrote under each tab in the Foldable. Begin with an introduction that expresses the main idea of your essay. In the body of your essay, be sure to compare and contrast at least one event with another. End with a conclusion about what happens when different peoples meet.

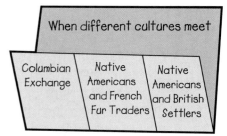

When different cultures meet

Columbian Exchange | Native Americans and French Fur Traders | Native Americans and British Settlers

Make a Diorama

Work with a partner to make a Native American diorama. Decide what your diorama will be. Examples include a Native American village, longhouse, trading post, or nature setting. Here's how to make your diorama.

1. Find a historical picture of your item to use as a model.

2. Use different materials, such as paper, paint, and markers, to make your diorama.

3. Your diorama can include things from nature like sand, rocks, and sticks.

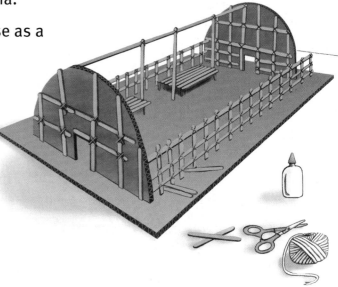

When you have finished your diorama, you and your partner should take turns presenting it to your class.

Creating a State

Unit 3

EXPLORE The Big Idea

Essential Question
Why do people take risks?

FOLDABLES Study Organizer

Cause and Effect
Make and label a Two-Tab Foldable Book before you read Unit 3. Across the top write **From Territory to State.** Label the two tabs **Cause** and **Effect**. Use the Foldable to organize information as you read.

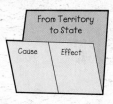

From Territory to State

Cause   Effect

LOG ON For more about the Unit 3, go to www.macmillanmh.com

Pioneers moved to the Indiana Territory in the early 1800s looking for more land and a different way of life.

89

PEOPLE, PLACES, AND EVENTS

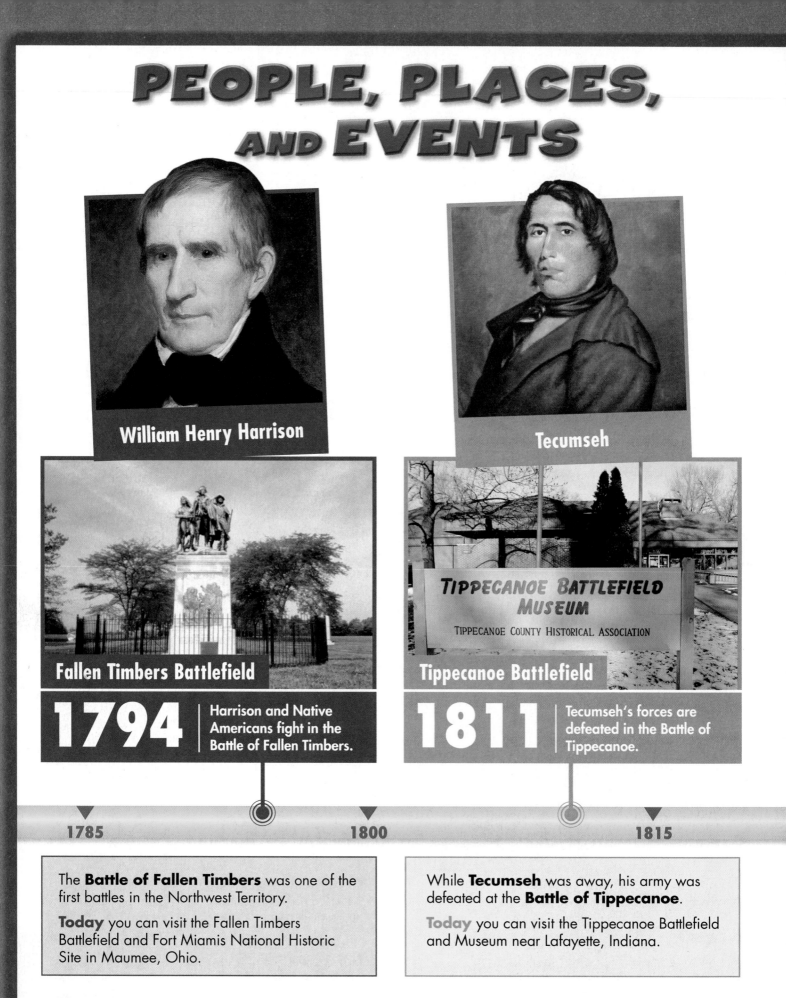

William Henry Harrison

Tecumseh

Fallen Timbers Battlefield

1794 Harrison and Native Americans fight in the Battle of Fallen Timbers.

TIPPECANOE BATTLEFIELD MUSEUM

TIPPECANOE COUNTY HISTORICAL ASSOCIATION

Tippecanoe Battlefield

1811 Tecumseh's forces are defeated in the Battle of Tippecanoe.

1785   1800   1815

The **Battle of Fallen Timbers** was one of the first battles in the Northwest Territory.

Today you can visit the Fallen Timbers Battlefield and Fort Miamis National Historic Site in Maumee, Ohio.

While **Tecumseh** was away, his army was defeated at the **Battle of Tippecanoe**.

Today you can visit the Tippecanoe Battlefield and Museum near Lafayette, Indiana.

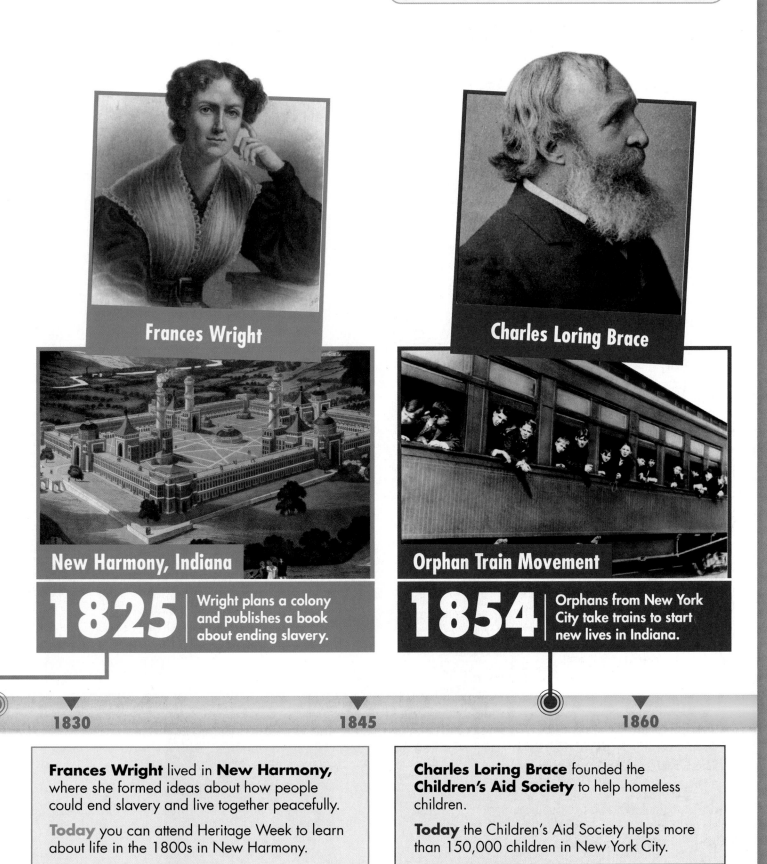

Frances Wright

New Harmony, Indiana

1825
Wright plans a colony and publishes a book about ending slavery.

Charles Loring Brace

Orphan Train Movement

1854
Orphans from New York City take trains to start new lives in Indiana.

1830   1845   1860

Frances Wright lived in **New Harmony,** where she formed ideas about how people could end slavery and live together peacefully.

Today you can attend Heritage Week to learn about life in the 1800s in New Harmony.

Charles Loring Brace founded the **Children's Aid Society** to help homeless children.

Today the Children's Aid Society helps more than 150,000 children in New York City.

Lesson 1

VOCABULARY

territory p. 93

pioneer p. 93

Battle of Fallen Timbers p. 94

Treaty of Greenville p. 94

READING SKILL

Cause and Effect
Copy the chart below. As you read, fill it in with causes and effects of establishing the Northwest Territory.

Cause	→	Effect
	→	
	→	
	→	

INDIANA ACADEMIC STANDARDS

4.1.3, 4.1.4, 4.1.15

THE NORTHWEST TERRITORY

Pioneers and Native Americans clash over land rights in the Northwest Territory.

Visual Preview

How did people adapt to the Northwest Territory?

A The Northwest Territory added land to the United States.

B Native Americans were forced to share land with the United States.

Ⓐ THE NORTHWEST TERRITORY

In 1783, Great Britain surrendered much of its land in North America to the United States. American settlers moved into this land. This angered Native Americans because they did not want settlers living on their land.

In 1787 the United States established a new **territory** in the West. A territory is land that is owned by a country but is not a state of that country. This new area was called the Northwest Territory. Today it includes Illinois, Indiana, Michigan, Ohio, eastern Minnesota, and Wisconsin. The country's borders now reached as far west as the Mississippi River.

Pioneers from the colonies began to move west into this new land. Pioneers are the first group of people to settle in a new region. The pioneers built homes along the Wabash and Ohio Rivers.

Native Americans were angry that the pioneers were taking their land. They began to attack American settlers to protect their lands. The pioneers and the United States Army joined together to fight Native Americans.

Many battles were fought before the two sides found a solution.

QUICK CHECK

Cause and Effect Why did Native Americans attack pioneers in the Northwest Territory?

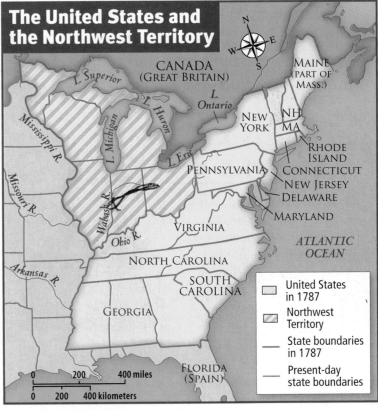

The United States and the Northwest Territory

CANADA (GREAT BRITAIN)
MAINE (PART OF MASS.)
L. Superior
L. Huron
L. Ontario
L. Michigan
L. Erie
NEW YORK
NH
MA
RHODE ISLAND
CONNECTICUT
NEW JERSEY
DELAWARE
MARYLAND
PENNSYLVANIA
Mississippi R.
Missouri R.
Wabash R.
Ohio R.
VIRGINIA
Arkansas R.
NORTH CAROLINA
SOUTH CAROLINA
GEORGIA
ATLANTIC OCEAN
FLORIDA (SPAIN)

0   200   400 miles
0   200   400 kilometers

United States in 1787
Northwest Territory
State boundaries in 1787
Present-day state boundaries

Map Skill

PLACE What body of water formed the western boundary of the Northwest Territory?

THE BATTLE OF FALLEN TIMBERS

One of the Native American groups that fought against the pioneers was the Miami. Little Turtle, a Miami chief, led a group of the Shawnee, the Delaware, and the Wyandotte against American soldiers.

In 1791, the United States Army attacked the Miami village of Kekionga. Little Turtle and more than 1,000 Native Americans defeated the American soldiers in the fight. Today the city of Fort Wayne is located where Kekionga once stood.

Anthony Wayne

American general Anthony Wayne, who had became a leader during the Revolutionary War, led part of the United States Army against the Native Americans. He built forts and trained the American army in western Ohio.

▲ Chief Little Turtle

His men called him "Mad Anthony" because he was not afraid to take risks. Little Turtle heard about General Wayne's strong leadership. He called Anthony Wayne "the chief who never sleeps."

In 1794, General Wayne's army fought the Miami without the leadership of Little Turtle. The **Battle of Fallen Timbers** took place along the Maumee River in Ohio at a spot where a tornado had knocked down many trees. General Wayne's army had many more soldiers than the Native Americans. Because of this, General Wayne's troops defeated the Native Americans in about an hour.

The Treaty of Greenville

The Battle of Fallen Timbers led Little Turtle and other Native American leaders to sign the **Treaty of Greenville** on August 3, 1795. The treaty required the Native Americans to agree to give up land in the eastern part of the Northwest Territory.

In return, the United States promised to let Native Americans live in the western part of the territory. They also agreed to pay the Native Americans for the land they were giving up.

PEOPLE

Chief Richardville was born in 1761 in Kekionga, Indiana, to a French father and a Native American mother. He was a chief of the Miami group. He signed the Treaty of Mississiniwas, which gave land that belonged to the Miami group in Indiana to the United States government. Unlike other members of the Miami group, Richardville did not have to leave Indiana. Instead, the U.S. government built him small estates and gave him livestock.

Chief Jean Baptiste Richardville

Many Native American leaders refused to sign the treaty. They had hoped to keep all of their lands. However, American settlers felt the Northwest Territory was safer after the treated was signed.

The Treaty of Greenville was important because it established a firm boundary between land belonging to Native Americans and the United States. The new land in the Northwest Territory was opened to American settlers.

QUICK CHECK

Cause and Effect **What did Native Americans agree to do as a result of the Treaty of Greenville?**

Native Americans were defeated by the United States Army at the Battle of Fallen Timbers.

Check Understanding

1. **VOCABULARY** Write a paragraph about the Northwest Territory using the terms below.

   pioneer

   Battle at Fallen Timbers

   Treaty of Greenville

2. **READING SKILL Cause and Effect** Use your chart from page 92 to write about the Northwest Territory.

Cause	→	Effect
	→	
	→	
	→	

3. **EXPLORE The Big Idea** **Write About It** Write about how the Treaty of Greenville affected Native Americans and American settlers.

Read Time Lines

VOCABULARY

chronology

time line

To understand history, you need to know when things happened. You also need to understand the **chronology**, or the order in which things happened. Sometimes it is not easy to remember what happened first, next, and last. A **time line** can help you organize historical events. A time line is a diagram that shows the chronology of events in history. It also shows the amount of time that passed between events. This helps give a sense of order to history.

Early Indiana History

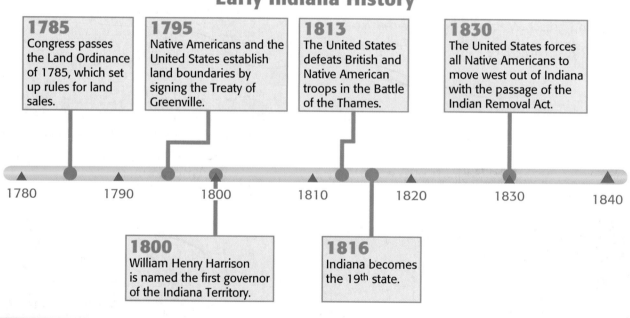

1785
Congress passes the Land Ordinance of 1785, which set up rules for land sales.

1795
Native Americans and the United States establish land boundaries by signing the Treaty of Greenville.

1813
The United States defeats British and Native American troops in the Battle of the Thames.

1830
The United States forces all Native Americans to move west out of Indiana with the passage of the Indian Removal Act.

1780   1790   1800   1810   1820   1830   1840

1800
William Henry Harrison is named the first governor of the Indiana Territory.

1816
Indiana becomes the 19th state.

Learn It

- Time lines are divided into parts. Each part represents a certain number of years. The time line on page 96 is divided into parts 10 years long. It tells of the events of Indiana's early history.

- Read the captions from left to right. You can see that the earliest event happened to the left and the latest event happened on the right.

Try It

Look at the time line on page 96 to answer the questions.

- Which event happened first, Indiana's statehood or the Battle of the Thames?

- Describe the significance of the events in Indiana between 1800 and 1816.

- Who was named as the first governor of the Indiana Territory in 1800?

Apply It

Use the time line on page 96 as a guide to create your own time line.

- Make a time line of your life. Talk with family members to find an important event for each year of your life. Draw a picture or place a photograph for each event.

- Make a time line of your day. Add events from both home and school. Make sure the time intervals are the same throughout the time line.

- Make a time line of your community's history. Include events such as when it was founded, its first mayor, and any other important events that have shaped your community.

Native Americans and American soldiers sign the Treaty of Greenville in 1795.

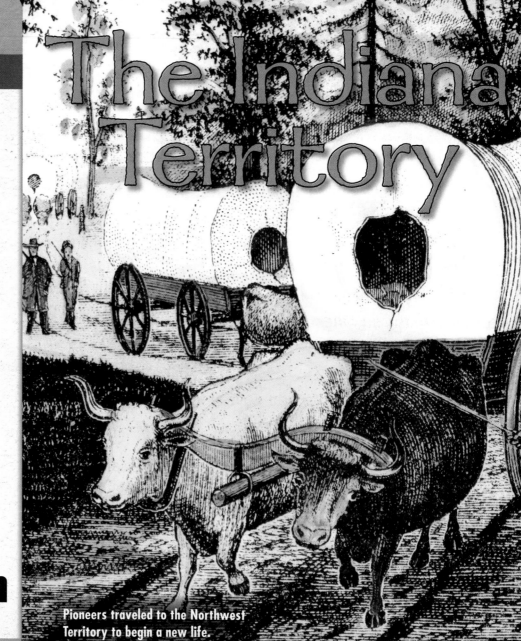

Lesson 2

The Indiana Territory

VOCABULARY

Land Ordinance of 1785 p. 99

Northwest Ordinance p. 99

slavery p. 99

population p. 103

census p. 103

READING SKILL

Cause and Effect

Copy the chart below. As you read, fill it in with the causes and effects of the ordinances of 1785 and 1787.

Cause	→	Effect
	→	
	→	
	→	

INDIANA ACADEMIC STANDARDS

4.1.3, 4.1.4, 4.2.6, 4.3.11

Pioneers traveled to the Northwest Territory to begin a new life.

Visual Preview

How did the lives of American settlers change in the Northwest Territory?

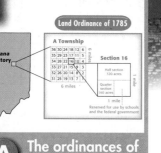

A The ordinances of 1785 and 1787 set up rules for the Northwest Territory.

B The Indiana Territory was created in the early 1800s.

C The population of the Indiana Territory grew quickly in the early 1800s.

DIVIDING THE NORTHWEST TERRITORY

A

When the Northwest Territory was formed in 1787, it was a large area of land. Over the years, the federal government broke up the territory into smaller pieces. The governor of the Indiana Territory signed treaties to gain more land occupied by Native Americans.

When a group of Native Americans signed the Treaty of Greenville in 1795, they gave up part of their land in the Northwest Territory. Pioneers began to settle in areas north of the Ohio River.

To divide the land in the territory, the government of the United States passed the **Land Ordinance of 1785**. This law set up rules for land sales. Land was divided into townships. Each township was separated into 36 one-mile squares, or sections. Each township set aside one section for a public school. The other 35 sections were to be sold to settlers.

The **Northwest Ordinance,** passed in 1787, set rules for governing the Northwest Territory.

It described the rights of settlers living in the area. It also made **slavery** illegal. Slavery is the practice of treating people as property and forcing them to work. Any part of the Northwest Territory that wanted to apply for statehood could not allow slavery.

QUICK CHECK

Cause and Effect How did the Treaty of Greenville affect the growth of the United States?

Land Ordinance of 1785

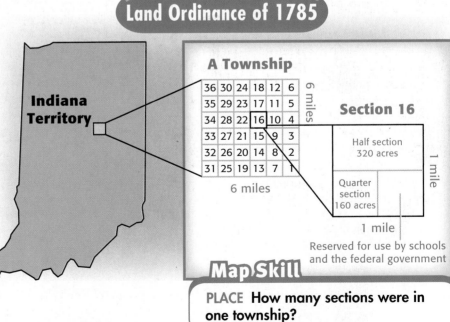

A Township

36	30	24	18	12	6
35	29	23	17	11	5
34	28	22	16	10	4
33	27	21	15	9	3
32	26	20	14	8	2
31	25	19	13	7	1

6 miles

6 miles

Indiana Territory

Section 16

Half section 320 acres

Quarter section 160 acres

1 mile

1 mile

Reserved for use by schools and the federal government

Map Skill

PLACE **How many sections were in one township?**

The Northwest Ordinance established the power of the United States government in the Northwest Territory. In 1800 the government divided the land into two parts. The eastern part became the Ohio Territory. The western part became the Indiana Territory.

The Indiana Territory stretched from the Ohio border in the east to the Mississippi River in the west. The northern edge of the territory reached all the way to Canada. The southern border of the territory was the Ohio River.

William Henry Harrison

The new Indiana Territory needed a leader. In 1800, President John Adams named William Henry Harrison as the territory's first governor.

▲ William Henry Harrison

The first log cabin in Indianapolis was built in 1820.

Harrison had proven himself as a leader when he fought in the Battle of Fallen Timbers. The first capital of the Indiana Territory was Vincennes. While he was governor, Harrison lived in Vincennes.

A Changing Territory

Harrison served as governor of the Indiana Territory from 1800 to 1812. The size of the territory changed twice during his time in office.

In 1805 a large section of the northern part of the territory was split off to create the Michigan Territory. Four years later, another large piece in the western section was split off. It became the Illinois Territory. This was the last time that the borders of Indiana changed.

QUICK CHECK

Cause and Effect How did the Indiana Territory change while Harrison was governor?

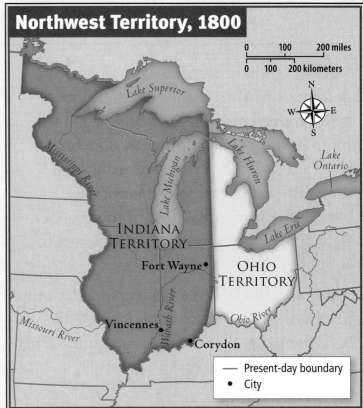

Northwest Territory, 1800

0 100 200 miles
0 100 200 kilometers

Lake Superior

Mississippi River

Lake Michigan

Lake Huron

Lake Erie

Lake Ontario

INDIANA TERRITORY

Fort Wayne •

OHIO TERRITORY

Missouri River

Vincennes •

Wabash River

• Corydon

Ohio River

—— Present-day boundary
• City

Divisions of the Northwest Territory, 1809

0 100 200 miles
0 100 200 kilometers

Lake Superior

Mississippi River

Lake Michigan

Lake Huron

Lake Erie

Lake Ontario

ILLINOIS TERRITORY

MICHIGAN TERRITORY

Fort Wayne •

OHIO

INDIANA TERRITORY

Wabash River

Missouri River

Vincennes •

• Corydon

Ohio River

—— Present-day boundary
• City

Map Skill

LOCATION How did the boundaries of the Indiana Territory change from 1800 to 1809?

THE TERRITORY GROWS

As the Indiana borders were formed, people from Virginia, Ohio, and other states moved into the area and began to build permanent settlements. The fear of attacks from Native Americans kept pioneers from exploring the northern part of the territory. Most of the pioneers built their homes in the southern part of Indiana.

Some of the land the pioneers wanted still belonged to the Native Americans. This soon led to conflict between the settlers and the Native Americans.

Bargaining for Land

In order to get the land for the settlers, Governor Harrison signed treaties with several Native American groups. Harrison promised the Native Americans money and goods in exchange for the land. He also used the threat of war to persuade Native American leaders to make deals.

Settlers who could speak the Native American languages helped make the treaties. One American who helped Harrison was William Conner. Conner knew the Native American languages because he used them during fur trades. His work with the Native Americans formed treaties that gave the pioneers the land they wanted. These treaties created the modern-day boundaries of Indiana.

The Population Grows

Harrison's treaties opened the southern part of Indiana and most of Illinois to American settlers. Harrison encouraged people to move into the area. The increase in the number of settlers meant that more land was needed for them. Native Americans were forced to give up millions of acres of land and had to find new places to live.

As the Native Americans were being forced to move, a group of diverse settlers moved into the territory. Many were of European descent. Some came from neighboring states in search of land. Others immigrated directly from Europe.

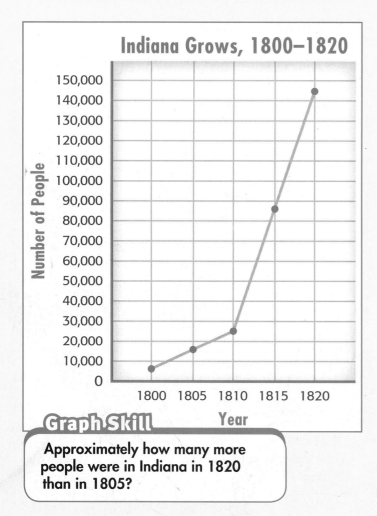

Indiana Grows, 1800–1820

Graph Skill

Approximately how many more people were in Indiana in 1820 than in 1805?

African American pioneers also came to the Indiana Territory. Most were farmers from Virginia and North Carolina. The African American **population** was 115 in 1800. Population is the number of people living in an area. By 1820, almost 1,500 African Americans lived in Indiana.

The Indiana Territory was growing quickly. A **census** taken in 1800 showed that the Indiana territory had 5,641 settlers. A census is a count of the people who live in a place. A census in 1815 showed a population of almost 64,000 people in the territory. In only 15 years, Indiana's population had grown to nearly 12 times what it had been.

QUICK CHECK

Cause and Effect **How did Indiana's new borders affect Native Americans?**

▼ At the Lincoln Pioneer Village in Rockport, Indiana, people can visit replicas of log cabins from the 1800s.

Check Understanding

1. **VOCABULARY** Write a paragraph about the Indiana Territory using the terms below.
   Land Ordinance of 1785
   Northwest Ordinance
   population

2. **READING SKILL Cause and Effect** Use your chart from page 98 to write about the Indiana Territory.

Cause	→	Effect
	→	
	→	
	→	

3. **Write About It** Write a paragraph about how the growth of the Indiana Territory affected Native Americans.

EXPLORE The Big Idea

VOCABULARY

Battle of Tippecanoe
p. 106

War of 1812 p. 107

Battle of the Thames
p. 107

Indian Removal Act
p. 109

READING SKILL

Cause and Effect
Copy the chart below. As you read, fill it in with the causes and effects of the Battle of Tippecanoe.

Cause	→	Effect
	→	
	→	
	→	

INDIANA ACADEMIC STANDARDS

4.1.3, 4.1.5, 4.3.10, 4.3.11

NATIVE AMERICANS FIGHT FOR LAND

Some Native Americans signed treaties to give up land, but others refused to do so.

Visual Preview

How did Native Americans try to hold on to land in Indiana?

A Tecumseh was a Native American leader.

B Native Americans lost the Battle of Tippecanoe.

C Native Americans were forced to leave Indiana.

104

TECUMSEH AND THE PROPHET

Native American leaders Tecumseh and Tenskwatawa did not sign the treaties that gave their land to American settlers. Tecumseh told Governor Harrison, "[Y]ou have taken our lands from us and I do not see how we can remain at peace with you if you continue to do so."

Many Native Americans were not in favor of the treaties that caused them to give up their lands. One such Native American was a Shawnee leader named Tecumseh. Tecumseh wanted Native Americans to stop selling their lands. He believed if different Native American groups joined together, they could stand up to the pioneers.

Tenskwatawa, Tecumseh's brother, became a religious leader for many Native Americans. They believed that Tenskwatawa could predict the future. They called him "the Prophet."

Tecumseh and Tenskwatawa's followers eventually began to gather at Prophetstown, a village on the Tippecanoe River. This worried many of the American settlers. They were afraid the Native Americans would attack them. They asked for protection from the United States government.

In 1810, Governor Harrison agreed to meet with Tecumseh at Vincennes. Tecumseh told Harrison that the

▲ Shawnee leader Tecumseh

treaties were not fair, and that the Native American leaders who had agreed to give the land away did not have the support of all the people. The two men could not come to an agreement on how to split the land fairly. The Vincennes meeting had failed.

QUICK CHECK

Cause and Effect What caused Tecumseh to meet with Governor Harrison in Vincennes?

BATTLE OF TIPPECANOE

B

After the failed meeting in Vincennes, Tecumseh and the Prophet gained more support for their cause from their people. At the same time, Harrison gathered a force of 1,000 troops and led them to a camp near Prophetstown. The governor knew that Tecumseh was away at the time. He believed the Native Americans would be weaker without their leader.

However, before they could attack, Harrison's forces were surprised by the Prophet and his forces. On November 7, 1811, the **Battle of Tippecanoe** began

when Tenskwatawa's warriors attacked Harrison's camp.

The battle did not go well for the Native Americans. The warriors believed that the Prophet's magic would protect them from enemy bullets. They were wrong. Many Native Americans died in the battle. After two hours, they had to abandon Prophetstown.

The battle was a great victory for Harrison. However, the victory came at a price. Nearly 20 percent of his men died or were wounded.

Battle of Tippecanoe, 1811

Map Skill

LOCATION **What fort or encampment is closest to Tippecanoe Battlefield?**

The War of 1812

After the defeat at Tippecanoe, Tecumseh was no longer able to unite the Native Americans. At the same time, the Americans and the British were fighting over control of the land and waterways in what is now Canada. The British navy attacked American ships at sea and kidnapped sailors from these ships. The Americans were angry and tried to stop trading with the British, but this only hurt the shipping industry in New England.

Eventually, the United States declared war on Britain, and the **War of 1812** began. While the United States lost many of the key battles, they had some success in the Northwest Territory.

Battle of the Thames

In 1813, Governor Harrison led the United States against Tecumseh and the British at the **Battle of the Thames**.

Harrison took his forces along the Thames River in Canada. Tecumseh tried to lead the British troops in battle. However, they were tired from other battles they had lost. When Tecumseh was killed on the battlefield, the Native Americans gave up their fight. The Americans won the battle easily.

QUICK CHECK

Cause and Effect What was the effect of the Battle of Tippecanoe on Native Americans?

Despite launching a surprise attack on American troops, Native Americans lost the Battle of Tippecanoe.

The Indian Removal Act forced thousands of Native Americans from their homes.

ⓒ THE INDIAN REMOVAL ACT

Harrison's victory in the Battle of the Thames made it easier for the United States to control the land in the Northwest Territory. The Native Americans had lost their leader. They were no longer united. They stopped fighting for their land.

In 1818 the Delaware and other Native American groups agreed to leave central Indiana. Other groups hoped they could remain in the state and live peacefully with the settlers.

Native American Communities

Native Americans across the country were experiencing similar struggles over land. Despite hard times, some Native American communities were doing well in the early 1800s. These groups were located in the Southeast and included the Cherokee, Choctaw, and Seminole groups. They had signed treaties with the federal government that gave them control of their lands and protection from new settlers.

The Native Americans developed schools and their own local governments. One of the achievements of this period was the development of the first written Native American alphabet. It was created by Sequoyah, a member of the Cherokee group. The alphabet used a system of Greek, Hebrew, and English symbols. Within months, thousands of Native Americans learned to read and write in their own language.

Forced to Leave

In 1830 the government of the United States passed the **Indian Removal Act**. This law allowed the President to remove Native Americans in all parts of the country from their homeland. Native Americans were forced to sign agreements with the federal government. In return for land they lost, the Native Americans were given land in what is now Oklahoma.

Some Native American groups tried to fight the Indian Removal Act. The Cherokee group said the law was unfair and argued to the Supreme Court. The Supreme Court agreed that the Native Americans had some rights to the land, but the President did not enforce the ruling.

Native Americans were forced to move to lands west of the Mississippi River. American soldier John G. Burnett said of the removal:

"[When] the bugle sounded and the wagons started rolling many of the children rose to their feet and waved their little hands good-by to their mountain homes, knowing they were leaving them forever."

Within ten years, most Native Americans had left Indiana.

QUICK CHECK

Cause and Effect How did the Indian Removal Act affect Native Americans in Indiana?

Indian Removal from Indiana to Kansas, 1838

NEBRASKA · IOWA · ILLINOIS · Twin Lakes · Lafayette · Quincy · Danville · Williamsport · Decatur · INDIANA · Huntsville · Independence · Missouri River · St. Louis · Osawatomie · KANSAS · MISSOURI · Ohio River · Mississippi River

0 100 200 miles
0 100 200 kilometers

Map Skill

PLACE Through which states did the Native Americans who left Indiana travel?

Check Understanding

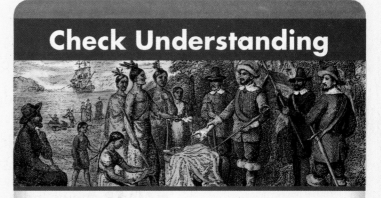

1. **VOCABULARY** Write one sentence for each of the vocabulary terms below.
   Battle of Tippecanoe   War of 1812
   Battle of the Thames

2. **READING SKILL Cause and Effect** Use your chart from page 104 to write about the Battle of Tippecanoe.

Cause	→	Effect
	→	
	→	
	→	

3. **Write About It** Write a paragraph about the risks associated with the Indian Removal Act.

Map and Globe Skills

Compare Maps at Different Scales

VOCABULARY

map scale

large-scale map

small-scale map

Maps cannot show places in the size they are in real life. All maps are drawn to scale. A **map scale** tells you the actual size of an area on the map. A map scale uses a unit of measurement to show a real distance. Sometimes one inch on a map represents 50 feet in real life. Other times, one inch on a map can represent 500 miles.

A **large-scale map** shows many details of a smaller area. A road map of Washington, D.C., is an example of a large-scale map. A **small-scale map** covers a large area, but it can't include many details. A world map is an example of a small-scale map.

Learn It

Look at the maps on page 111.

- Map A shows Corydon, Indiana, in the 1800s. This is a large-scale map. It shows a small area of the state with a lot of specific detail. You can see where the roads and buildings of the town were located.

- Map B shows Indiana in 1816, the year it became a state. This is a small-scale map. It shows a large area without any specific detail. You can see where each county was, and you can measure the size of each county.

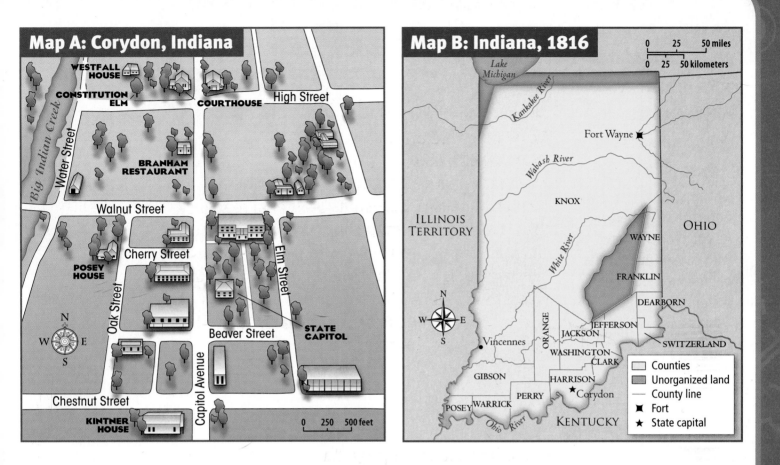

Map A: Corydon, Indiana

WESTFALL HOUSE
CONSTITUTION ELM
COURTHOUSE
High Street
Water Street
Big Indian Creek
BRANHAM RESTAURANT
Walnut Street
Cherry Street
POSEY HOUSE
Oak Street
Elm Street
Beaver Street
STATE CAPITOL
Capitol Avenue
Chestnut Street
KINTNER HOUSE

N W E S

0 250 500 feet

Map B: Indiana, 1816

0 25 50 miles
0 25 50 kilometers

Lake Michigan
Kankakee River
Fort Wayne
Wabash River
KNOX
ILLINOIS TERRITORY
OHIO
WAYNE
White River
FRANKLIN
DEARBORN
N W E S
ORANGE
JACKSON
JEFFERSON
Vincennes
SWITZERLAND
WASHINGTON
CLARK
GIBSON
HARRISON
Corydon
PERRY
POSEY WARRICK
Ohio River
KENTUCKY

Counties
Unorganized land
— County line
✖ Fort
★ State capital

Try It

- Compare the map scale for Map A to the map scale for Map B. Which map scale represents a small distance? Which map scale represents a large distance?

- What county is Corydon in? How did you know which map to use to find the answer?

- Using the scale on Map A, what is the distance from the State Capitol to the Courthouse?

Apply It

- Suppose your family is taking a vacation. Which type of map would you use to drive from Indianapolis to Washington, D.C.?

- Draw a large-scale map of your neighborhood. Then draw a small-scale map of Indiana, and indicate where your city or town is in the state. Which map would be more useful to a new student at your school?

Statehood

Lesson 4

VOCABULARY

resident p. 113

delegate p. 113

READING SKILL

Cause and Effect
Copy the chart below. As you read, fill it in with causes and effects of Indiana's journey to statehood.

Cause	→	Effect
	→	
	→	
	→	

INDIANA ACADEMIC STANDARDS

4.1.4, 4.1.6, 4.2.2, 4.2.6

Visual Preview

What risks did Indiana take when it became a state?

Citizens of Indiana gather at the capitol building in Corydon in 1816.

A Residents of Indiana wrote the first state constitution.

B Indiana became the nineteenth state in 1816.

112

A APPLYING FOR STATEHOOD

"All power is inherent in [belongs to] the people." In 1816 the leaders of the Indiana Territory included these words in the first constitution for the state of Indiana.

When the population of a territory reached 60,000, the people in a territory could apply for statehood. By 1815, the Indiana Territory had enough **residents** to apply for statehood. A resident is a person who lives in a specific place.

A territory also had to have a constitution to become a state. The people of Indiana chose 43 **delegates** to write their constitution. A delegate is a person who is chosen to speak for a group.

The delegates gathered at Corydon, the territory's new capital, on June 10, 1816. They met in the Harrison County Courthouse. They elected Jonathan Jennings as president of the meeting. Jennings had represented the Indiana Territory in the government of the United States since 1809.

Indiana's constitution was based on the United States Constitution. It had three parts. The General Assembly made the laws. The state governor made sure the laws were followed. And the state supreme court decided if the laws passed were fair.

▲ Jonathan Jennings

Jennings helped write a constitution that gave control of the government to the people. They now chose their leaders by voting. The constitution protected freedom of speech, religion, and the press. It also called for free public education from elementary school through college.

QUICK CHECK

Cause and Effect **What caused the delegates to write a constitution for Indiana?**

INDIANA BECOMES A STATE

Citizenship

Being a Leader

A few years ago, students from Spencer, Indiana, noticed that the copper dome of the Owen County courthouse was falling apart. They collected jars of pennies, held bake sales, and sold aluminum cans to recycling centers to raise money to save the dome. They told the city council that saving the dome was important to the history of the area. The council members voted to repair the dome. The students who led the fund-raising project were invited to speak at a ceremony at the courthouse.

Write About It Write about a way a group could bring change in your community.

One issue that had divided the delegates was slavery. The Northwest Ordinance had made slavery illegal in the Northwest Territory. However, some people still brought enslaved workers into Indiana.

Some of the delegates wanted to allow each county to decide whether slavery would be legal. Other delegates, including Jonathan Jennings, did not want to allow slavery at all. After many debates, the constitution stated that slavery was not allowed in Indiana.

Another issue facing the delegates was that of voting rights. At the time, only white men who owned property in Indiana were allowed to vote. Indiana's constitution stated that any white man who lived within Indiana's borders was allowed to vote. However, women, African Americans, and Native Americans were not allowed to vote.

Becoming a State

After almost three weeks of work, the delegates completed their plan of government on June 29, 1816. The delegates sent the document to Washington, D.C., for the nation's leaders to approve it.

On December 11, 1816, President James Madison signed a law that made Indiana a state. It was the nineteenth state to join the nation. Indiana voters elected Jonathan Jennings as the first state governor.

EVENT

In 1917 the Indiana General Assembly adopted the state flag. The flag was designed by Paul Hadley of Mooresville, Indiana. The blue field has nineteen stars and a flaming torch. The torch stands for liberty and enlightenment. The thirteen stars of the outer circle represent the thirteen original colonies. The five stars of the inner circle represent the additional states admitted to the nation before Indiana. The large star above the torch represents Indiana.

The Indiana State Flag

Moving the State Capital

Corydon had been the capital of Indiana since 1813. It was in the southeastern part of the territory. In 1820 the state government chose a group to find a new location for the capital.

Leaders thought that the new capital should be centrally located. They picked a spot and named it Indianapolis, which means "the city of Indiana." It took more than a week to move state documents and offices over the rough roads from Corydon to Indianapolis.

Indianapolis became the new state capital on December 10, 1825. The government worked in the Marion County Courthouse until the capitol was completed in 1831.

QUICK CHECK

Cause and Effect **How did Jonathan Jennings help Indiana achieve statehood?**

Check Understanding

1. **VOCABULARY** Write a sentence about how Indiana's state constitution was written using following vocabulary words. **resident** **delegate**

2. **READING SKILL Cause and Effect** Use your chart from page 112 to write about how Indiana became a state.

Cause	→	Effect
	→	
	→	
	→	

3. **Write About It** Write a paragraph about the obstacles Indiana overcame to become a state.

PIONEER LIVING

VOCABULARY

ferry p. 117

lean-to p. 118

log cabin p. 118

READING SKILL

Cause and Effect
Copy the chart below. As you read, fill it in with the causes and effects of pioneer life.

Cause	→	Effect
	→	
	→	
	→	

INDIANA ACADEMIC STANDARDS

4.1.4, 4.3.10

Some pioneers traveled to Indiana on flatboats.

Visual Preview

What risks did the pioneers of Indiana take?

A Pioneers traveled to Indiana in search of land and a better life.

B Pioneers learned to adjust to their environment as they built their lives in Indiana.

A   A LONG JOURNEY

After the Indiana Territory became a state in 1816, many people moved there. New settlers built homes, hunted, and farmed in Indiana. They worked together to build better lives.

In 1816, Indiana had a great deal of open land available for sale. Thousands of pioneers looking for a better life moved to the new state. Most traveled from nearby states, including Kentucky, Ohio, and Virginia. Indiana's population rose from 24,000 in 1810 to more than 340,000 by 1830.

Many pioneers traveled to Indiana by horse and wagon. Others had to cross the Ohio River. At that time there were no bridges over the river. To cross the river, pioneers had to hire a **ferry**. A ferry is a boat used to carry people and goods across a body of water. Once the settlers crossed the river, they had to walk through Indiana's thick forests to find a place to call home.

The Land Ordinance of 1785 had set up a system for buying and selling land.

It also divided land into sections known as townships. Abraham Lincoln, a future President of the United States, moved from Kentucky to Indiana with his parents and sister in 1816. Lincoln's father, Thomas, bought land in Indiana under the Ordinance of 1785. Like other pioneer families, the Lincolns began to settle into their new surroundings.

QUICK CHECK

Cause and Effect How did the Land Ordinance of 1785 affect Indiana's population?

▼ Pioneers traveled in groups known as wagon trains. This group stops to rest during their journey to Indiana.

B BUILDING A HOME

The new state residents needed shelters to live in. Because houses took a while to build, many settlers put up a **lean-to**. A lean-to was a simple shelter that had three walls made of tree branches and twigs. The fourth side usually faced south and was open to allow for the most sunlight to come in during the day to warm the shelter.

Most settlers built a **log cabin** for their permanent home. A log cabin is a home made of logs from large trees that the settlers cut down. The logs were stacked to form the cabin walls. The spaces between the logs were filled with mud and clay.

PLACE

Hoosier National Forest is in southern Indiana. The land was originally used by early Indiana settlers. They cleared the trees, sold them to sawmills, and used the land for farming. Today, people can hike through the park to enjoy the land's natural beauty.

Hoosier National Forest

▼ This painting shows Lincoln at work cutting logs. This type of early work earned him the nickname of "railsplitter" when he entered politics.

Log cabins usually had only one room, which was used as a kitchen, living room, and bedroom. Children often slept above the main room in a loft. Food was also stored in the loft.

Living Off the Land

The settlers hunted rabbits, deer, and wild turkeys to feed their families. They also made their own clothes, medicine, and furniture.

Many settlers were also farmers. Before they could plant their crops, they had to clear the thick forests. They chopped down trees with an ax and used the trees to build their shelters.

Corn was the most important crop the pioneers grew. They learned about corn from Native Americans. They used it to feed their families. They also fed it to the livestock. Sometimes a family killed one of their livestock to make sure they would have enough food for the winter.

Pioneer families worked together on the Indiana frontier.

Working Together

Every member of a pioneer family had to help with jobs such as farming, cooking, gardening, making clothes, and keeping house. Settlers also shared in the work of building homes, barns, and harvesting crops.

Hardships on the Frontier

Many pioneer families faced hardships and losses. Pioneer women gave birth to many children, but very few lived into adulthood. Some died from disease or in accidents. Others were killed by wild animals. Pioneer families had to adjust to these hardships as they settled into their lives in Indiana.

QUICK CHECK

Cause and Effect **How did log cabins affect the way settlers lived?**

Check Understanding

1. **VOCABULARY** Write a sentence using the vocabulary terms listed below.

   ferry   lean-to   log cabin

2. **READING SKILL Cause and Effect** Use your chart from page 116 to write about why the pioneers traveled to Indiana in different ways.

Cause	→	Effect
	→	
	→	
	→	

EXPLORE
The Big Idea

3. **Write About It** Write about the obstacles pioneers faced and how they overcame them.

Lesson 6

VOCABULARY

preacher p. 121

Harmonist p. 121

Owenite p. 122

READING SKILL

Cause and Effect

Copy the chart below. As you read, list actions taken by Johan George Rapp and Robert Owen and the effects of those actions.

Cause	→	Effect
	→	
	→	
	→	

INDIANA ACADEMIC STANDARDS

4.1.6

Life in Harmony

Harmonie was built on the banks of the Wabash River.

Visual Preview

What risks did the citizens of New Harmony take?

A Harmonie, Indiana, was a place where people had religious freedom.

B People in New Harmony worked together to create a new way of life.

Ⓐ THE HARMONISTS

Many early settlers came to Indiana looking for freedoms they did not have in other places. In Indiana, people had the freedom to practice their religion and speak as they wished. These freedoms attracted two colonial leaders and their followers.

Johan George Rapp was a **preacher** in Germany. A preacher is a person who speaks about a religious subject. One subject Rapp spoke about was how people should behave:

[People should] strongly entertain the desire 'to do good to all men,' and even to those who think themselves his enemies.

Rapp did not have the freedom to preach about his beliefs in Germany. The government did not allow him to hold meetings with others who shared his beliefs. He moved to the United States in 1803 because Americans had religious freedom. Many Germans moved with him.

Rapp and his followers moved from Pennsylvania to the Indiana Territory in 1814. Rapp's followers were called **Harmonists** because they wanted to live in harmony. Harmony occurs when people live together in friendly agreement or cooperation. The Harmonists built a town on the Wabash River. They named it Harmonie. It is located near present-day Evansville.

The Harmonists worked hard. They built their own homes and community buildings. They also planted corn, fruit trees, and grapes. They harvested and sold these crops to other people in the area. By doing so, they became wealthy.

Some people in Indiana were jealous of the Harmonists and thought they had become too wealthy. Indiana became a less friendly place for George Rapp and his followers. The Harmonists moved away in 1825.

QUICK CHECK
Cause and Effect **What caused the Harmonists to leave Indiana?**

Ⓑ THE OWENITES

A man named Robert Owen bought the land and buildings that the Harmonists had left behind. Owen, who was born in Wales but had been living in Scotland, was a wealthy man who believed that people could work together and live good, honest lives. Owen wanted to create a town where people knew right from wrong and would work together.

Owen moved to Indiana so that he could practice his beliefs. He changed the name of the town he bought from George Rapp from Harmonie to New Harmony. Robert Owen wanted this new town to be a place where people worked together to try new ideas.

▲ Robert Owen

People from all over the United States and Europe moved to New Harmony in search of a better way of life. They were called **Owenites**. Some of the Owenites

Primary Source

"This Institute should be solely and only applied to the **diffusion** of Useful Knowledge by mutual instruction amongst the producing classes who labor with their hands, and gain their bread by the sweat of their brow."

The mission statement of the Working Men's Institute in New Harmony

diffusion: the spreading of

✎ **Write About It** Rewrite the mission statement in your own words.

were teachers and scientists. They set up a library and printed their own books. One of Indiana's oldest public libraries is in New Harmony. It was founded in 1838 by William Maclure as a place for learning. Owenites also started schools, including one of the first preschools in the United States.

The Owenites spent much more time coming up with new ideas than they did farming. They soon ran out of food. In 1827 most Owenites left Indiana. Robert Owen went back to Scotland.

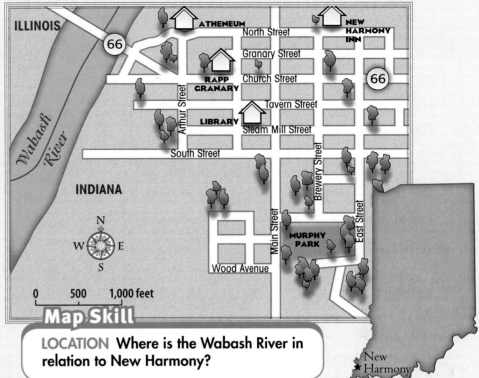

NEW HARMONY, INDIANA

Map Skill

LOCATION Where is the Wabash River in relation to New Harmony?

QUICK CHECK

Cause and Effect Why did the Owenites set up a library and schools?

Historic New Harmony had a central town hall surrounded by houses, community buildings, and small gardens.

Check Understanding

1. **VOCABULARY** Write a paragraph using each of the vocabulary terms listed below.
   Harmonist   **Owenite**

2. **READING SKILL Cause and Effect** Use your chart from page 120 to explain why New Harmony is important.

Cause	→	Effect
	→	
	→	
	→	

3. **Write About It** Write about the risks the Harmonists and Owenites took to establish their communities.

INDIANA ON THE MOVE

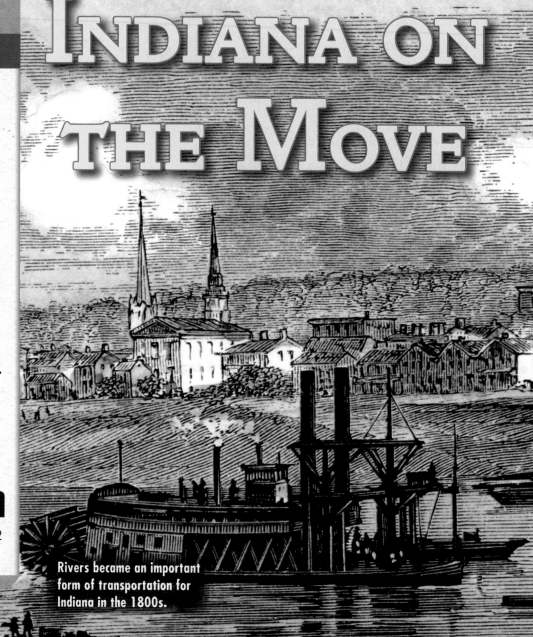

Rivers became an important form of transportation for Indiana in the 1800s.

VOCABULARY

transportation p. 125

flatboat p. 126

steamboat p. 126

navigable p. 126

canal p. 126

READING SKILL

Cause and Effect
Copy the chart below. As you read, fill it in with the causes and effects of changes in transportation.

Cause	→	Effect
	→	
	→	
	→	

INDIANA ACADEMIC STANDARDS

4.1.6, 4.1.9, 4.3.3, 4.3.9, 4.3.12

Visual Preview

What risks did early settlers take to travel to Indiana?

A Early pioneers used roads to travel to Indiana.

B Rivers and canals became important methods of transportation.

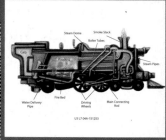

C The steam engine was one form of new transportation used in Indiana.

124

A ROADS LEADING WEST

Travel was difficult in Indiana's early history. Roads were very bumpy. In the 1820s, people in Indiana started making their roads better. Steamboats, canals, and railroads also improved **transportation***, or the moving of goods and people.*

Most early pioneers who came to Indiana followed traces, which are trails in the forest made by animals. These trails were good for traveling by foot or on horseback, but they were too narrow for wagons.

Covered wagons were a common form of transportation in the early 1800s, but they could be difficult to drive. Many of Indiana's early roads were dirt trails. Tree stumps could be found in the middle of roads. Wagons often became stuck in muddy roads.

To fix this problem, people built corduroy roads. Corduroy roads were bumpy roads made from logs laid across trails. Settlers later cut the logs into flat planks, which made the roads smoother and easier for travel.

In the 1820s, Hoosiers completed the Michigan Road. It connected northern and southern Indiana.

Today, U.S. Route 421 follows much of the old Michigan Road. Hoosiers also helped to build the National Road. Work on this road started in Maryland in 1811 and reached Indiana in the 1830s. The road ended in Illinois. Today, U.S. Route 40 follows the route of the National Road.

QUICK CHECK

Cause and Effect **How did changing the structure of corduroy roads affect travel in Indiana?**

▼ Settlers built corduroy roads to help improve transportation in Indiana.

TRAVEL BY WATER

Roads were not the only method of transportation. In the 1700s, goods in the Indiana Territory were often shipped on rivers. This was faster and less costly than shipping over land.

Farmers taking their goods to market placed their goods on **flatboats**. A flatboat is a large, flat-bottomed boat with square ends made from wood. Flatboats could only travel in the same direction as the river's current. The farmers who arrived at the market by flatboat had to find other ways to return home. Flatboats were often taken apart once they traveled downstream.

In the 1820s, **steamboats** became the fastest way to travel or ship goods. Steamboats had steam engines and could travel up or down a river. Because of steamboats, businesses thrived in towns along rivers.

Steamboats needed **navigable** rivers. Navigable rivers are wide and deep enough for boats to use without getting stuck. Indiana had few navigable rivers in the 1850s. Only the people who lived near these rivers could benefit from steamboats.

Because many Indiana farmers lived far away from large rivers, they had to find a better form of transportation. They decided to build **canals**. A canal is a waterway people dig through the land. Canals provided a way to get to the rivers

Flatboats remained important forms of transportation, even as steamboats were introduced.

more easily. In 1853 the Wabash and Erie Canal opened. At 468 miles long, it was the longest canal in America. Look at the map on this page. Which cities were on the canal's route?

Canals had some problems. They were often too shallow in the summer, and they froze in the winter. People soon realized that improvements in transportation were needed.

QUICK CHECK

Cause and Effect Why did people use boats to transport goods?

Indiana Canals and River Routes

Lake Michigan

MICHIGAN

Lake Erie

Toledo

Fort Wayne

Logansport

Peru

ILLINOIS

INDIANA

OHIO

Lafayette

Hagerstown

Whitewater River

Terre Haute

Connersville

Brookville

Washington

KENTUCKY

Ohio River

Wabash River

Evansville

N W E S

| 0 | 50 | 100 miles |
| 0 | 50 | 100 kilometers |

— Wabash and Erie Canal
— Whitewater Canal
— River navigable by steamboat

Map Skill

MOVEMENT How long is the Whitewater Canal?

THE STEAM RAILROAD

People had been traveling by trains pulled by horses for many years, but this form of transportation was slow. In the early 1800s, trains powered by steam engines changed this. Train tracks could go almost anywhere. As more people started using trains, canals became less important.

Steam engines work by burning coal to release its heat energy. Coal is put into a fire. The fire heats a large, closed container of water called a boiler. When the water boils, it changes into steam. The steam builds up pressure. It is released into pipes that are connected to the engine.

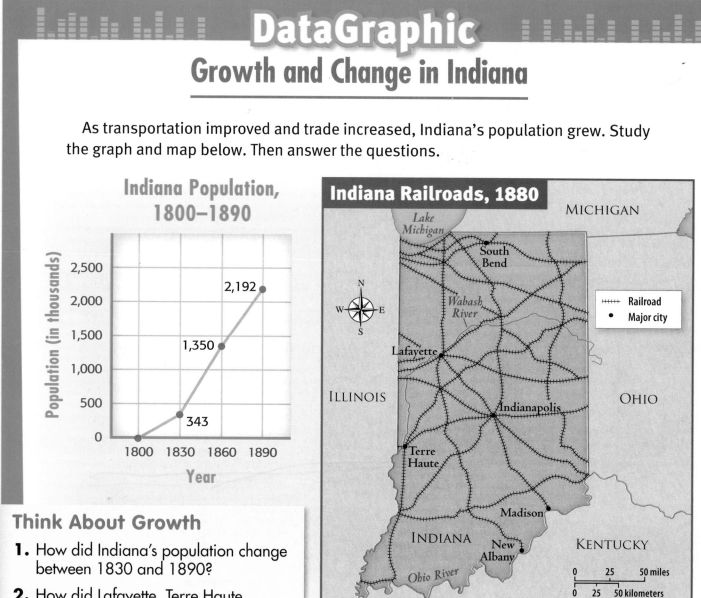

DataGraphic
Growth and Change in Indiana

As transportation improved and trade increased, Indiana's population grew. Study the graph and map below. Then answer the questions.

Indiana Population, 1800–1890

Indiana Railroads, 1880

Think About Growth

1. How did Indiana's population change between 1830 and 1890?

2. How did Lafayette, Terre Haute, Madison, and New Albany benefit by being located near rivers?

The engine is connected to the wheels by steel rods. When there is enough pressure, the engine moves the rods, which makes the wheels turn. This makes the train move. The speed of a train depended on how much steam pressure it could make.

In 1847 the first train line in Indiana ran from Indianapolis to Madison, which is located on the Ohio River. Other train routes connected several towns in the state. These routes also linked Indiana to other states. The state capital became known as the "Crossroads of America."

As the number of roads and train routes in Indiana increased, travel became easier, businesses grew, and more people traveled to Indiana.

QUICK CHECK

Cause and Effect How did the addition of the steam engine affect transportation in Indiana?

Check Understanding

1. **VOCABULARY** Write a paragraph about the growth of transportation in Indiana using each of the vocabulary terms listed below.

   flatboat   canal   steamboat

2. **READING SKILL Cause and Effect** Use your chart from page 124 to explain how the canal system affected transportation in Indiana.

Cause	→	Effect
	→	
	→	
	→	

3. **Write About It** Write about the risks involved with creating and using new forms of transportation.

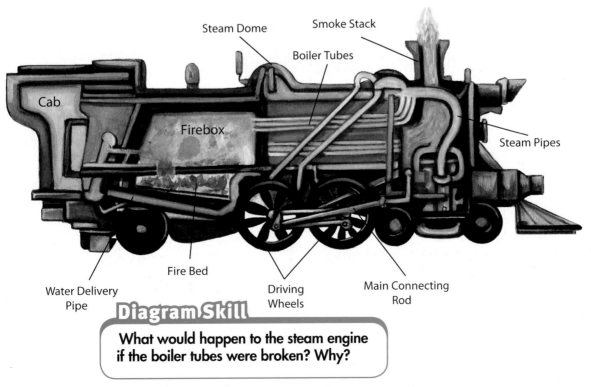

Smoke Stack

Steam Dome

Boiler Tubes

Cab

Firebox

Steam Pipes

Water Delivery Pipe

Fire Bed

Driving Wheels

Main Connecting Rod

Diagram Skill

What would happen to the steam engine if the boiler tubes were broken? Why?

Unit 3 Review and Assess

Vocabulary

Copy the sentences below. Use the list of vocabulary words to fill in the blanks.

Battle of the Thames   **population**

territory   **transportation**

1. Covered wagons and flatboats were two forms of _____ in the 1800s.

2. Tecumeh was killed on the battlefield during the _____.

3. Before it became a state, Indiana was a _____.

4. Indiana had to have a _____ of at least 60,000 before it could apply for statehood.

Comprehension and Critical Thinking

5. Why was the Treaty of Greenville important?

6. How did pioneers establish their new lives in Indiana?

7. **Reading Skill** What effect did developments in transportation have on Indiana?

8. **Critical Thinking** Why did Native Americans fight against American settlers in the early 1800s?

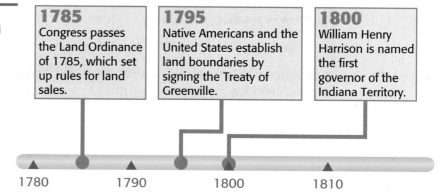

Skill

Read a Time Line

Use the time line to answer each question.

9. When was the Treaty of Greenville signed?

10. What event happened in 1800?

Early Indiana History

1785
Congress passes the Land Ordinance of 1785, which set up rules for land sales.

1795
Native Americans and the United States establish land boundaries by signing the Treaty of Greenville.

1800
William Henry Harrison is named the first governor of the Indiana Territory.

1780   1790   1800   1810

Indiana Statewide Test Practice

Read the passage below. Then choose the best answer or write a short response to each of the following questions.

> Jonathan Jennings was born in New Jersey in 1784. He moved to the Indiana Territory in 1806 and began to represent the territory in the United States Congress in 1809. He was one of the delegates who helped to write the Indiana constitution. He worked to make sure the constitution stated that slavery was not allowed in the state.
>
> Once Indiana became a state, the people elected Jennings as their first governor. He served Indiana from 1816 until 1822, when he was elected to the United States Congress. He died in July 1834.

1 **Which of these sentences best sums up the main idea of the first paragraph?**

Ⓐ Jennings was the first governor of Indiana.

Ⓑ Jennings represented the state of Indiana in Congress.

Ⓒ Jennings was a representative of the Indiana territory and helped write its constitution.

Ⓓ Jennings was the first governor of New Jersey.

2 **What caused Jennings to end his term as the governor of Indiana?**

Ⓐ He was elected to the United States Congress.

Ⓑ He was no longer needed to serve Indiana.

Ⓒ He moved out of the state to become a delegate for other territories.

Ⓓ He did not like that Indiana did not allow slavery.

3 **Suppose you were writing about Indiana's early history. Explain why Jennings would be an important person to include in your paper.**

Write your answer on the separate piece of paper.

The Big Idea Activities

Why do people take risks?

Write About the Big Idea

Narrative Essay
Use the Unit 3 Foldable to help you write a narrative essay. Use the Big Idea question, *Why do people take risks?* Begin with an introductory paragraph, stating how past events and the risks that people took influenced Indiana today. How did those risks cause events that shaped the present? Your final paragraph should summarize the main ideas of your essay and give ideas about how the events discussed have shaped our state.

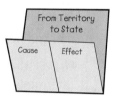

Make a 3-D Time Line

Work in small groups to make a three-dimensional time line of the events that took Indiana from part of the Northwest Territory to a state.

1. Decide the time range for your time line. Write the starting year on one index card, and the ending year on a separate index card.

2. Tape each card onto a piece of poster board. Draw a line to connect the start date with the end date.

3. Choose four or five major events that occurred in Indiana during your time range.

4. Decorate each event card with a picture to illustrate the event. Write each event on a separate index card.

5. Tape the cards onto the poster board in the correct order. Draw a line from each card to the time line.

Indiana Grows

Unit 4

EXPLORE The Big Idea

Essential Question
How does change affect people's lives?

FOLDABLES™ Study Organizer

Fact and Opinion
Make and label a Concept Map Foldable before you read Unit 4. Across the top, write **How change affects people's lives.** Label the three tabs **End of Slavery, New Technology,** and **Growth of Industry.** Use the Foldable to organize information as you read.

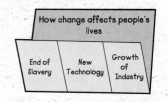

How change affects people's lives

| End of Slavery | New Technology | Growth of Industry |

LOG ON For more about the Unit 4, go to www.macmillanmh.com

Union army troops fighting Confederate troops in the Civil War

133

PEOPLE, PLACES, AND EVENTS

Levi Coffin

Fountain City

1826
Levi Coffin helps people escape slavery on the Underground Railroad.

Oliver P. Morton

Camp Morton

1861
Oliver P. Morton provides money to train Indiana troops for the Civil War.

1800   1820   1840

Levi Coffin was a Quaker who helped enslaved Africans find freedom through the **Underground Railroad**.

Today you can visit the house where Coffin worked for freedom in Fountain City, Indiana.

Oliver P. Morton supported 150,000 soldiers, many of whom were trained at **Camp Morton**, a training camp named after him.

Today Morton is remembered at the Indiana Soldiers' and Sailors' Monument.

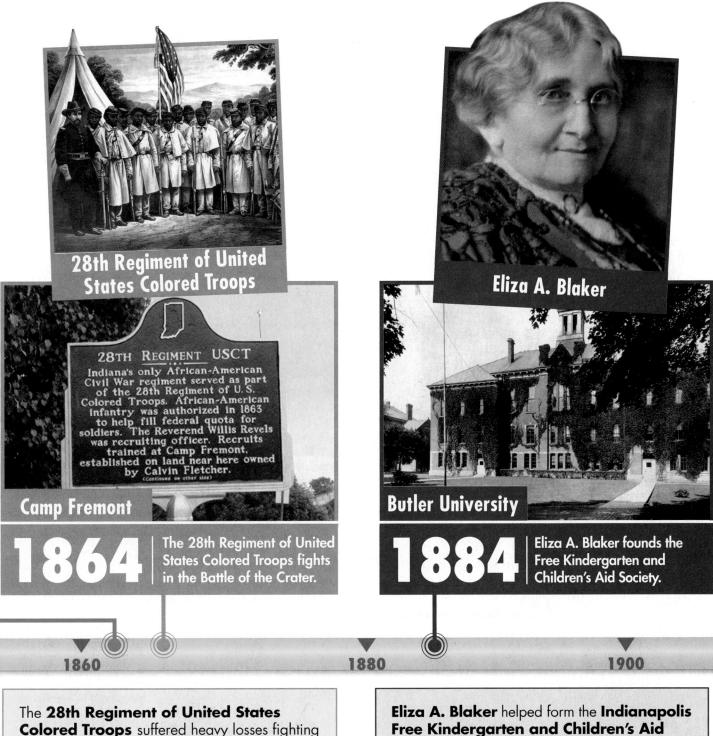

28th Regiment of United
States Colored Troops

28TH REGIMENT USCT
Indiana's only African-American
Civil War regiment served as part
of the 28th Regiment of U.S.
Colored Troops. African-American
infantry was authorized in 1863
to help fill federal quota for
soldiers. The Reverend Willis Revels
was recruiting officer. Recruits
trained at Camp Fremont,
established on land near here owned
by Calvin Fletcher.
(Continued on other side)

Camp Fremont

1864 The 28th Regiment of United
States Colored Troops fights
in the Battle of the Crater.

Eliza A. Blaker

Butler University

1884 Eliza A. Blaker founds the
Free Kindergarten and
Children's Aid Society.

1860   1880   1900

The **28th Regiment of United States
Colored Troops** suffered heavy losses fighting
Confederate soldiers in the Battle of the Crater.

Today the 28th Regiment is remembered with
a historical marker near **Camp Fremont**.

Eliza A. Blaker helped form the **Indianapolis
Free Kindergarten and Children's Aid
Society** to provide free kindergarten schools.

Today the Society's school for training teachers
is now part of Butler University.

135

Slavery and Indiana

Lesson 1

VOCABULARY

abolition p. 137

plantation p. 137

Underground Railroad p. 138

READING SKILL

Fact and Opinion

Copy the chart below. As you read, fill it in with facts and opinions about slavery.

Fact	Opinion

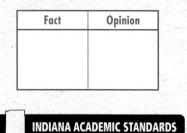

INDIANA ACADEMIC STANDARDS

4.1.7, 4.1.17, 4.2.5, 4.2.6, 4.2.7

Enslaved Africans on the Underground Railroad

Visual Preview

How did slavery affect people in Indiana?

A Some people in Indiana wanted to end slavery everywhere in the United States.

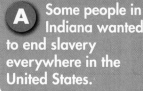

B Some Hoosiers helped enslaved people escape to freedom through the Underground Railroad.

A LIFE UNDER SLAVERY

By the early 1800s, most Northern states had banned slavery. Many people there believed that slavery was wrong. Most Southern states allowed slavery. They felt their farm economies would not survive without enslaved workers.

Indiana became a part of the United States in 1816. It did not allow slavery. Some people in Indiana wanted **abolition**, or an end to slavery in all states. Both whites and African Americans worked to end slavery.

In 1852 Harriet Beecher Stowe, an abolitionist, published a novel called *Uncle Tom's Cabin*. This book was about people who escaped slavery and fled North. It was written in response to the Fugitive Slave Law of 1850. This law made it illegal to help enslaved people escape.

Still, some Hoosiers wanted to help people escape. Life was harsh for people in slavery. Most worked in the South on large farms called **plantations**. They had no rights. Parents and children were often sent to different plantations. The work was hard and the hours were long. Enslaved workers were not paid and did not own much. They lived in small cabins that were often falling apart. Sometimes slaveholders beat enslaved workers.

Even though trying to escape slavery could be very dangerous, some people fled this horrible life. They tried to escape to free states in the North. Because Indiana did not allow slavery, many formerly enslaved people settled here.

QUICK CHECK

Fact and Opinion **What opinion would abolitionists have had about the Fugitive Slave Law?**

▼ A Southern plantation in 1855

Primary Sources

"I was willing to receive and aid as many **fugitives** as were [able] to come to my house. I knew that my wife's feelings . . . were the same as mine. . . .

[We] found it necessary to keep a **team** and a wagon always at command, to [carry] the fugitive slaves on their journey. . . . These journeys had to be made at night, often through deep mud and bad roads. . . . Every [effort] to **evade pursuit** had to be used, as the hunters were often on the track."

A section from *Reminiscences of Levi Coffin* by Levi Coffin, 1876

fugitives: runaways
team: horses harnessed together to pull a wagon
evade pursuit: keep from being caught

Write About It Suppose you worked helping people escape slavery. Describe a day of work.

Members of a religious group called the Quakers (also known as the Society of Friends) lived in southern and eastern Indiana. Starting in the winter of 1826, two Quakers, Levi and Catherine Coffin, helped enslaved people escape to freedom. Read Levi Coffin's description of the dangers of this work on this page.

The Underground Railroad

Some people risked their lives to free enslaved people. They helped enslaved people travel to freedom in Northern states and Canada along secret routes called the **Underground Railroad**. The Underground Railroad was not a real railroad, but the name for the system of secret escape routes. People known as conductors helped lead escapees along these routes. Safe hiding places were called stations. Because of his work, some people called Levi Coffin the president of the Underground Railroad.

Free African Americans also helped people escape slavery. A preacher named Chapman Harris lived in Eagle Hollow, near the Ohio River. He and his family helped many people cross the river to freedom.

Liberia Colonization Movement

Some people believed setting up a colony for African Americans would bring an end to slavery. In 1816 both African Americans and whites founded the American Colonization Society.

▲ Freed African Americans arriving in Liberia in 1832

Members of this group helped free African Americans move to a colony in Africa called Liberia.

Indiana followed with its own Liberian colonization society in 1829. Many African Americans and abolitionists were divided on the issue of Liberian colonization. Many saw colonization as a way to remove free African Americans from the United States and thus strengthen slavery.

In Indiana, antislavery Quakers were against colonization. They felt the American Colonization Society was founded to unfairly remove African Americans from the United States. The Society of Friends said that:

"[colonization] as a condition to the slaves being set [free], is unjust."

QUICK CHECK

Fact and Opinion **What opinion did Quakers have about the colonization of Liberia?**

Check Understanding

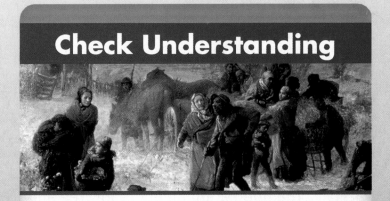

1. Write a paragraph about slavery using the terms below.

   abolition   **Underground Railroad**

   plantation

2. **READING SKILL Fact and Opinion** Use your chart from page 136 to write about slavery.

Fact	Opinion

 3. **Write About It** Write an essay about how slavery affected people in Indiana.

✗ Workbook page 33

139

Read Bar Graphs

VOCABULARY
bar graph

  In the last lesson, you read about slavery and the Underground Railroad. Even though Indiana was a free state, some African Americans in our state were enslaved illegally in the early 1800s. You can learn more about slavery by reading **bar graphs**. Bar graphs use bars to show information in a way that is easy to understand. You can use bar graphs to compare amounts, such as populations.

Learn It

- When studying any graph, you should read the title first. The bar graph on this page shows the population of African Americans in Indiana from 1800 to 1840.

- Read the labels. The labels along the bottom show the years 1800 to 1840. The labels on the left show the population numbers for free and enslaved African Americans in Indiana during this time period.

- Use the lines in the graph to put the information together. For example, in 1810 about 300 enslaved African Americans lived in Indiana.

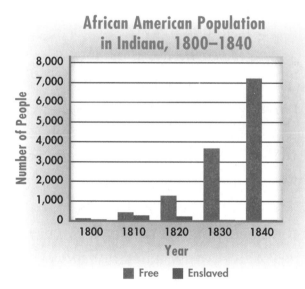

African American Population in Indiana, 1800–1840

Workbook page 34

Now look at the bar graph below to answer the questions.

- What does the bar graph show?

- About how many free African Americans lived in the United States in 1840?

- In 1820, about how many more enslaved African Americans than free African Americans lived in the United States?

- Research the population of Indiana over a period of at least 50 years. Then make a bar graph to show the information. Decide which information will go along the bottom and side of the graph. Give your graph a title.

African American Population in the United States, 1800–1840

Number of People — Year

Free   Enslaved

INDIANA AND THE CIVIL WAR

Lesson 2

Confederate soldiers firing on Union-held Fort Sumter in South Carolina

Visual Preview

How did the Civil War affect people's lives?

A Southern states seceded from the Union over the issues of slavery and states' rights.

B Both the North and the South had strengths and weaknesses during the war.

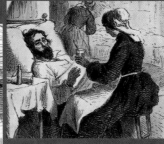

C Men and women in Indiana volunteered to help defeat the Confederacy.

D The Emancipation Proclamation freed enslaved people living in Confederate states.

Ⓐ THE CIVIL WAR BEGINS

*By the 1850s, divisions between the North and the South had grown. Southern states believed the only solution was to **secede**. To secede means to break away from a nation or organization. Newly elected President Abraham Lincoln said this was illegal.*

Abraham Lincoln became President in 1861. Two key issues he faced were slavery and **states' rights**. Supporters of states' rights thought the states should make their own laws about any issue not stated as belonging to Congress by the U.S. Constitution. Many Southerners supported the idea of states' rights.

Some Southern states decided to secede from the United States. These states called themselves the Confederate States of America, or the **Confederacy**. President Lincoln felt that the United States was a **Union** of states that should not be broken. If necessary, he would fight a war to keep the nation whole.

On April 12, 1861, Confederate soldiers fired on the Union-held Fort Sumter in South Carolina. The Union troops at the fort surrendered. President Lincoln called for an army of 75,000 volunteers to stop the South from seceding. This started a **civil war** in the United States. A civil war is a war that is fought among people in the same country.

Lincoln fought the Civil War because he wanted to keep the United States one nation. However, he was also against slavery. In a letter he wrote in 1859, he said:

> Those who deny freedom to others, deserve it not for themselves.
>
> —ABRAHAM LINCOLN

QUICK CHECK

Fact and Opinion Is the sentence "Southern states seceded from the Union" a fact or an opinion? Why?

STRENGTHS AND WEAKNESSES

B

Both sides in the Civil War had strengths and weaknesses. These strengths and weaknesses helped decide the outcome of the war.

Resources of the South

The South's greatest strength was its army. Men in the South knew how to ride horses and hunt, which were good skills for soldiers. The South also had many well-trained officers. Robert E. Lee, one of these officers, became the commander of the Confederate army.

▼ In 1863 the Union army won a major victory at Gettysburg, Pennsylvania.

One of the South's greatest weaknesses was that the farms there grew mostly cotton, not food. The South got most of its food from states in the North. It also had less than half the population of the North, less money, and only one factory making cannons.

Union and Confederacy

OR
CA
MN
WI
IA
KS
MO
OK
TX
AR
LA
MI
IL
IN
OH
KY
TN
MS
AL
GA
FL
WV
VA
NC
SC
PA
NY
ME
VT
NH
MA
RI
CT
NJ
DE
MD

PACIFIC OCEAN

ATLANTIC OCEAN

Union state
Confederate state
Territory
— Boundary between United States and Confederate States

0   200   400 miles
0   200   400 kilometers

Map Skill

LOCATION **Which side had more states, the Confederacy or the Union?**

Resources of the North

The North had a much larger population than the South, but the people did not have fighting skills. The North also had more army supplies because most of the country's factories were there. The factories made weapons and uniforms. The North also grew most of the country's food. Plus, the North had more railroads. Railroads could be used to move troops and supplies.

The North's greatest weakness was that most of the battles took place in Confederate states. Southern soldiers knew the land much better than Northern soldiers. People in the South were also defending their homes.

A Modern War

The Civil War has been called the first modern war because of the new **technology** used. Technology is the use of skills, ideas, and tools to meet people's needs. The Gatling machine gun, ironclad battleships, and mines all made the Civil War more deadly than any war before it.

Another important new technology was the telegraph. The telegraph sent messages across the country in minutes. It was used by both sides during the war to plan attacks and send information.

QUICK CHECK

Fact and Opinion **What was the South's greatest strength in the Civil War?**

C THE WAR IN INDIANA

Oliver P. Morton became governor of Indiana in 1861—the same year Lincoln became President. Morton was a strong ally of the President. From the start of the Civil War, the new governor provided money to train Indiana troops. Camp Morton in Indianapolis was named after him.

Early in the war, Indiana soldiers trained at Camp Morton. Later, the camp served as a prison and hospital for Confederate soldiers.

The Iron Brigade

Almost 200,000 Hoosiers fought in the Civil War. The 19th Indiana Volunteer Infantry Regiment joined other regiments from the Midwest to become the Iron Brigade. Soldiers in the Iron Brigade fought against such great odds in battle that they seemed to be made of iron. One general called the brigade the "best troops in the world."

Benjamin Harrison

Some famous Hoosiers also volunteered to fight in the Civil War. A grandson of President William Henry Harrison, Benjamin Harrison, was colonel of the 70th Indiana Volunteer Infantry Regiment. Harrison soon became a general and commanded a brigade. While Harrison was a war hero, he is better known as the 23rd President of the United States. During his campaign in 1888, Harrison spoke of the power of truth: "The bud of victory is always in the truth."

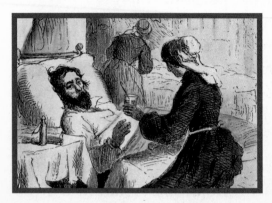

◄ Women nursed the wounded and sick during the Civil War.

Women and the War

Many women living in Indiana at the time contributed to the war effort. They nursed the sick, made bandages, and cooked meals.

Life was difficult for the wives of soldiers. They had to earn money, care for their families, and run their households. Even so, some found time to make clothes for soldiers. Some became nurses. Others worked in factories that made war equipment.

Morgan's raid on Corydon

One woman, Mary Wise, dressed like a man so she could serve in an Indiana regiment. She fought in a battle in Tennessee and suffered a wound before officials found out she was a woman. Troops called Lovina Streight the "Mother of the 51st Regiment" because she took care of injured soldiers. Mary Ann Shadd Cary helped to enlist African American troops in Indiana.

Morgan's Raid

Only a few Civil War battles took place in the North. One of these battles took place in Corydon, in Harrison County, on July 8, 1863. Against orders, Confederate general John Hunt Morgan staged a raid into Northern states.

At Corydon, 400 Union soldiers fought Morgan's 2,500 troops. The Confederate army captured many of the Union troops. Morgan's men then burned down the capitol. They also told business owners they would burn their businesses if Morgan was not paid $1,000.

Later that same day, Morgan's men left Corydon and continued to cross the Indiana countryside, stealing fresh horses and money. Morgan then turned towards Ohio. Union forces later caught General Morgan in Ohio.

QUICK CHECK

Fact and Opinion **What opinion would a Northerner have of Morgan's Raid?**

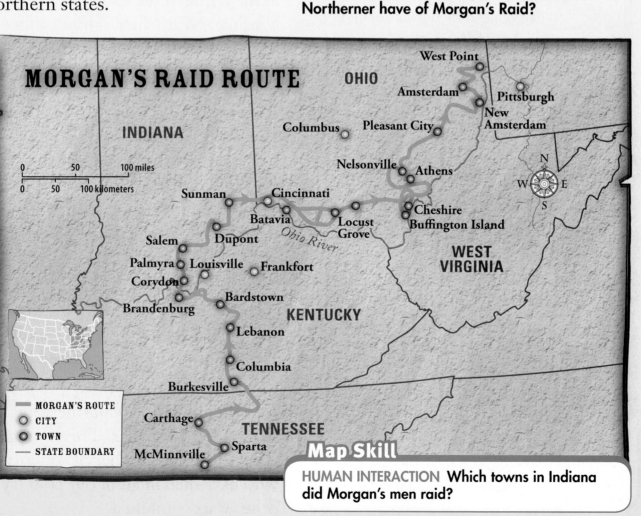

MORGAN'S RAID ROUTE

OHIO

INDIANA

West Point
Amsterdam   Pittsburgh
New Amsterdam
Columbus   Pleasant City
Nelsonville   Athens

0   50   100 miles
0   50   100 kilometers

Sunman   Cincinnati
Batavia   Locust Grove   Cheshire
Salem   Dupont   Buffington Island
Palmyra   Louisville   Ohio River
Corydon   Frankfort   WEST VIRGINIA
Brandenburg   Bardstown

KENTUCKY

Lebanon
Columbia
Burkesville

MORGAN'S ROUTE
◦ CITY
◦ TOWN
— STATE BOUNDARY

Carthage
McMinnville   Sparta   TENNESSEE

Map Skill

HUMAN INTERACTION **Which towns in Indiana did Morgan's men raid?**

Primary Source

"A proclamation was issued by the President of the United States, containing, among other things, the following, to [know]:

That on the 1st day of January, in the year of our Lord 1863, all persons held as slaves within any State or **designated** part of a State, the people whereof shall then be in rebellion against the United States, shall be then, **thenceforward**, and forever free; and the Executive Government of the United States, including the military and naval authority thereof, will **recognize** and maintain the freedom of such persons, and will do no act or acts to **repress** such persons, or any of them, in any efforts they may make for their actual freedom."

A section from *The Emancipation Proclamation,* issued by Abraham Lincoln, September 22, 1862

designated chosen

thenceforward from now on

recognize respect

repress hold back

Write About It Write about what you think the Emancipation Proclamation meant to enslaved people in Confederate states.

On September 22, 1862, President Lincoln issued the Emancipation Proclamation. It freed enslaved people in the Confederate states. It also changed the reasons for fighting the war. Now, the war was more about slavery and freedom than Southern independence or saving the Union. Read an excerpt from Lincoln's Emancipation Proclamation on this page.

The Fighting 28th

Some freed African Americans enlisted in the 28th Regiment of the United States Colored Troops. These soldiers fought at the Battle of the Crater in Petersburg, Virginia. Nearly half of the regiment's soldiers were killed or wounded. After the war, the 28th returned to Indianapolis and were given a celebration in their honor.

The Cost of War

More than 7,000 Indiana soldiers died in battle in the Civil War. Nearly 18,000 died from illness and infection. About 1 in 8 of the state's soldiers did not return home.

Raids by General Morgan's army and other Confederate armies destroyed some railroad lines, bridges, and farms in Indiana. Still, Indiana suffered less than other parts of the country.

In all, about 620,000 Americans died during the Civil War. This total is almost half the number of Americans who have died in all of our country's other wars combined.

Lincoln Is Shot

Five days after the war was over, President and Mrs. Lincoln were watching a play at Ford's Theater in Washington, D.C. Suddenly a gunshot rang out. John Wilkes Booth, a supporter of the Confederacy, had shot the President. The next morning, April 15, 1865, President Lincoln died. The poet Walt Whitman expressed the country's sadness:

> **❝O CAPTAIN! My Captain! our fearful trip is done; The Ship has weather'd every storm, the prize we sought is won.❞**

Whitman's "prize" was many things. It was an end to the war and to slavery. It was a new beginning for the United States, which was united once again.

Check Understanding

1. Write a paragraph about the Civil War using the terms below.

   secede   Confederacy
   states' rights   Union

2. **READING SKILL Fact and Opinion** Use your chart from page 142 to write a paragraph about the Civil War.

Fact	Opinion

3. **Write About It** Write an essay about how the Civil War affected people in Indiana.

QUICK CHECK

Fact and Opinion What facts changed after the Emancipation Proclamation was issued?

▼ Abraham Lincoln's funeral procession in New York City

149

RECONSTRUCTION

VOCABULARY

Reconstruction p. 151

discrimination p. 152

Freedmen's Bureau p. 152

depression p. 153

sharecropping p. 153

READING SKILL

Fact and Opinion
Copy the chart below. As you read, fill it in with facts and opinions about Congress during Reconstruction.

Fact	Opinion

INDIANA ACADEMIC STANDARDS

4.1.8, 4.2.5, 4.3.10

Many Southern cities needed to be rebuilt after the war.

Visual Preview

What changed for African Americans during Reconstruction?

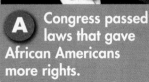

A Congress passed laws that gave African Americans more rights.

B The Freedmen's Bureau provided services to help African Americans.

REBUILDING AFTER THE WAR

Even though the war was over, bitter feelings still existed between the North and the South. Thousands of soldiers had been killed. Cities and farms across the South were destroyed. The nation faced the task of rebuilding.

On April 9, 1865, the war ended. Still, the North and South did not agree on many issues. Before Lincoln died, he had said he did not want to punish the South. He wanted Americans to put away their malice, or desire to harm, with these words: "with malice toward none, with charity for all."

Reconstruction Begins

After Lincoln's death, Vice President Andrew Johnson became the new President. His task was to continue the job of **Reconstruction**. Reconstruction was the period following the Civil War in which the United States Congress passed laws that would help to rebuild the country and bring the Southern states back into the Union.

Constitutional Amendments

During Reconstruction, Congress passed amendments, or additions, to the Constitution that guaranteed rights to African Americans. In 1865 the Thirteenth Amendment abolished slavery everywhere in the United States. In 1868 the Fourteenth Amendment made African Americans citizens of the United States and guaranteed them the same legal rights as whites. In 1870 the Fifteenth Amendment made it illegal for states to deny a man's right to vote.

QUICK CHECK

Fact and Opinion Why do you think Lincoln did not want to punish the South?

EVENT

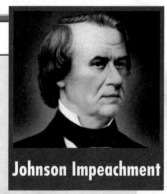

Johnson Impeachment

Many members of Congress were against Andrew Johnson's Reconstruction plan and replaced it with their own plan. However, Johnson refused to recognize many of the new laws that Congress passed. For example, Johnson removed government officials without Congress's approval. In 1868 Congress voted to impeach Johnson. To impeach means to charge a government official with wrongdoing. Johnson is one of only two Presidents ever to be impeached.

NEW BEGINNINGS IN INDIANA

Before and after the war, most African Americans faced **discrimination**, or unfair treatment. The Indiana Constitution of 1851 stated that no African American could enter or settle in the state. In 1866 the constitution was changed. Newly freed African Americans could now move to Indiana, but they still faced discrimination in many areas, including jobs and housing.

Freedmen's Bureau

Just before the war ended, the United States Congress set up a government agency called the **Freedmen's Bureau**. It provided food, clothing, shelter, medical care, jobs, and legal help to freed African Americans. The bureau also helped some white farmers to rebuild their farms.

The most important thing the bureau did, though, was to create schools. Now African American children could learn the skills they needed. Most of the teachers were women. Some of them had even been enslaved workers. Much like you do today, children in these schools studied reading, writing, math, and geography.

▼ The Freedmen's Bureau started many schools such as this one in Richmond, Virginia.

Hard Times

Some newly freed African Americans moved to Northern cities to work. However, there were not many jobs after the Civil War. Our nation entered a **depression**. A depression is a time when people have little money and there are not enough jobs.

The "Long Depression," as it was called, lasted from 1873 to 1896. During this time, 18,000 businesses failed. Workers without jobs reached 14 percent of the population.

Making a Living

To make a living, some African Americans and poor whites worked on farms they did not own. Landowners paid workers in shares of crops. This system of farming was known as **sharecropping**. A landowner provided a cabin, mules, tools, and seed. The sharecropper farmed the land and used part of the crop to pay for rent and farming supplies.

Sharecropping offered African Americans the freedom to work for pay. Yet few people got ahead in sharecropping. Sharecroppers often had to borrow money to buy supplies. Crops were often poor and prices were low. Every year most sharecroppers slipped deeper into debt.

QUICK CHECK

Fact and Opinion **What was the most important thing the Freedmen's Bureau did?**

PEOPLE

Ulysses S. Grant was the leading Union general during the Civil War who accepted the surrender of Confederate general Robert E. Lee. He became President of the United States in 1868 and was a strong supporter of Congress during Reconstruction. He was also President during the Long Depression. Today, he is known among historians as a strong supporter of civil rights for African Americans.

Ulysses S. Grant

Check Understanding

1. Write a paragraph about Reconstruction using the terms below.

   Reconstruction   **Freedmen's Bureau**
   discrimination   **sharecropping**

2. **READING SKILL** **Fact and Opinion** Use your chart from page 150 to write a paragraph about Reconstruction.

Fact	Opinion

3. **Write About It** Write an essay about how Reconstruction affected African Americans.

workbook page 36

FARM LIFE

Lesson 4

VOCABULARY

self-sufficient p. 155

reaper p. 155

Grange p. 157

READING SKILL

Fact and Opinion

Copy the chart below. As you read, fill it in with facts and opinions about farm technology.

Fact	Opinion

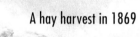

INDIANA ACADEMIC STANDARDS

4.1.9, 4.4.1, 4.4.2, 4.4.3

A hay harvest in 1869

Visual Preview

How did changes in farming affect farmers' lives?

A Technology made farmwork easier and more productive.

B More money meant farmers could buy the things they needed.

154

A FARMERS AND FARM LIFE

In the late 1800s, new farming tools and methods improved the lives of farmers. These new methods increased the amount of food farmers could grow. They sold the extra food and used the money to buy goods that made their lives easier.

Unlike today, Indiana farmers in the early 1800s were **self-sufficient**. This means they provided for almost all their own needs. The farm family grew or made what it needed. Each member of the family had a set of tasks. Men tended the fields. Women took care of the house, the cooking, the cleaning, the sewing, and the children. In planting and harvest seasons, everybody worked in the fields.

Technology Brings Change

In the late 1800s, farm life changed. New technology made farmwork easier. One new tool was the **reaper**. This horse-drawn machine cut and bundled grain. With a reaper, farmers could harvest more quickly than when they had to work by hand.

Another useful new tool was an improved plow made of steel. Hoosier James Oliver first invented his chilled plows in the 1850s. A chilled plow is made from metal that is cooled rapidly, hardening the surface of the metal. Oliver's plow did not break

▼ 1850s steel plow

as easily as wood and iron models had. It also cut more cleanly through damp soil. In the 1860s, many farmers bought James Oliver's plows.

Crop Rotation

Farmers also developed new methods that made farming more productive. They learned how to rotate their crops. That is, they planted a different crop in the same field each year. This rotation kept the soil fertile.

Another important change was an increase in the use of horses. Horses pulled reapers and plows. As a result, farmers could work more land.

QUICK CHECK

Fact and Opinion Why do you think most farmers today are not self-sufficient?

New machines and the increased use of horses made farms larger and more productive. By the 1880s, Indiana was the fourth-largest producer of corn in the nation.

Many Indiana farmers also raised hogs. In Indianapolis and Madison, workers butchered the hogs, earning Madison the nickname "Porkopolis."

▼ Poster from the 1885 Indiana State Fair

Money

Farm life changed in another way. Money became a bigger part of farm families' lives. They got money for selling their crops. They used that money to buy goods, such as new stoves, pots, and pans. Family members could also now buy clothes instead of making them.

Farm families did not have to travel to stores to buy these goods. New companies had formed that published catalogs showing all the goods they had for sale. Catalogs contained many different products, from clothing to farm tools. Anything that farm families wanted could be ordered from a catalog and delivered to the farm.

Having Fun

Farm families had some fun, too. They held dances, shooting matches, and quilting bees. In a quilting bee, a group of women would help each other make quilts. While they worked, they socialized and caught up on each other's lives. Trips to town and county fairs were also big events for farm families because they got to visit with their neighbors.

Painting of a quilting bee in the 1800s

The Grange

Farmers also came together at meetings of the **Grange**. The Grange is a farmers' group that was founded in 1867. At Grange meetings, farmers learned about new ways of farming. They also relaxed and socialized.

The Grange fought for the rights of farmers. For example, the Grange pushed for rural mail deliveries. They also worked to improve the education system in farming communities. Today the Grange has about 300,000 members.

QUICK CHECK

Fact and Opinion **How did money change farm life in the 1800s?**

Check Understanding

1. Write a paragraph about farm life using the terms below.
   self-sufficient   **reaper**   **Grange**

2. **READING SKILL Fact and Opinion** Use your chart from page 154 to write a paragraph about farm technology.

Fact	Opinion

3. **Write About It** Write about how changes in farming affected people's lives.

The Growth of Cities

Lesson 5

VOCABULARY

industry p. 160

public service p. 162

READING SKILL

Fact and Opinion
Copy the chart below. As you read, fill it in with facts and opinions about the growth of Indiana in the 1800s.

Fact	Opinion

INDIANA ACADEMIC STANDARDS

4.1.9, 4.3.9, 4.3.10, 4.4.1, 4.4.3

Cities in Indiana grew in the late 1800s.

Visual Preview

How did Indiana's growth in the 1800s affect people?

A Immigrants from Europe and others came to Indiana's cities to work in factories.

B Railroads created jobs and connected Hoosiers to the rest of the nation.

C As cities grew, public services such as fire and police departments were set up.

Ⓐ BOOMING CITIES

While farm life was changing, Indiana's cities were growing. Railroads spread to new areas. Where the tracks went, factories were built. The factories attracted people, who came from the South, from Europe, and from Indiana's farms.

Between 1850 and 1880, Indiana's urban population grew. While many Hoosiers still lived in rural areas, by 1880, about two out of every ten people in the state lived in cities. Urban centers such as Indianapolis, South Bend, Evansville, Fort Wayne, and Gary had department stores, theaters, amusement parks, schools, and libraries.

Why Cities Grew

After the Civil War, many African Americans moved from the South to the North to start new lives. At the same time, millions of immigrants came to the United States from Europe. Some African Americans and immigrants from Germany, Ireland, Russia, Hungary, England, Scotland, Poland, and Yugoslavia came to Indiana hoping to work in the growing factories. They settled in Indiana's cities, where the factories were located. Many farmers looking for work also moved to the cities.

Resources and Growth

Some cities grew because there were important resources nearby. For example, east central Indiana had large reserves of natural gas. The energy supply attracted factories. Kokomo, Muncie, Anderson, Elwood, Marion, and Gas City all thrived.

QUICK CHECK

Fact and Opinion List three facts about why Indiana grew during the 1800s.

PLACE

In 1892 **Gas City** discovered a huge natural gas reserve in its fields. Within three months, eight factories had moved to Gas City. As well, a bank, hotels, and many business offices were built. The population of the town grew from 150 people in 1890 to 3,622 in 1900.

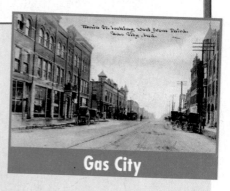
Gas City

The first railroad in Indiana ran from Madison to Indianapolis. It was completed in 1847. In time, other rail lines were built. The earliest lines connected inland areas to the Ohio River. By 1854, 18 railroad companies had laid more than 1,400 miles of track in Indiana.

The Economy Grows

Railroads helped boost the state's economy. They made it easier and cheaper to ship goods. The rail lines also connected Hoosiers with the rest of the nation.

The railroad led to the growth of many Indiana cities. Indianapolis became an important national rail center because rail lines traveling from east to west passed through the city.

Factories

The railroads brought raw materials to factories. Companies also used rail lines to ship products. As a result, many cities became centers for **industry**. An industry is all the businesses that make one kind of product or provide one kind of service.

Railroads brought people and industry to Indiana in the 1800s.

South Bend had two major factories. James Oliver made his plows there. By 1880, his company was making more plows than any other company in the world. Henry and Clement Studebaker built wagons in the 1850s. Some pioneer families moving to the West used Studebaker wagons. In the early 1900s, Studebaker began making automobiles.

Singer Manufacturing Company made sewing machines in Fort Wayne. Terre Haute grew because coal, iron ore, and oil were nearby. People used iron to build bridges and railroad cars.

QUICK CHECK

Fact and Opinion **What opinion would a factory owner have about the expansion of railroads?**

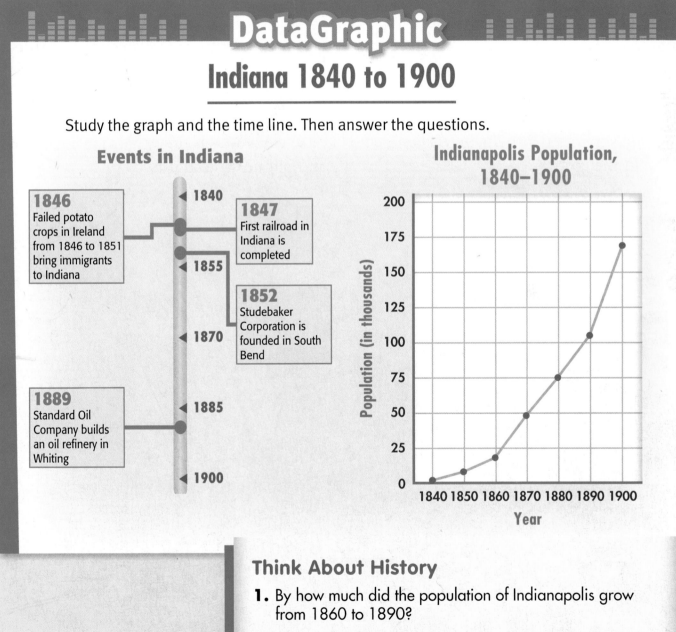

DataGraphic
Indiana 1840 to 1900

Study the graph and the time line. Then answer the questions.

Events in Indiana

1846 Failed potato crops in Ireland from 1846 to 1851 bring immigrants to Indiana

◄ 1840

1847 First railroad in Indiana is completed

◄ 1855

1852 Studebaker Corporation is founded in South Bend

◄ 1870

1889 Standard Oil Company builds an oil refinery in Whiting

◄ 1885

◄ 1900

Indianapolis Population, 1840–1900

Population (in thousands) — Year: 1840 1850 1860 1870 1880 1890 1900

Think About History

1. By how much did the population of Indianapolis grow from 1860 to 1890?

2. What helped Indiana's population grow starting in 1847?

The growing populations of Indiana's cities caused problems. Some cities became crowded. Many immigrants had no choice but to live in crowded, poorly kept apartment buildings.

Growing cities brought new challenges, such as fires and unsafe drinking water. One person or family could not solve these problems, so people had to work together. The idea of **public services** took hold. A public service is an act, such as firefighting or garbage collection, that helps people. City governments began to provide services that helped everyone who lived in the city.

Protection from fire was the first of these new services. Many buildings in the cities were wooden, so fire was a major danger. Firefighters in the 1800s had to carry water to a fire on a horse-drawn fire wagon. Volunteers formed the first firefighting companies. In time, cities hired full-time firefighters.

Government leaders and workers in large cities in Indiana also tried to protect people. To enforce laws, cities set up police forces. They took control of water and sewer systems so that people could have clean water. They also paved streets and put up streetlights.

▼ Indianapolis in the 1870s

Fire trucks were pulled by horses in the 1800s (above), and streetcars were the first form of public transporation in Edinburg, Indiana (right).

As the cities grew, many people settled near others who were from the same ethnic group. Cities were home to many different groups of people. Each group had its own neighborhoods with stores, clubs, and places of worship.

Many immigrants could not speak English. This was a great challenge for both adults and children. Parents often learned English through their children.

Soon settlement houses were built to help immigrants. A settlement house offered education, hot meals, and other types of services.

QUICK CHECK

Fact and Opinion **What opinion would a person living in a city have about public services? Why?**

Check Understanding

1. Write a paragraph about Indiana's growth using the terms below.

   industry   **public service**

2. **READING SKILL** Fact and Opinion Use your chart from page 158 to write about the growth of Indiana in the 1800s.

Fact	Opinion

EXPLORE The Big Idea

3. **Write About It** Write an essay about how growth affected people in Indiana in the 1800s.

Map and Globe Skills

Use Special-Purpose Maps: Population Maps

VOCABULARY
population map

Special-purpose maps are maps that show information such as climate and products. Another kind of special-purpose map is a **population map**. A population map shows the number of people that live in a certain area.

The map on page 165 shows you where most people were living in Indiana in 1900. It shows the most populated and least populated counties in the state.

Learn It

Use the steps below to learn how to read a population map.

- Population maps show where the most or fewest number of people live in a certain area.

- Read the title of the map. The map on the next page shows Indiana's population by county in 1900.

- In order to understand a population map, first study the map legend, or key. The legend in the map has five different colors. Next to each color is a label that tells you a range of how many people that color represents.

- Use the legend and the map together. For example, you can use the map and legend on page 165 to determine how many people lived in the area around South Bend.

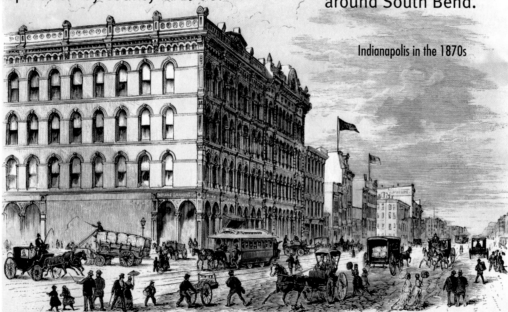

Indianapolis in the 1870s

Read the map below and answer the questions.

- What does the color yellow mean on this map?

- How many people were living in the area around Evansville?

- Compare the population of the area around Gary with the population of the area around Indianapolis. Which area had a larger population?

- What information about population is not shown on this map?

- Make a different population map by dividing the map below into the most populated and least populated counties. Make a legend with two colors and give a population range for each color.

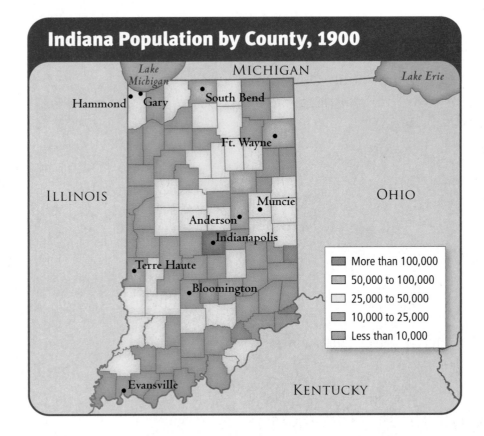

Indiana Population by County, 1900

Legend:
- More than 100,000
- 50,000 to 100,000
- 25,000 to 50,000
- 10,000 to 25,000
- Less than 10,000

Lesson 6

VOCABULARY

labor union p. 170

strike p. 170

READING SKILL

Fact and Opinion
Copy the chart below. As you read, fill it in with facts and opinions about education and unions.

Fact	Opinion

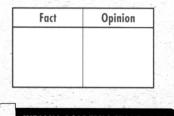
INDIANA ACADEMIC STANDARDS

4.1.9, 4.2.2, 4.2.5, 4.4.2

Education and Labor

Children working in a vegetable cannery

Visual Preview

How did education and unions affect people's lives?

A In 1851 Indiana began offering free public education to children.

B Students at Indiana universities can study a variety of subjects, including medicine.

C Labor unions improved working conditions for many Indiana workers.

166

A EDUCATION LAWS

Even though the Indiana State Constitution of 1816 called for free public education, the state government did not provide much money to pay for it. As a result, most schools were private. Many Hoosiers could not afford to pay for these schools.

Indiana government leaders believed education was important. In school, children could learn the basic skills they needed to live a productive life.

In 1851 a new state constitution called for new taxes to pay for public schools. Between 1852 and 1858, more than 2,700 schoolhouses were built in Indiana. Due to discrimination, however, African American children were not allowed to attend. They attended their own private schools.

Child Labor

Many Hoosiers believed children should spend most of their time in school. However, new technology meant that factories began using machines that could be operated by children as well as adults. Child workers were usually paid less. In 1867 Indiana passed a law limiting the number of hours children could work in factories. In 1879 a law required all children between the ages of 8 and 14 to go to school at least 12 weeks per year.

Expanding Education

In 1884 Eliza A. Blaker helped form a group to provide free kindergarten schools for poor children ages 3 to 8. The schools were so successful that Blaker began a training school for teachers. That school eventually became a part of Butler University.

QUICK CHECK

Fact and Opinion **What opinion did Eliza A. Blaker and Indiana government leaders share?**

▲ A kindergarten class at the Blaker training school

GROWTH OF HIGHER EDUCATION

Indiana is known as the "Brain Bank of the Midwest" because Indiana's colleges and universities attract the largest number of out-of-state students in the Midwest. The growth of higher education has given students the skills they need to run businesses and work more productively.

There are more than 40 colleges and universities throughout Indiana. Vincennes University was established in 1801 by William Henry Harrison. It was the first university established in Indiana. It began when Indiana was still a territory.

In 1820 the state founded Indiana University as its public university. The first campus was in Bloomington. Today, there are eight campuses across the state. Students at Indiana University can study a variety of subjects, including international business, medicine, and law.

1801 VINCENNES UNIVERSITY
Vincennes University is one of two universities founded by a President of the United States. The first campus was built on William Henry Harrison's farm.

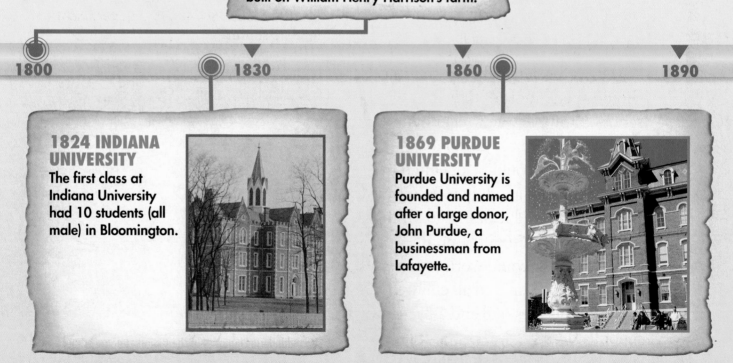

1800   1830   1860   1890

1824 INDIANA UNIVERSITY
The first class at Indiana University had 10 students (all male) in Bloomington.

1869 PURDUE UNIVERSITY
Purdue University is founded and named after a large donor, John Purdue, a businessman from Lafayette.

President Abraham Lincoln wanted to establish agricultural colleges throughout the United States. In 1862 he signed a law that would turn over government land to any state that agreed to use the money from its sale to establish an agricultural college. Purdue University was established from this law in 1869.

Indiana also has many private colleges. Butler University is a small college in Indianapolis. There are about 4,500 students there, compared to the 94,000 students at the Indiana University. The University of Notre Dame is also in Indiana. It has about 8,400 students. Notre Dame was founded in 1842.

QUICK CHECK

Fact and Opinion **What opinion did Lincoln have about colleges teaching agriculture?**

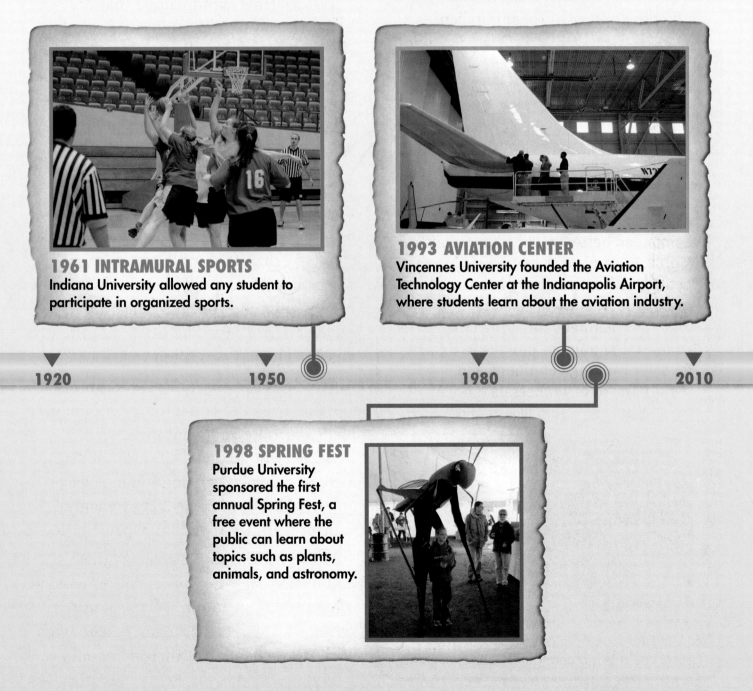

1961 INTRAMURAL SPORTS
Indiana University allowed any student to participate in organized sports.

1993 AVIATION CENTER
Vincennes University founded the Aviation Technology Center at the Indianapolis Airport, where students learn about the aviation industry.

1920   1950   1980   2010

1998 SPRING FEST
Purdue University sponsored the first annual Spring Fest, a free event where the public can learn about topics such as plants, animals, and astronomy.

The growth of railroads helped promote industry. Railroads and the new manufacturing companies held great power. Farmers who felt that the railroads were too powerful began to fight against that power. Workers formed groups to try to protect their rights. In some cases, the state government stepped in to try to control the power of these companies.

Citizenship

Mobilizing Groups

Factory workers in Indiana started a movement to form labor unions that demanded better working conditions. Mobilizing groups is one way to organize people. Movements have been used throughout history to call attention to unfair treatment and bring change. Today, labor unions continue to fight for safer working conditions and fair treatment of workers. Is there a movement you would like to join?

Write About It Write about a way a group could bring change in your community.

Powerful Railroads

Local railways linked farmers and rural businesses to major rail lines and markets. One railroad company usually controlled all of these local railways. That company could raise its prices because the farmers needed its services.

Many farmers complained that the high prices were unfair. Farmers used the Grange to push for changes in railroad rates. In 1905 the state set up the Indiana Railroad Commission. This government agency had the power to set shipping prices and make sure they were fair.

Factory Workers

Meanwhile, manufacturing was becoming a bigger part of the state's economy than farming. Some factory workers enjoyed good lives, but many others suffered, working 7 days a week for 12 hours a day. The work was often unsafe. The pay was often very low.

Faced with poor working conditions, workers began to come together. They formed groups called **labor unions**. Workers who joined a labor union had a greater chance of gaining better wages and working conditions. They wanted shorter workdays and better pay.

Most business owners fought these unions. People who joined unions were often fired. One union weapon was to **strike**. In a strike, workers refuse to work until the owners meet their demands.

Men striking for better working conditions

When unions organized a strike, owners hired strikebreakers, or nonunion workers who replaced the striking workers. In 1877 a major strike stopped trains in Indiana and across the nation.

Unions slowly won improved conditions for their members and pushed for changes in child labor laws. The United Mine Workers Union was the largest workers' group in the state. In 1898 this union won an eight-hour workday for its workers. Today, about 42 percent of miners are union members.

QUICK CHECK

Fact and Opinion List three facts about why labor unions were created.

Check Understanding

1. Write a paragraph about the labor unions using the terms below.
   labor union   strike

2. **READING SKILL Fact and Opinion** Use your chart from page 166 to write about education and unions in the 1800s.

Fact	Opinion

 3. **Write About It** Write an essay about how education and unions affected people in Indiana in the 1800s.

Unit 4 Review and Assess

Vocabulary

Copy the sentences below. Use the list of vocabulary words to fill in the blanks.

abolition   technology

secede   strike

1. Workers sometimes _____ in order to get better working conditions.

2. Southern states voted to _____ from the Union in 1861.

3. Some people in Indiana wanted the _____ of slavery.

4. The use of ideas, skills, and tools to meet people's needs is called _____.

Comprehension and Critical Thinking

5. Why did some Southern states leave the Union after Abraham Lincoln became President of the United States?

6. Why did some workers form labor unions?

7. **Critical Thinking** Why did cities in Indiana grow during the 1800s?

8. **Reading Skill** What opinion did abolitionists have of slavery?

Skill

Use Special Purpose Maps: Population Maps

9. About how many people live in the area around Indianapolis?

10. Which has a larger population, the area around Fort Wayne or the area around Muncie?

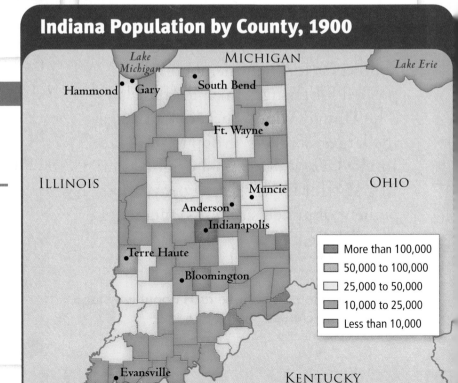

Indiana Population by County, 1900

More than 100,000
50,000 to 100,000
25,000 to 50,000
10,000 to 25,000
Less than 10,000

TEST PREP

Indiana Statewide Test Practice

Read the passage below. Then choose the best answer or write a short response to each of the following questions.

> African Americans were very important to the Underground Railroad operations that ran through Indiana. Many middle-class African Americans worked hard to help rescue and protect people escaping slavery. They raised money for supplies and helped organize rescue efforts.
>
> African American communities along the Ohio River were of special importance. They made sure people escaping slavery crossed the river safely and sent word to other stations when people were on their way. The station houses in these communities gave people shelter, food, and clothing until the routes they would follow farther North became safe.

1 What is the main idea of the passage?

Ⓐ African Americans raised money for the Underground Railroad.

Ⓑ The Underground Railroad helped people escape slavery.

Ⓒ The Underground Railroad helped people cross rivers safely.

Ⓓ African Americans helped the Underground Railroad operate.

2 How did African Americans who did not live along the Ohio River help people escape slavery?

Ⓐ They raised money and helped organize rescue efforts.

Ⓑ They made sure people escaping slavery crossed the river safely.

Ⓒ They sent word to other stations when people were on their way.

Ⓓ They worked in station houses.

3 What did African American communities along the Ohio River do to help people escaping slavery?

Write your answer on a separate piece of paper.

How does change affect people's lives?

Write About the Big Idea

Persuasive Essay

Use the Unit 4 Foldable to help you write a persuasive essay that answers the Big Idea question, *How does change affect people's lives?* Use the notes you wrote under each tab in the Foldable. You may choose to write about one of the Foldable topics. Begin with an introduction that expresses the main idea of your essay. In the body of your essay, be sure to use facts and opinions, and persuasive language. End with a conclusion about how change affects people's lives.

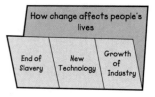

How change affects people's lives

End of Slavery | New Technology | Growth of Industry

Civil War Museum Exhibit

Work with a group to make a Civil War exhibit. Decide what your Civil War topic will be. Examples include Camp Morton, the Battle of Corydon, Indiana soldiers, or women on the home front. Here's how to make your exhibit.

1. Research your topic.

2. Make or find five objects that represent your topic.

3. Build your exhibit. Write a sentence on a card explaining each object.

When everyone has finished, set up a tour of all the Civil War exhibits. A member from each group should explain the objects in each exhibit.

Indiana in Modern Times

Unit 5

Essential Question
What causes a society to grow?

FOLDABLES
Study Organizer

Draw Conclusions
Use an Accordion Book Foldable to take notes as you read Unit 5. Label book faces with **Inventions and Entrepreneurs, A Changing World, Difficult Times, The Civil Rights Movement, Cold War Conflicts,** and **Modern Wars.**

Indiana in a Changing World

Inventions and Entrepreneurs

A Changing World

Difficult Times

The Civil Rights Movement

Cold War Conflicts

Modern Wars

LOG ON

For more about Unit 5, go to
www.macmillanmh.com

Downtown Indianapolis and Central Canal

PEOPLE, PLACES, AND EVENTS

Elwood Haynes

Madam C.J. Walker

Automobile Heritage Museum

1894
Elwood Haynes test-drives a gas-powered automobile in Kokomo, ___na.

Walker Building

1927
The Walker Building opens as a community center and business headquarters.

1895

1910

1925

Elwood Haynes's inventions include one of the first gasoline-powered automobiles, stainless steel, and thermostats.

Today you can explore automotive history at the **Automobile Heritage Museum.**

Madam C.J. Walker became the first female African American millionaire after starting her own hair-care business.

Today the **Walker Building** in Indianapolis houses the Madam Walker Theatre Center.

Robert L. Brokenburr

Ernie Pyle

Crispus Attucks High School

1942
Robert L. Brokenburr ends segregation of high school sports tournaments.

Ernie Pyle State Historic Site

1944
Ernie Pyle wins a Pulitzer Prize for his articles about World War II soldiers.

1940

1955

1970

State lawmaker **Robert L. Brokenburr** worked to allow sports teams of all races to play together in state tournaments.
Today Crispus Attucks High in Indianapolis displays the school's cultural history in a museum.

Journalist **Ernie Pyle** wrote newspaper articles from the battlefields of Europe during World War II.
Today you can see World War II artifacts at the **Ernie Pyle State Historic Site** in Dana.

Inventions and Entrepreneurs

Lesson 1

Orville Wright poses at the controls of the airplane he and his brother Wilbur invented.

Visual Preview

How did new inventions change the lives of people in Indiana?

A In the early 1900s, new technologies like the radio made communication easier.

B Indiana is home to many inventors and entrepreneurs.

C Transportation is an important part of Indiana's economy.

A NEW INVENTIONS

The early 1900s was an exciting time for Indiana. New inventions changed people's lives. New businesses and industries added to the growth of the economy and made communication easier.

Between 1900 and 1930, many **inventions** changed American culture. An invention is a newly created product. Farmers had new machinery that made work easier. Electric lights made it possible for people to work indoors and at night. A cheaper way was found to make steel. Soon, steel was used to improve railroad tracks. Other forms of transportation, like the automobile and the airplane, made traveling easier.

Communication also improved in the early 1900s. Communication is the exchange of information between people. Improvements to the telephone made it easier for people to talk to doctors, order groceries, and stay in touch with one another. Radios brought people information. Farmers could hear crop reports. People listened to news from around the world.

EVENT

First Flight

Wilbur Wright was born near Millville, Indinana, on April 16, 1867. In 1903, he made the first successful airplane flight with his brother, Orville. Wilbur later wrote a letter to the U.S. Patent Office telling them about his flying machine. The Wright Brothers were granted a patent for their invention in 1906.

▼ People of all ages listened to radio shows, including comedies, adventure shows, and music.

QUICK CHECK

Draw Conclusions **What were the advantages of improved communication?**

INVENTORS AND ENTREPRENEURS

As we have read, new inventions made life easier in Indiana. Inventors created new products, and some came up with ways to make existing products less expensive to manufacture. **Entrepreneurs** were also important to Indiana's economy. An entrepreneur is a person who starts a business.

The charts below highlight some of Indiana's inventors and entrepreneurs. Inventors such as Stanley Hayes and the Duesenberg Brothers had ideas that improved transportation. James Oliver invented a plow made of chilled steel that made farm work easier. C. Francis Jenkins made the first movie projector.

GEORGE BALL

INDIANA INVENTORS

INVENTOR	INVENTION
Marion Donovan	Disposable diapers
The Duesenberg Brothers	8-cylinder engine
Elwood Haynes	Gasoline-powered automoblile
Stanley Hayes	Train rails
Andrew J. Moyer	Penicillin made from moldy cantaloupe
C. Francis Jenkins	Motion-picture projector
James Oliver	Steel farming plow
Wilbur Wright	Airplane

Some inventors were also entrepreneurs. Many of these entrepreneurs came up with better ways to make or sell existing products. These entrepreneurs started businesses to sell their new products. For example, George Ball and his brothers invented ways to manufacture and sell glass jars. Madam C. J. Walker, who made hair-care products, was the first female African American millionaire.

The contributions of inventors and entrepreneurs added to the growth of Indiana's economy. The businesses they started provided jobs for many people in the state. Also, their products made daily life for people a little easier.

QUICK CHECK

Compare **How are inventors and entrepreneurs alike?**

INDIANA ENTREPRENEURS

ENTREPRENEUR	BUSINESS
William S. Culbertson	Kentucky-Indiana Railroad Bridge Co.
The Ball Brothers	The Ball Corporation (glass jars)
Jonas Gaar	Gaar Scott Steam Engine Company
Eli Lilly	Eli Lilly and Company Pharmaceuticals
Hamilton Smith	Cannelton Cotton Mill Company
The Studebaker Brothers	The Studebaker Corporation (automobiles)
Madam C.J. Walker	The Madam C.J. Walker Company (hair-care products)
Marie Webster	Practical Patchwork Company (quilting supplies)

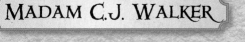

MADAM C.J. WALKER

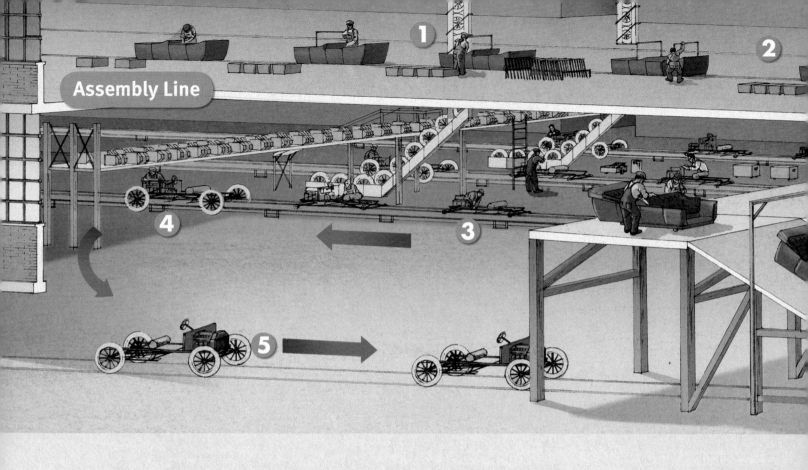

Assembly Line

C AUTOMOBILES

In 1894, Elwood Haynes built the first gas-powered car made in Indiana. Haynes joined with others to build the first auto factory in Indiana. The Studebaker Company and the Duesenberg Company started making cars, too.

Soon, auto manufacturing became one of the state's top industries. By 1913, many automobile factories began creating cars through **mass production**. This is the manufacturing of many products at one time. Car factories made thousands of cars on an **assembly line**, or a line of workers and machines that put together products in steps. The assembly line was developed by Henry Ford. On an assembly line, each worker or machine does one task again and again.

Another invention also made travel easier. Hoosiers created an electric railroad system. Although the first electric train was developed in Europe, engineers in Indiana came up with a system to connect many electric railways at once. They called this electric train system the inter-urban railway. The trains connected many of Indiana's larger cities. The name *inter-urban* means "between cities."

1. Car body is placed on assembly line.
2. Seats, top, and sides are attached to car body.
3. Gas tank and engine are attached to frame.
4. Wheels and steering wheel are attached to frame.
5. Frame moves along line to meet body.
6. Car body is attached to frame.

Diagram Skill

As the car body moved, the seats, sides and tops were added, then the engine and wheels were attached to the car frame. What was the last step?

The first electric train line opened in 1900 and ran from Indianapolis to Greenwood. Soon, railway stations were crowded with people traveling to neighboring cities. By 1920, nearly every large city in Indiana was part of an inter-urban railway system.

QUICK CHECK

Draw Conclusions **How did improved transportation help cities grow?**

◄ This inter-urban railcar was one of several railway lines that ran between Indiana's large cities.

Check Understanding

1. **VOCABULARY** Write an advertisement for a new invention you have created. Be sure to include the following vocabulary words.
   **invention   communication
   mass production**

2. **READING SKILL** Draw Conclusions Use your chart from page 178 to write about the automobile industry.

Text Clues	Conclusion

3. **Write About It** Write a paragraph about how new inventions improved communications.

Lesson 2

VOCABULARY

decade p. 185

Allied Powers p. 186

rationing p. 187

suffrage p. 188

Roaring Twenties
p. 190

READING SKILL

Draw Conclusions

Copy the chart below. Use it to draw conclusions about the early 1900s.

Text Clues	Conclusion

INDIANA ACADEMIC STANDARDS

4.1.10, 4.1.11, 4.1.12, 4.2.2, 4.2.5

A Changing World

This painting shows a Roaring Twenties dance club.

Visual Preview

How did changes in the world affect the people of Indiana?

A Many people moved to cities to work in new factories.

B World War I was fought in Europe.

C Women won the right to vote.

D The Roaring Twenties was a time of riches and growth.

A INDIANA CITIES GROW

Several important changes took place around the 1920s that affected the daily lives of Americans. Many items we use today were introduced during this time. Changes around the world brought conflict as Americans, and Hoosiers, went to war.

Between 1910 and 1920, automobile factories boosted the state's economy. This **decade**, or 10-year period, introduced inventions and machines that did the work faster and cheaper than it had previously been done.

Mass production made it easier to make automobiles. People moved to northern cities like South Bend to find work. Indiana auto factories and independent car companies produced over 25 percent of the cars sold in the United States.

Another important industry for Indiana's economy was the steel industry. Small steel mills across the country combined to form a large steel company based in Gary, Indiana. This collection of steel foundries became the United States Steel Corporation. At one time, the steel foundries based in Gary produced more steel than any other steel company in the country.

▲ This painting shows the inside of a steel mill.

These steel mills provided jobs for many people in Indiana. Even today, nearly 30,000 Hoosiers work in the steel industry.

QUICK CHECK

Making Inferences **What was an advantage of moving to a large northern city?**

In 1914, the world changed. Archduke Franz Ferdinand, a European nobleman who was going to be the next ruler of Austria-Hungary, was shot and killed by an assasin. His death sparked the beginning of a war we now call World War I. It is called a world war because countries from all over the world fought in it.

United States President Woodrow Wilson wanted our nation to stay out of the war. But when German submarines attacked ships in the Atlantic Ocean carrying American passengers, he realized that we could no longer stay out of the war.

The USS *Indiana* was an active battleship during World War I.

On April 6, 1917, the United States joined the **Allied Powers**, or the Allies. The Allied Powers included Great Britain, France, Russia, and Italy. They fought against the Central Powers, which included Germany, Austria-Hungary, and present-day Turkey.

Hoosiers supported the war effort. More than 130,000 soldiers fought in the war, and more than 3,000 died in battle. At home, people made bandages that doctors used to treat the wounded. Factory workers in Indiana made military supplies, weapons, and vehicles. When men went to war, some women had to work outside the home. Many worked in factories making weapons.

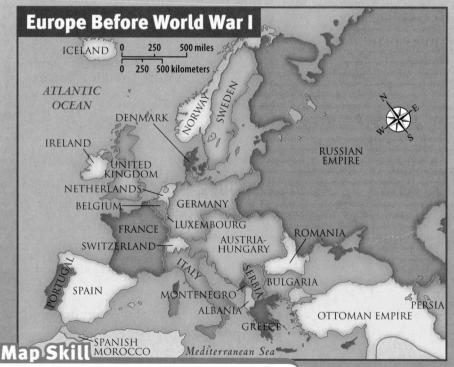

Europe Before World War I

ICELAND

0   250   500 miles

0   250   500 kilometers

ATLANTIC OCEAN

NORWAY

SWEDEN

DENMARK

IRELAND

UNITED KINGDOM

NETHERLANDS

BELGIUM

GERMANY

LUXEMBOURG

FRANCE

SWITZERLAND

ITALY

PORTUGAL

SPAIN

MONTENEGRO

ALBANIA

GREECE

SERBIA

AUSTRIA-HUNGARY

ROMANIA

BULGARIA

RUSSIAN EMPIRE

OTTOMAN EMPIRE

PERSIA

Mediterranean Sea

SPANISH MOROCCO

Map Skill

LOCATION **Where is Romania located in relation to the Russian Empire?**

Many people helped raise the money needed to carry on the war. Hoosiers also lived with **rationing**. To ration means to give things out in limited portions. During the war, Americans had only limited supplies of some goods because large amounts were reserved for soldiers.

The war ended in 1918 when the Central Powers surrendered. Indiana soldiers returned home. Major celebrations were held in Indianapolis, as well as throughout Indiana and the rest of the nation.

QUICK CHECK

Draw Conclusions **What were two ways that Hoosiers supported the war effort?**

The poster above was one of many asking men to join the war effort. The painting below shows soldiers in Belgium during World War I.

C FIGHTING FOR EQUAL RIGHTS

Many Hoosiers faced discrimination in the 1900s. Discrimination happens when certain groups of people are treated differently or unfairly. African Americans and women were two groups that suffered discrimination. They fought for equal rights.

Women's Right to Vote

Before 1900, women could not vote. Many women at this time fought for **suffrage**, or the right to vote. In 1878, May Wright Sewall helped start the Indianapolis Equal Suffrage Society. She was also a leading member of the National Woman Suffrage Association with Ida Husted Harper. Harper used her skill as a writer to promote the cause. Along with many others, May Sewall and Ida Harper fought for equality for women not only in Indiana but across the country.

In 1920, the Nineteenth Amendment to the U.S. Constitution was adopted. This law gave women the right to vote. Indiana changed its constitution to grant this right to its citizens soon thereafter. Women had gained suffrage and had earned their right to vote.

▲ This painting shows women voting for the first time. The portrait to the left shows May Wright Sewall, who worked for suffrage.

Violence Against Many

Many African Americans had moved to Indiana cities during the Great Migration to work in steel mills, automobile factories, and other industries. From 1910 through the 1920s, over one million African Americans left the South. They wanted to escape violence, discrimination, and low wages in the southern states. There were also few factory jobs in the southern states. However, African Americans often faced discrimination in northern cities, too.

Some white people were unhappy about the number of African Americans who were moving north and taking jobs there. Some of these people joined a group called the Ku Klux Klan.

The Ku Klux Klan used violence against people they saw as different from themselves. They discriminated against many groups in addition to African Americans. The groups the Ku Klux Klan targeted included Catholics, Jews, and immigrants. The Klan grew powerful around the United States and throughout the state of Indiana.

In 1924, Indiana Klan leader D.C. Stevenson was arrested for murder. This arrest brought attention to the violent acts that many Klan members had committed. By the end of the 1920s, the Ku Klux Klan had little power in Indiana. The Klan lost its popularity across the country, and many people left the organization. Many Hoosiers joined the fight for equal rights.

QUICK CHECK

Draw Conclusions **In what way was the Great Migration unsuccessful for African Americans?**

Ku Klux Klan members in front of the Capitol in Washington, D.C.

The years after World War I were good for most Americans. Many businesses enjoyed success. People had jobs and money to buy new products that made life easier and more enjoyable. Because life was changing rapidly in exciting ways, this period was called the **Roaring Twenties**.

Automobiles, which were once a luxury, became affordable for many people. The increasing number of cars created a need for highways, gas stations, motels, and restaurants. Many modern household items, such as vacuum cleaners and electric stoves, were also affordable. People started spending money on things to make their lives more convenient. They had more time and money to spend on entertainment because new inventions made their work easier.

The poster to the left advertises one of the many movies that people could enjoy in their free time. The photograph below shows the Capitol Theater, formerly the Old Park Theatre, in Indianapolis.

▶ In the 1920s, dance competitions were popular. This photo shows dancers with trophies after winning a competition.

Movie theaters became a popular and affordable form of entertainment in the 1920s. New inventions in the film industry made it possible for many movies to be made. Movie theaters were able to offer motion pictures for less than 20 cents per person. By the end of the 1920s, Muncie, Indiana, had 9 movie theaters, while Indianapolis had more than 50 theaters.

Another form of entertainment that became popular in the 1920s was music. Musicians started playing a type of music called jazz. Jazz has its roots in the African tradition. Indiana songwriter Noble Sissle became a famous jazz singer and composer. He and his partner, Eubie Blake, wrote the first African American musical to become a box office success.

Dancing to jazz music became the latest craze in the 1920s. Dances that were popular included the Charleston, the Swing, and the Lindy Hop. Hoosier Marian Harris was a well known dancer who performed many swing dances during this era.

QUICK CHECK

Draw Conclusions Why was there time for entertainment in the 1920s?

Check Understanding

1. **VOCABULARY** Use the following vocabulary to create a time line of events you read about in this lesson.

   decade   Allied Powers   suffrage

2. **READING SKILL Draw Conclusions** Use your chart from page 184 to write about Indiana and changes after World War I.

Text Clues	Conclusion

EXPLORE The Big Idea

3. **Write About It** Write a newspaper article about new types of entertainment during the Roaring Twenties.

Read Line Graphs

VOCABULARY

line graph

Some information that you may read shows a change over time. One way to learn how the information has changed is to look at a graph. Graphs are diagrams that show information in a visual way. **Line graphs** show how one type of information changes over time.

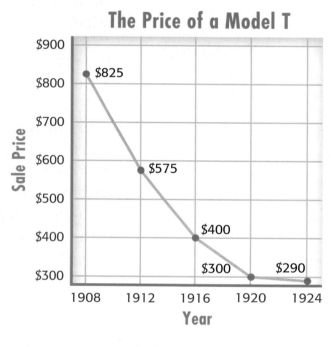

The Price of a Model T

Learn It

Look at the line graph.

- The title of a line graph tells what information has changed.

- Labels on the graph tell the length of time and the amount of what has changed.

- Line graphs often show an increase or decrease in number. A flat line means no change or a small change. A slanted line means there was a large change.

- The title tells that the graph shows a change in the price of the Model T car. The Ford Company used new technology in the early 1900s to produce an inexpensive car that everyone could buy.

- The bottom of the line graph is divided into a length of time that represents a certain number of years. The length of time for this line graph is four years. The Model T automobile rolled off the assembly line for the first time in 1908.

- The left side of the line graph shows dollar amounts. The Ford Company was able to offer the Model T for $825 in 1908. The cost of buying things is much higher today, so $825 in 1908 would be about $20,000 by today's standards.

Look at the line graph to questions below.

- What was the price of the Model T in 1912?

- In what length of time did the price of the Model T decrease the most?

- What was the smallest decrease in price?

- In a group, research the cost of a Studebaker car in the early 1900s. Use the Internet and the information in Unit 5 to help you. Create a line graph of the change in price of the Studebaker over several years. How does the price of the Studebaker compare to the prices of the Model T shown on the graph?

This painting shows an automobile assembly line in 1910.

DIFFICULT TIMES

VOCABULARY

stock p. 195

Great Depression p. 195

drought p. 196

New Deal p. 197

dictator p. 198

Axis Powers p. 198

READING SKILL

Draw Conclusions
Copy the chart below. Use it to draw conclusions about the Great Depression and World War II.

Text Clues	Conclusion

INDIANA ACADEMIC STANDARDS

4.1.10, 4.1.11, 4.2.6, 4.2.7, 4.4.1

One of many soup kitchens that operated in the 1930s.

Visual Preview

How did changes affect Indiana in the late 1920s, 1930s, and 1940s?

A The Great Depression swept the country at the end of the 1920s.

B Roosevelt's New Deal eased some of the hardships of the Depression.

C The United States entered World War II.

D Many Hoosiers supported the war effort at home.

194

A THE GREAT DEPRESSION

The Great Depression brought hard times to many Hoosiers. People lost their savings and their jobs. The New Deal provided some help. In 1941 the United States entered another world war.

By late 1929, the United States economy was facing serious problems. Mass production had led to more goods than people needed. Also, many people had gotten into trouble by purchasing items on credit. Buying on credit means to borrow money to pay for things.

Many Americans had bought **stocks** in the 1920s. Stocks are certificates that show that the people who own them have a share in a company. Businesses grew, and stock prices rose for years. In October 1929, stock prices fell sharply. Some people panicked. They sold their stock and stopped buying goods. This made stock prices fall even more. When prices collapsed, the stock market crashed. Many stocks became worthless. People who had borrowed money to buy stocks could not repay their debts. Many banks closed because they had no money.

Soon the whole economy suffered a long period of decline called the **Great Depression**, which lasted through the 1930s. Banks failed, companies stopped producing goods, and many people lost their jobs. People around our state and around the country had little money. The United States was facing the worst economic disaster in its history. Many people, including many Hoosiers, could not afford food. They had to wait in long lines to get food.

QUICK CHECK

Cause and Effect How did mass production hurt businesses in the late 1920s?

▼ By 1932, more than one in four workers were jobless.

The stock market crash hurt not only banks and businesses but everyday workers and their families. More than one in four workers lost their jobs. Many people lost their homes as well. Some people were forced to live in shacks and tents. Soon tent cities sprang up across Indiana and across the country. These tent cities were known as "Hoovervilles." The tent cities were named after Herbert Hoover, the President in 1929, because many Americans blamed him for the Depression.

▲ Franklin D. Roosevelt, pictured here with a family friend, created programs called the New Deal.

John Steinbeck's novel, *The Grapes of Wrath*, tells the story of Dust Bowl farmers who left their homes for a chance at a better life in California.

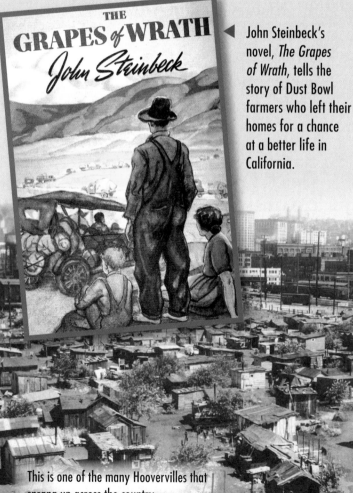

This is one of the many Hoovervilles that sprang up across the country.

Farmers in Indiana and across the country also had a hard time after the stock market crash. Many farmers had borrowed money from banks to buy machines. When the farmers could not pay back their loans, they lost their farms.

To make matters worse, for several years beginning in 1930, a severe **drought** affected states in the Midwest and Southwest. A drought is a long period of little rain. High winds blew away millions of acres of soil. This area came to be known as the Dust Bowl. Many farm families were forced to leave their land to look for jobs in the West.

▲ New Deal dam project

New Deal Programs	
Civilian Conservation Corps (CCC)	put people to work planting trees and fighting forest fires
Agricultural Adjustment Act (AAA)	helped farmers get higher prices for their crops
Federal Deposit Insurance Corporation (FDIC)	insured banks and protected people's money
Tennessee Valley Authority (TVA)	brought electricity to rural areas of Tennessee and bordering states

Chart Skill

What program listed on the chart helped to improve crop prices?

In 1933, Franklin D. Roosevelt became President. He had a plan to help the nation recover from the Great Depression. He started a series of programs called the **New Deal**.

The New Deal used federal tax money to pay for programs to create jobs. The new programs helped businesses, banks, and farmers. It also created programs to build roads, schools, and parks.

One important New Deal program was the Civilian Conservation Corps, or the CCC. This program hired young men to work in forests. Three CCC companies were formed in Indiana. These men helped rebuild Indiana's state forests.

Governor Paul McNutt of Indiana also helped Hoosiers during the Depression. He started many programs for the needy, which were paid for by state tax dollars. One program provided money to elderly people who had little savings.

QUICK CHECK

Main Idea and Details **How did the Civilian Conservation Corps create jobs?**

U.S. troops prepare for war.

Ⓒ WORLD WAR II BEGINS

The United States was not the only country suffering during the Great Depression. Other countries around the world, including Germany, were hurting as well. A man named Adolf Hitler took advantage of this situation. Hitler became dictator of Germany in 1933.

A **dictator** is a person who rules a country alone. Hitler convinced many people in Germany that certain groups of people, especially Jews, were responsible for Germany's problems.

Eventually, Hitler led Germany into World War II. This war began in September 1939. Germany and Italy formed the **Axis Powers** in Europe. They fought against the Allied Powers of Great Britain, France, and the Soviet Union.

At first, the United States stayed out of this new war. Then, on December 7, 1941, Japan attacked American ships at Pearl Harbor, Hawaii.

American World War II bomber

The next day, the U.S. Congress declared war on Japan. Soon after, Germany and Italy declared war on the United States. The United States joined the war on the side of the Allies.

The new war gradually pulled the country out of the Depression. The war created new jobs and work for many Americans. Women worked in factories, building tanks and airplanes. African Americans continued to move from the South to work in mills and factories in Northern cities.

Once again, the people of Indiana helped their country. More than 360,000 men and women served in the armed forces. More than 10,000 Hoosiers died fighting for our country. Members of the Indiana National Guard fought bravely in the Philippines.

PEOPLE

By 1942, some baseball teams had stopped playing ball because many of the players were sent overseas to fight. In 1943, the All-American Girls Professional Baseball League was formed. Young women were recruited for the baseball league, and many played in the Midwest. The Fort Wayne Daisies was one of three Indiana teams. In 1945 the Daisies had a winning season, winning 62 of the 109 games they played.

Fort Wayne Daisies

▼ During World War II, many women worked in the military in noncombat roles.

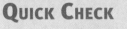

QUICK CHECK

Draw Conclusions
What ended the Great Depression?

Citizenship
Working for the Common Good

To keep food on the table during World War II, people in Indiana and across the country planted victory gardens. They grew food in backyards, in empty lots, and even on city rooftops. Many times, vegetables from the garden provided meals for many in the community. Today there are people who are less fortunate than most and struggle to buy food. Some people rely on shelters to provide food, clothing, and a place to sleep. You can work for the common good in your community by volunteering at a food bank or a community garden. You can also help work in a soup kitchen to feed the hungry or homeless.

Write About It Create a plan for a project at your school that will show you and your class working for the common good.

Hoosiers at home helped out, too. Miners dug large amounts of coal for fuel. Farmers grew more food than before. People rationed rubber, gasoline, and metal for the war effort. They cut back on eating things such as meat and sugar so that there would be enough for the soldiers. Children collected paper and cooking fat to recycle into items that could be used in the war.

Many Indiana factories stopped producing automobiles and started building weapons for the war. Workers built army base camps or helped at the prisoner-of-war camp in Edinburgh.

Hoosier Ernie Pyle was a famous reporter during World War II. He joined American soldiers in Europe at the front.

▲ A teacher directs her students during a national air raid drill.

Ernie Pyle (center) talks to soldiers overseas.

Check Understanding

Pyle wrote stories describing the dangers soldiers faced. He wrote many newspaper articles about everyday soldiers fighting in Europe and Japan. People across the United States read his articles.

In 1945 the Allies won World War II. Soldiers returned home to an era of hope. After the war, thousands of people moved to Indiana looking for jobs. They found higher wages in Indiana's factories than in many other areas of the country.

QUICK CHECK

Summarize **How did Hoosiers help win the war at home and in Europe?**

1. **VOCABULARY** Create a World War II poster. Include the following vocabulary words:

   dictator   **Axis Powers**

2. **READING SKILL** Draw Conclusions Use your chart from page 194 to write about economic changes in the 1930s.

Text Clues	Conclusion

EXPLORE The Big Idea

3. **Write About It** Write a newspaper article about New Deal programs that helped Indiana.

Map and Globe Skills

Use a Historical Map

VOCABULARY

historical map

Maps can be used to show many different things, such as landforms, roadways, or where things are located. Maps can also show things that happened in the past. A **historical map** shows where events from the past took place. Historical maps can show how the population of an area changed over time, where battles occurred, or how landforms have changed.

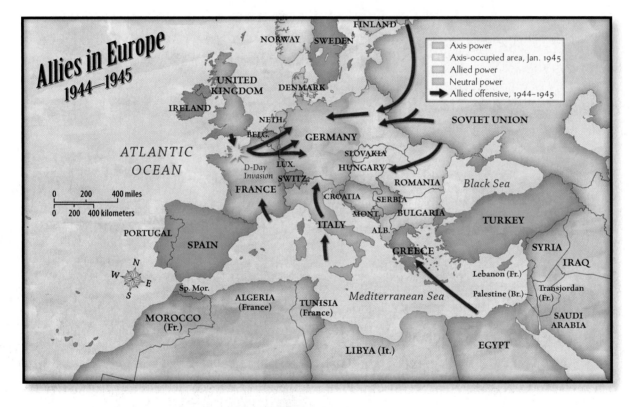

Learn It

- Most historical maps have a title and dates. What is the title of this map? What are the dates for this map?

- Use the map key to find the meaning of symbols or color shading on the map. On this map, the map key is in the top right-hand corner.

Try It

Use the map on page 202 to answer the following questions.

● What color represents the countries that were Neutral Powers? List the countries.

● In what direction did Allied forces move from the Soviet Union to Hungary?

● In what month and year did the Axis Powers occupy Finland?

● Some of the countries on this map no longer exist today. Can you name one of those countries?

Apply It

● As you read the rest of this unit, look for other historical maps.

● Compare the information that is given in those maps with the information that you read in each lesson.

● Find vocabulary words in the lessons to help you understand the maps.

● Create a historical map of your community from 50 years ago. How have things changed over time? Use the map to tell your area's history.

American soldiers land on the coast during the invasion of Normandy in France.

THE CIVIL RIGHTS MOVEMENT

Lesson 4

VOCABULARY

segregation p. 205

integration p. 205

civil rights p. 206

protest p. 206

READING SKILL

Draw Conclusions
Copy the chart below. Use it to draw conclusions about the civil rights movement.

Text Clues	Conclusion

INDIANA ACADEMIC STANDARDS

4.1.11, 4.1.13, 4.1.17, 4.2.2, 4.2.5, 4.2.6, 4.2.7

Marchers carry anti-segregation signs at the March on Washington.

Visual Preview

What risks do people take to gain equal rights?

A Many Americans fought against discrimination in schools.

B The civil rights movement worked for equality.

C Many different groups have fought for equal rights.

A SEPARATE BUT NOT EQUAL

In the 1940s and 1950s, African Americans were not treated equally in many ways. In both Indiana and the nation, many people worked for equality for all citizens of the United States.

In many parts of the United States, African Americans were not treated equally. By the early 1950s, there was **segregation** across the country. Segregation is the practice of keeping ethnic groups separated. African Americans could not go to the same restaurants as white people. They were forced to use separate restrooms and drinking fountains in public places. They had to attend separate schools and sporting events.

Several Hoosiers fought for **integration**. Integration is the act of making something open to people of all ethnic groups. One Hoosier who fought for integration was Robert Brokenburr. In 1942 he wrote a law that integrated high school sports tournaments. The law allowed teams of all races to play together in the same tournaments.

Another person who fought for school equality was Henry Richardson. He wrote a law to make segregated schools illegal. He also worked to stop discrimination in other public places. Due to the work of these people and others, in 1957, Indiana passed laws banning segregation in public schools.

QUICK CHECK
Draw Conclusions **Why did people feel that they had to change Indiana laws?**

▼ Protesters march in the Ten Mile March for Freedom.

RAISING A COLLECTIVE VOICE

B

In the 1950s, many Americans, including many people from our state, fought for **civil rights**. Civil rights are the rights of all citizens to be treated equally under the law.

Many civil rights groups held **protests** to help create laws making discrimination illegal. A protest is a complaint against an unfair practice. The civil rights movement won a victory when the Voting Rights Act became law in 1965. This law banned practices used to keep African Americans from voting.

▲ This political cartoon shows an artist's opinion about desegregation in schools. Why do you think the artist showed desegregation as a door needing to be opened?

Many civil rights groups in cities all across Indiana organized marches and protests in support of the Voting Rights Act. For example, the Ten Mile March for Freedom was held in Indianapolis on July 4, 1964. People marched in support of the Voting Rights Act.

After the Voting Rights Act became law, many African Americans were able to exercise their right to vote. They began to seek political office as well. In 1967 Richard Hatcher became one of the first African Americans to be mayor of a large city when he became mayor of Gary. As mayor, he promoted cooperation between different ethnic groups and was a champion for equality and fairness.

Dr. Martin Luther King, Jr.

In the late 1950s and 1960s, Dr. Martin Luther King, Jr., was a leader in the civil rights movement across the nation. He believed in using peaceful ways to bring about change. Dr. King organized many peaceful protests.

In 1963 Dr. King joined more than 250,000 people in a march in Washington, D.C., to support the civil rights movement. A group of civil rights supporters from Indiana traveled by bus to join Dr. King in the march. Those who could not attend were able to watch the many speeches and demonstrations on television, as this was one of the first large events to be nationally broadcast.

Many people around the country respected Dr. King for his peaceful views on promoting change. In 1968, Dr. King was shot and killed. There were riots in cities across the country when people heard of Dr. King's death. Fortunately, this did not happen in Indiana. A senator named Robert Kennedy, who was speaking to a large crowd in Indianapolis, broke the news about Dr. King's death. Kennedy urged people to continue to fight for justice in peaceful ways.

QUICK CHECK

Draw Conclusions **How was Indiana affected by the civil rights movement?**

The photograph on the right shows Dr. Martin Luther King, Jr., at the Indianapolis Airport. The photograph below is from the 1963 March on Washington.

Primary Sources

"I have a dream that one day this nation will rise up and live out the true meaning of its **creed**: 'We hold these truths to be self-evident, that all men are created equal' . . . I have a dream that my four little children will one day live in a nation where they will not be judged by the color of their skin but by the content of their character . . . .

This will be the day when all of God's children will be able to sing with a new meaning: 'My country, 'tis of thee, sweet land of liberty, of thee I sing. Land where my fathers died, land of the pilgrim's pride, from every mountainside, let freedom ring!'"

From the "I Have a Dream" speech given by Dr. Martin Luther King, Jr., on August 28, 1963, in Washington, D.C.

creed   **a stated belief**

Write About It Write a speech about a dream that you have for the future.

The struggle for equality continued in Indiana and across the country. People organized protests for improved working conditions and equal pay.

One group that protested was migrant farm workers. Migrant farm workers travel across the country to harvest crops. These workers often face unhealthy working conditions for little pay. In the late 1960s and early 1970s, groups of migrant workers fought for better working conditions and higher wages.

Another group that fought for equal rights was women. In the late 1960s, the National Organization for Women (NOW) fought to make discrimination against women in the workplace illegal. In 1972 a law was passed that gave women equal rights in education and expanded women's sports programs in schools.

▼ César Chávez (front right) marched for farm workers' rights.

▶ Women's rights leaders marching in Washington, D.C.

▼ President George H. W. Bush signs the Americans with Disabilities Act in 1990.

For years, millions of Americans with disabilities faced discrimination in the workplace. In 1990, the Americans with Disabilities Act made it illegal for workplaces to discriminate against people who are disabled. The law also requires that certain public places must provide ramps and widen doorways so that disabled people can enter public buildings more easily.

QUICK CHECK

Making Inferences **How can fighting for equality improve working conditions?**

Check Understanding

1. **VOCABULARY** Write three sentences about the civil rights movement. Use one these vocabulary words in each sentence.

   segregation　　**integration**　　**protest**

2. **READING SKILL** Draw Conclusions
   Use the chart from page 204 to write about civil rights activists.

Text Clues	Conclusion

EXPLORE The Big Idea

3. **Write About It** Write a letter to the principal of your school. Suggest ways that your class could honor equality.

Lesson 5

VOCABULARY

communism p. 211

Cold War p. 211

arms race p. 211

satellite p. 212

truce p. 213

READING SKILL

Draw Conclusions

Copy the chart below. Use it to draw conclusions about the Cold War.

Text Clues	Conclusion

INDIANA ACADEMIC STANDARDS

4.1.11, 4.1.13, 4.1.16, 4.2.7, 4.3.12

COLD WAR CONFLICTS

The Berlin Wall in Germany became a symbol of the Cold War. It was torn down in 1989.

Visual Preview

How did world events from 1945 to 1975 affect Indiana?

A Tensions grew between the United States and the Soviet Union.

B Conflicts over communism led to the Korean War.

C The war in Vietnam divided the United States.

210

A A NEW WORLD POWER

After World War II, the United States and the Soviet Union were two of the most powerful nations in the world. After 1945, tensions started to grow between these former allies.

After World War II, the Soviet Union took control of much of Eastern Europe. It forced these countries to follow its economic system, called **communism**. In this system, the government controls all property and resources.

As the Soviet Union's power grew, the United States worried that communism would spread even farther. Many Americans believed the spread of communism would harm the United States. The growing tension between the two nations became known as the **Cold War**. It was called "cold" because the two nations did not attack each other. Instead they fought with ideas, words, and money.

During the 1950s, the United States and the Soviet Union each developed nuclear weapons. Both nations spent enormous amounts of money on these weapons. They thought that if they were evenly matched in weapons, neither country would be the first to attack the other, because each side would be afraid the other would fight back.

Such a buildup of weapons between two competing countries is called an **arms race**. Millions of dollars were spent to test and store nuclear weapons. Today there are several empty missile storage sites in Indiana.

During the arms race, U.S. missiles were built to carry nuclear weapons called warheads.

QUICK CHECK

Summarize **What led the United States and the Soviet Union into the Cold War?**

COMMUNISM SPREADS

In addition to the arms race, the United States and the Soviet Union competed in the space race. It began in 1957 when the Soviet Union launched a **satellite** that circled Earth. A satellite is an object that circles another object. Meanwhile, the United States worked on its own space program. In 1969 the program had a huge success when Neil Armstrong became the first person to walk on the moon.

In October of 1962, another conflict called the Cuban Missile Crisis caused concern in America. Cuba, a small island country near the Florida coast, became a communist country and stored nuclear missiles for the Soviet Union. Many people feared the Soviet Union would launch missiles from Cuba. President

John F. Kennedy addressed America's concerns when he said:

"...we shall...meet any hardship, support any friend...in order to assure the survival and success of liberty."

Still, concern over a communist attack was part of everyday life. Schools held drills to prepare students for possible attacks. Some American families built bomb shelters in their homes. Nuclear warheads and other missiles were stored in sites across the country.

The Korean War

In the late 1940s and the early 1950s, the fear of communism led to another war. The nation of Korea was divided in two by a border at the 38th parallel of latitude. North Korea was a communist country with ties with the Soviet Union and China. South Korea was a republic with allies in the United States and other countries.

EVENT

During World War II, the United States used atomic bombs on Japan. After that, the testing of large nuclear weapons began around the world. The United States, Russia, Great Britain, and France began testing hydrogen bombs and thermonuclear devices between 1945 and 1968. In the United States, most testing took place in remote locations in Nevada, New Mexico, and Utah. Throughout the Cold War, many countries signed treaties to stop nuclear testing.

Nuclear Testing

When North Korea invaded South Korea, American and other troops fought to drive them back. The Korean War ended in 1953 when a **truce** was signed. A truce is an agreement to stop fighting. This truce left the border between North Korea and South Korea where it had been before the invasion. North Korea remained a communist country. South Korea remained a republic.

QUICK CHECK

Draw Conclusions **Why did the Soviet Union and the United States take opposite sides in the Korean War?**

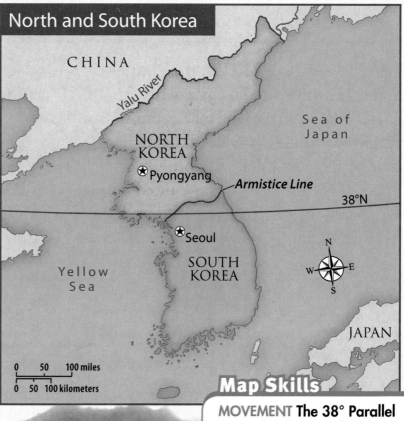

North and South Korea

CHINA

Yalu River

NORTH KOREA

★ Pyongyang

Sea of Japan

Armistice Line

38°N

★ Seoul

SOUTH KOREA

Yellow Sea

JAPAN

N W E S

| 0 | 50 | 100 miles |

| 0 | 50 | 100 kilometers |

Map Skills

MOVEMENT **The 38° Parallel is one dividing line for North Korea and South Korea. What is another dividing line between the two countries?**

A battle during the Korean War

C CONFLICTS NEAR AND FAR

In the 1960s and 1970s, the United States continued to struggle with the Soviet Union. The fear that communism would spread to many small countries around the world led to another war. From 1965 until 1975, the United States fought forces in North Vietnam to keep it from controlling South Vietnam.

North Vietnam was a communist nation supported by the Soviet Union and China. South Vietnam, a republic, was supported by the United States. When North Vietnamese troops attacked military bases in South Vietnam, President Lyndon Johnson sent planes to bomb North Vietnam.

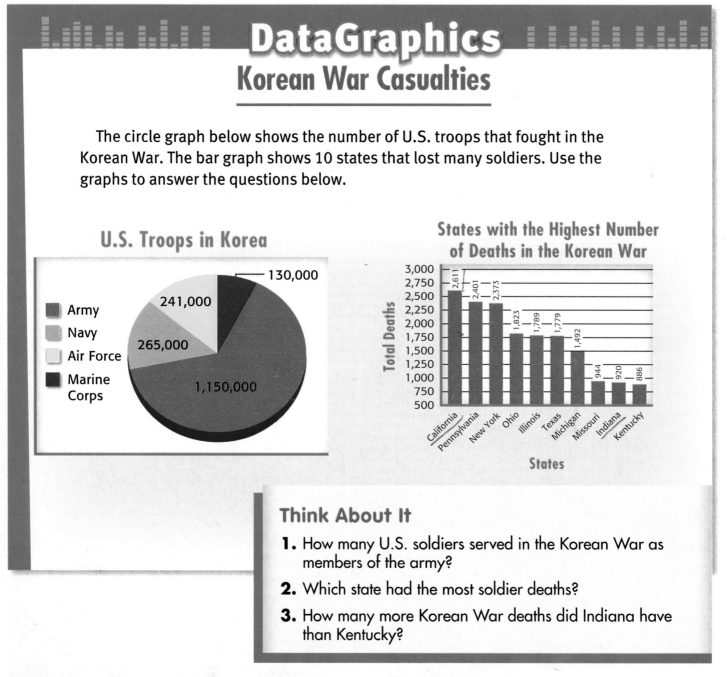

DataGraphics
Korean War Casualties

The circle graph below shows the number of U.S. troops that fought in the Korean War. The bar graph shows 10 states that lost many soldiers. Use the graphs to answer the questions below.

U.S. Troops in Korea

- Army
- Navy
- Air Force
- Marine Corps

130,000
241,000
265,000
1,150,000

States with the Highest Number of Deaths in the Korean War

Total Deaths

California 2,611
Pennsylvania 2,401
New York 2,373
Ohio 1,823
Illinois 1,789
Texas 1,779
Michigan 1,492
Missouri 944
Indiana 920
Kentucky 886

States

Think About It

1. How many U.S. soldiers served in the Korean War as members of the army?

2. Which state had the most soldier deaths?

3. How many more Korean War deaths did Indiana have than Kentucky?

Protesting the War

The Vietnam War caused conflict in the United States. Some Americans supported the war. Others did not believe that our country should be fighting in a war where our own safety was not threatened.

Thousands of people took part in war protests across the country. In Indiana, there were protests against the war on some college campuses. There were marches on other Indiana campuses that supported the war.

When the Vietnam War ended, over 57,000 American troops had died. Of that amount, 1,500 were from Indiana.

QUICK CHECK

Making Inferences **Why was there conflict in the United States about the Vietnam War?**

Vietnam Today

CHINA

MYANMAR (BURMA)

Red R.

Hanoi

LAOS

Gulf of Tonkin

Mekong R.

THAILAND

VIETNAM

CAMBODIA

South China Sea

Gulf of Thailand

Ho Chi Minh City (Saigon)

Mekong Delta

0   100   200 miles
0   100   200 kilometers

Map Skill

LOCATION **What two countries border Vietnam to the west?**

Check Understanding

1. **VOCABULARY** Write a paragraph about the Cold War. Use the following vocabulary words:

   communism   **Cold War**   **arms race**

2. **READING SKILL** Draw Conclusions Use the chart from page 210 to write about the Cold War.

Text Clues	Conclusion

3. **Write About It** Research the Vietnam War. Write a newspaper article about it. Make sure to describe how people from our state felt about the war.

Soldiers in South Vietnam wade through a canal during the Vietnam War.

Lesson 6

VOCABULARY

terrorism p. 217

Department of Homeland Security p. 218

READING SKILL

Draw Conclusions

Copy the chart below. Use it to draw conclusions about modern wars after 2000.

Text Clues	Conclusion

INDIANA ACADEMIC STANDARDS

4.1.13, 4.1.17, 4.2.6, 4.3.2

MODERN WARS

Firefighters walk through the rubble of New York City streets after the terrorist attacks of September 11, 2001.

Visual Preview

How do modern wars affect the people of Indiana?

A Many people helped after the September 11, 2001, attacks.

B U. S. soldiers were sent to Afghanistan and Iraq to fight against terrorism.

SEPTEMBER 11, 2001

On September 11, 2001, the World Trade Center in New York City and the Pentagon in Washington, D.C., were attacked. People from Indiana and across the nation responded to the crisis.

On September 11, 2001, our country changed forever. Terrorists took over four U. S. airplanes and used them to attack the United States. The men who hijacked these planes committed acts of **terrorism**. Terrorism is using violence or threats to achieve a political goal. Over 3,000 people died in this attack, which was the worst terrorist attack in history on American soil.

The attacks of September 11, 2001, shocked Americans and people from all over the world. Rescue workers acted quickly to help in the crisis. Firefighters and medical workers from cities all around the country offered their services. The crisis brought a new sense of patriotism to the nation.

Citizens from Indiana also did their part to help. A group called the Indiana Task Force traveled to New York City to join other rescue teams at the scene of the disaster. Many Hoosiers donated blood, raised money, or collected supplies for victims and rescue workers.

QUICK CHECK

Draw Conclusions **How did American citizens respond to the terrorist attacks?**

▼ The Indiana Task Force was honored with a mural for responding to the attacks.

Responding

Indiana Task Force 1's team of 62 search-and-rescue specialists left Indianapolis shortly after 5 p.m. on Sept. 11 for the 16-hour trip to New York with three semi-trailer trucks carrying tools and equipment along with two command vehicles.

Several Indiana **communities** were represented. The team, organized by the Federal Emergency Management Agency, was made up physicians, paramedics, engineers and damage structure specialists as well as search-dog handlers. The team was the first to try out remote-control robots that use cameras to search through wreckage.

MIDDLE EAST TERRORISM

There have been many acts of terrorism in American history. Since World War II, most terrorist attacks on Americans have been carried out by groups from the Middle East. The attacks of September 11, 2001, were carried out by a terrorist group called al-Qaeda. This group had support from other terrorist groups in Afghanistan. In October 2001, the United States and its allies invaded Afghanistan.

President George W. Bush was concerned that terrorists might obtain weapons of mass destruction, such as nuclear bombs. One country that concerned President Bush was Iraq. The President and government officials feared Iraq might help terrorists attack the United States. In 2003 the United States and its allies invaded Iraq. No weapons of mass destruction were found, however. Many people in the United States and around the world argued about whether or not Iraq should have been invaded.

President Bush wanted to protect the American people from other terrorist attacks. He asked congress to create the **Department of Homeland Security**. This is a federal agency developed to protect the United States against acts of terrorism. The agency has started many programs to try to improve the security of our nation.

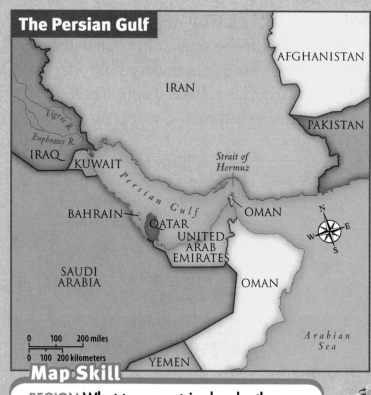

The Persian Gulf

AFGHANISTAN

IRAN

PAKISTAN

Tigris R.

Euphrates R.

IRAQ

KUWAIT

Strait of Hormuz

Persian Gulf

BAHRAIN

QATAR

OMAN

UNITED ARAB EMIRATES

SAUDI ARABIA

OMAN

YEMEN

Arabian Sea

0 100 200 miles
0 100 200 kilometers

Map Skill

REGION **What two countries border the Persian Gulf to the north?**

▶ American troops in Iraq

The Department of Homeland Security has taken many actions to keep America and Indiana safe. One of these actions was to increase security at airports around the country, as shown in the photo above.

Here in Indiana, the Indiana Department of Homeland Security was created. This department organizes fire and police departments to help them practice for emergencies. These emergency drills will help Hoosiers in the event of a disaster.

As with the war in Iraq, not all Americans agree that the increased security measures have been good. Some people believe that we have had to give up too much freedom in exchange for more security.

QUICK CHECK

Draw Conclusions **How did terrorist attacks affect Indiana?**

▲ Airport security has increased since the attacks on September, 11, 2001.

Check Understanding

1. **VOCABULARY** Write a sentence for each vocabulary word listed below.

   terrorism

   Department of Homeland Security

2. **READING SKILL** Draw Conclusions Use the chart from page 216 to write about American conflicts in the Middle East.

Text Clues	Conclusion

3. **Write About It** Write about whether you think it is good to give up some freedoms in exchange for security.

Unit 5 Review and Assess

Vocabulary Review

Copy the sentences below. Use the list of vocabulary words to fill in the blanks.

invention   decade

communism   civil rights

1. The second _____ of the 1900s was known as the Roaring Twenties.

2. After 1945, many people began fearing the spread of _____.

3. The _____ movement fought for equality.

4. The radio was an _____ that improved communication.

Comprehension and Critical Thinking

5. What are two ways Hoosiers contributed to the war effort during World War II?

6. Reading Skill How did the national government help Indiana during the Great Depression?

7. Reading Skill Why was segregation unfair to African Americans?

8. Critical Thinking What inventions changed agriculture in the early 1900s?

Skill

Read Historical Maps

Write a complete sentence to answer each question.

9. According to the map, which states were part of the Dust Bowl?

10. Why would people living in the Dust Bowl most likely have moved west?

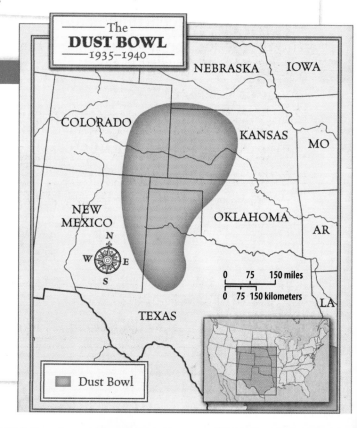

The
DUST BOWL
1935–1940

NEBRASKA   IOWA

COLORADO

KANSAS   MO

NEW MEXICO

OKLAHOMA

AR

0   75   150 miles
0   75   150 kilometers

LA

TEXAS

Dust Bowl

Read the passage below. Then choose the best answer or write a short response to each of the following questions.

> Tensions were building between the United States and the Soviet Union during the Cold War. Both countries wanted to show their strength and power. Between 1957 and 1975, they competed in the space race. In this competition, each country wanted to be the first to send rockets into space.
>
> In 1957 the Soviet Union launched *Sputnik*. This was the first man-made satellite to circle the Earth. Meanwhile, the United States continued working on its own space program. The first American satellite was called *Project SCORE*. This was a communications satellite that was launched in 1958.
>
> In 1969, the program had a huge success when Neil Armstrong walked on the moon. In recent years, the Soviet Union and the United States have joined together. Both countries have teams that do scientific research on the International Space Station.

1 **What was the first satellite successfully launched into space?**

Ⓐ the space race

Ⓑ *Sputnik*

Ⓒ *Project SCORE*

Ⓓ the International Space Station

2 **In recent years, how has the space race competition between the United States and the Soviet Union changed?**

Ⓐ The Soviet Union does not send rockets into space.

Ⓑ There are few satellites in space.

Ⓒ The United States no longer has a space program.

Ⓓ Both countries work together on joint space projects.

3 **How has the technology of both space programs helped our knowledge of space?**

Write your answer on a separate piece of paper.

The Big Idea Activities

What causes a society to grow?

Write About the Big Idea

FOLDABLES™
Study Organizer

Persuasive Essay

Use the Unit 5 Foldable to help you write a persuasive essay. Use the Big Idea question, *What causes a society to grow?* Think about the changes in society between 1900 and 2000 and the contributions that people made to bring about those changes.

Pick an event from this unit to write about. Think about the people surrounding the event and the contributions that they made to bring about change. Your essay should try to persuade the reader that the contributions helped society grow.

Create a Salt Map

Create a map of one country that you read about in Unit 5.

1. Research the geography and history of the country.

2. Look through atlases, globes, and Internet sites to find ideas.

3. Create a paper map of the country you have chosen.

4. Create a salt map of your country. Label major cities.

5. Write a paragraph about the country, and display it with the map.

When everyone has finished their salt maps, they should present them to the class. Display each map on a table in the classroom.

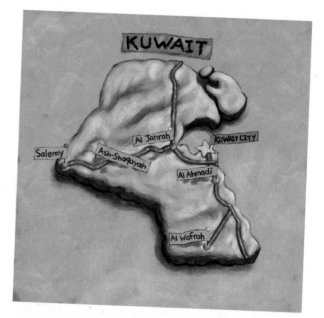

INDIANA TODAY

Unit 6

EXPLORE The Big Idea

Essential Question
How do government and the economy affect people's lives?

FOLDABLES™ Study Organizer

Summarize
Make and label a Two-Tab Book Foldable before you read Unit 6. On the top tab write **How government affects people's lives**. On the bottom tab write **How the economy affects people's lives**. Use the Foldable to organize information as you read.

How government affects people's lives

How the economy affects people's lives

LOG ON
For more about Unit 6, go to www.macmillanmh.com

The Indy 500 has made Indiana the racing capital of the world and a center for the motorsports industry.

223

PEOPLE, PLACES, AND EVENTS

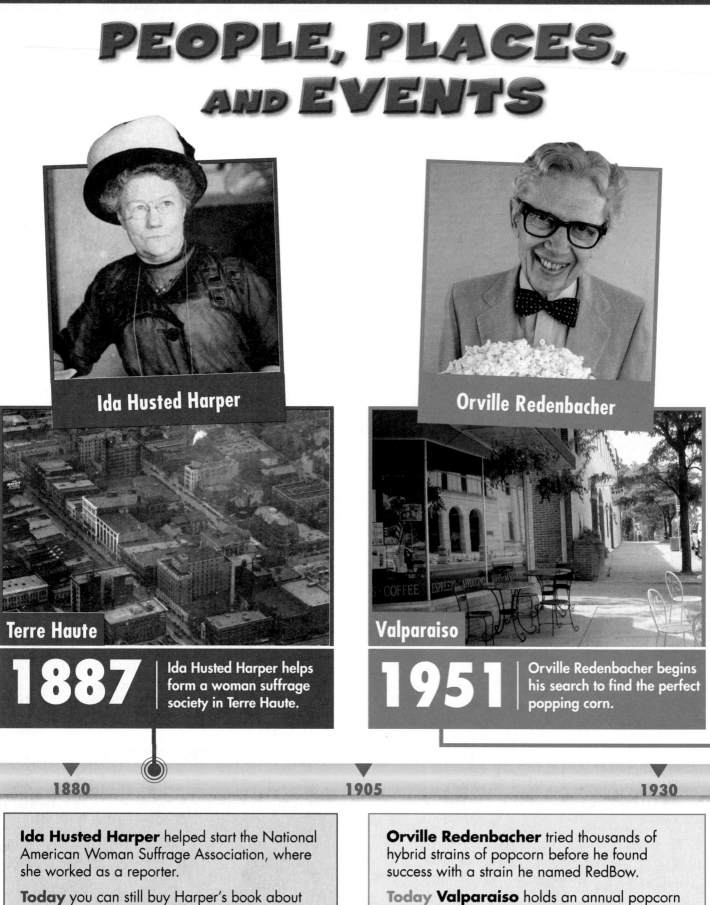

Ida Husted Harper

Terre Haute

1887
Ida Husted Harper helps form a woman suffrage society in Terre Haute.

Orville Redenbacher

Valparaiso

1951
Orville Redenbacher begins his search to find the perfect popping corn.

1880   1905   1930

Ida Husted Harper helped start the National American Woman Suffrage Association, where she worked as a reporter.

Today you can still buy Harper's book about the suffrage movement, *History of Woman Suffrage*.

Orville Redenbacher tried thousands of hybrid strains of popcorn before he found success with a strain he named RedBow.

Today **Valparaiso** holds an annual popcorn festival to honor America's popcorn king.

LOG ON

For more about People, Places, and Events, visit
www.macmillanmh.com

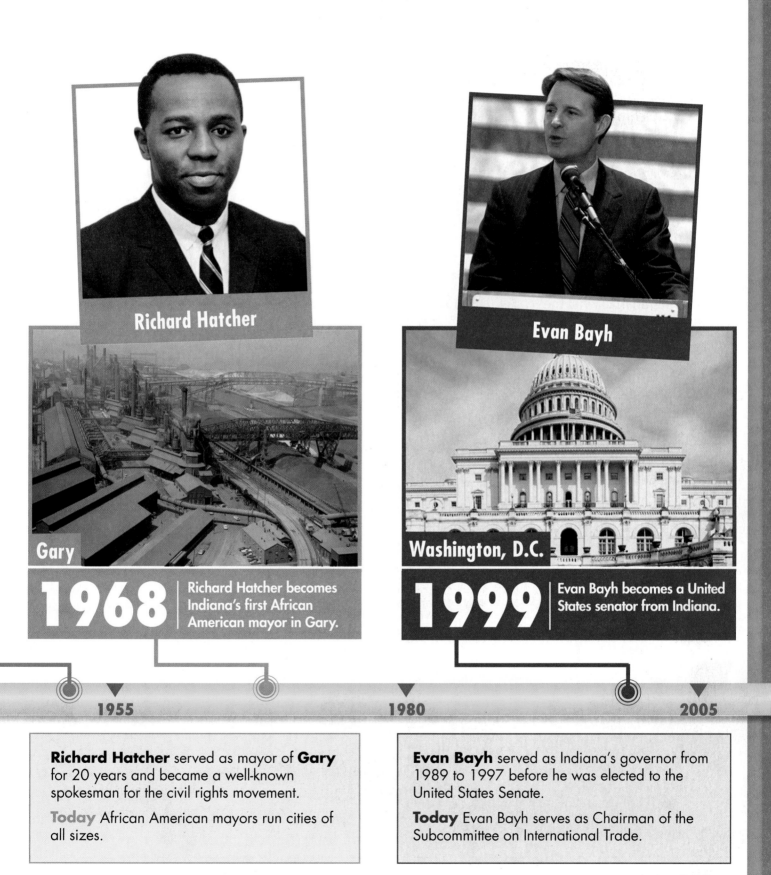

Richard Hatcher

Evan Bayh

Gary

Washington, D.C.

1968
Richard Hatcher becomes Indiana's first African American mayor in Gary.

1999
Evan Bayh becomes a United States senator from Indiana.

1955   1980   2005

Richard Hatcher served as mayor of **Gary** for 20 years and became a well-known spokesman for the civil rights movement.

Today African American mayors run cities of all sizes.

Evan Bayh served as Indiana's governor from 1989 to 1997 before he was elected to the United States Senate.

Today Evan Bayh serves as Chairman of the Subcommittee on International Trade.

Lesson 1

VOCABULARY

democratic republic p. 227

executive branch p. 228

legislative branch p. 228

judicial branch p. 229

checks and balances p. 229

READING SKILL

Summarize

Copy the chart below. Use it to summarize what the branches of our national government do.

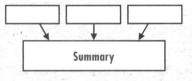

Summary

INDIANA ACADEMIC STANDARDS

4.2.2, 4.2.3, 4.2.4

National laws are created in the United States Capitol in Washington, D.C.

Visual Preview

What role do citizens play in our national government?

A Citizens elect people to represent them in national government.

B Hoosiers have served in all three branches of national government.

A UNITED STATES GOVERNMENT

In 1863, President Abraham Lincoln said that we have a "government of the people, by the people, for the people." His words remind us that the United States government serves its citizens.

The plan for our national government is based on the United States Constitution. As you read in Unit 2, the first leaders of our nation wrote this document in 1787. The Constitution states that our country is a **democratic republic**, or democracy. In a democratic republic, the citizens rule by electing representatives to run the country. To elect is to choose by voting. These representatives act in the interest of the people who voted for them.

Bill of Rights

The first ten amendments to the Constitution are called the Bill of Rights. These laws promise basic rights to citizens. They include freedom of religion and freedom of speech.

Government Services

The United States government provides important services for all citizens. One of these services is defense. Our government runs the armed forces. It uses tax dollars to pay for ships, planes, and weapons

▲ The original hand written Constitution is displayed at the National Archives in Washington, D.C.

that defend our country. It also pays hundreds of thousands of people in military service.

Other government services include the Federal Emergency Management Agency (FEMA). FEMA helps people recover from disasters when local and state governments cannot meet the needs of survivors.

QUICK CHECK

Summarize **What is a democratic republic?**

Primary Sources

"What makes America special [is that] the Oath [pledge] of Allegiance to our country is really the Oath of Allegiance to an idea, to a dream, to a promise that for more than 200 years has said to everyone in this country who has wanted to work hard and dream big and **sacrifice** to make those dreams come true, that you can make it. You can have a life that's filled with more opportunity, more hope, more freedom, more **justice**. That's what makes the United States of America the special place that it is."

From a speech by Evan Bayh, May 21, 2006 DePauw University, Greencastle, Indiana

sacrifice to give up something wanted for the sake of something else
justice fair treatment

Write About It Write a speech about a sacrifice you have made to make a dream come true.

Washington, D.C., is the home of our nation's government. Our government has three branches—executive, legislative, and judicial.

The Executive Branch

Voters elect the President of the United States to run the **executive branch**. A President is elected every four years. He or she carries out the nation's laws, meets with leaders of other countries, and heads the military. The President also chooses people to run national departments, such as the Department of Defense.

The Legislative Branch

Congress is the **legislative branch** of the government. Congress writes and passes laws for the entire country. Congress has two parts—the House of Representatives and the Senate.

Voters in each state elect two senators. However, the number of representatives elected depends on each state's population. States with more people get to elect more representatives. Indiana elects nine people to the House of Representatives. Representatives serve for two years, and senators serve for six years.

Congress begins each day with the Pledge of Allegiance. The pledge is a promise to be loyal to our country's government. Read the passage from a speech by Senator Evan Bayh of Indiana about the Pledge of Allegiance on this page.

The Judicial Branch

The **judicial branch** of is made up of judges and courts. The highest court in our country is the U.S. Supreme Court. It decides if the laws passed by Congress follow the rules of the U.S. Constitution.

Checks and Balances

Our national government has a system of **checks and balances** so that one branch does not have too much power. For example, the President is allowed to order the army into battle, but only Congress can declare war. So Congress has a check on the President's powers.

Hoosiers in Government

Hoosiers have played an important part in our national government. Benjamin Harrison served as our country's President. Over the years, five Hoosiers have served as Vice President.

▲ Benjamin Harrison (left) served as President from 1889 to 1893. Vice President Dan Quayle (center) served from 1989 to 1993. Virginia Jenckes (right) served in the U.S. House of Representatives from 1933 to 1939.

Check Understanding

1. **VOCABULARY** Write a paragraph about our nation's government using the terms below.

democratic republic
checks and balances

2. **READING SKILL Summarize** Use your chart from page 226 to write an essay about the three branches of government.

Summary

3. **Write About It** Write a song about the United States Constitution.

QUICK CHECK

Summarize **What does the judicial branch of government do?**

Lesson 2

VOCABULARY

appoint p. 232

budget p. 234

READING SKILL

Summarize

Copy the chart below. Use it to summarize how state government works.

↓ ↓ ↓

Summary

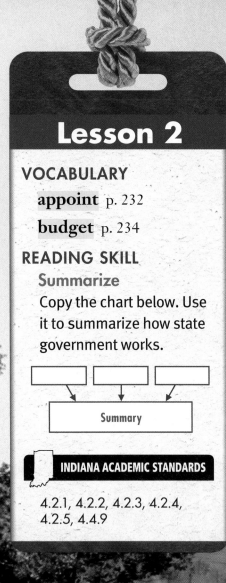

INDIANA ACADEMIC STANDARDS

4.2.1, 4.2.2, 4.2.3, 4.2.4, 4.2.5, 4.4.9

STATE GOVERNMENT

The Indiana State House in Indianapolis

Visual Preview

How does the state government serve its citizens?

A The Indiana constitution is a plan for how the state government works.

B Checks and balances limit the powers of each branch of government.

C A state budget shows citizens how their tax dollars are spent.

230

A INDIANA'S CONSTITUTION

The introduction to Indiana's constitution states that its goal is to see "that justice be established [and] public order maintained." Like the United States Constitution, our state constitution also gives people rights and defines the powers of government.

Our state government is located in Indianapolis, the capital of Indiana. The state capitol is also called the State House. It is where many of our government leaders work. Most of the state's services are planned and put into action in this building.

Our state constitution has 16 separate sections called articles. The first article is called the Bill of Rights. The rights include freedom of religion and freedom of speech. Article One also states that citizens have the right to a trial by jury and the right to bear arms.

Article Two explains the rules for holding elections. It states that all elections shall be free and equal. Citizens who are at least 18 years of age and who have been living in Indiana for at least 30 days have the right to vote. It also states that general elections will be held on the first Tuesday in November.

Article Eight explains how public schools will be run and calls for public education for all:

"Knowledge and learning . . . being essential to the preservation of a free government; it should be the duty of the General Assembly to encourage . . . and provide, by law, for a general and uniform system of Common Schools . . . without charge, and equally open to all."

QUICK CHECK

Summarize Summarize Indiana's state constitution.

PLACES

In November 1816, the first General Assembly met in the **Corydon capitol**. When the capital was moved to Indianapolis in 1825, the capitol became what it was intended to be, the Harrison County courthouse. Today, you can tour the old capitol and learn about Indiana's early history.

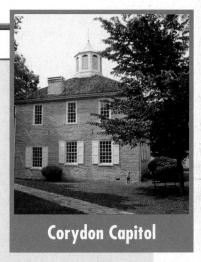

Corydon Capitol

Like the U.S. Constitution, our state constitution divides the government into three branches —executive, legislative, and judicial. Each branch has some power over the other two.

Executive Branch

A state's laws are carried out by the executive branch of the government. The people of the state elect a governor to run this branch. The governor serves a term of four years. He or she also **appoints**, or chooses, people to run state departments, such as the Department of Health.

Legislative Branch

The Indiana General Assembly is the legislative branch of state government. It makes the laws for our state. The General Assembly has two parts—the House of Representatives and the Senate. The House has 100 members, who are elected to two-year terms. The Senate has 50 members, who are elected to four-year terms. Representatives and senators vote on bills. A bill is a written idea for a law. Look at the chart below to see how a bill becomes a law.

How a Bill Becomes a Law

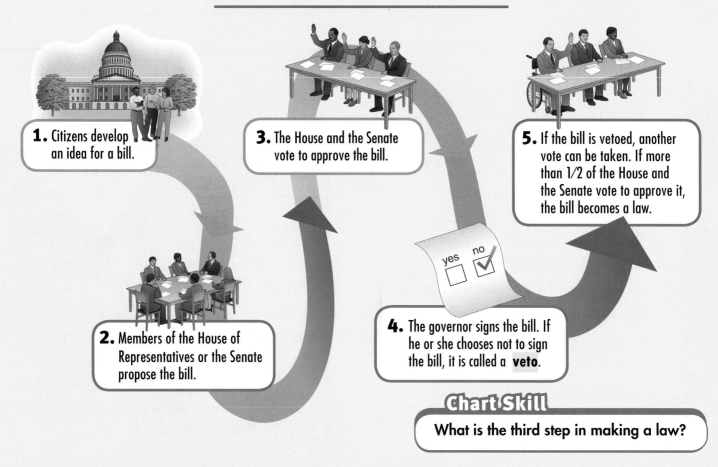

1. Citizens develop an idea for a bill.

2. Members of the House of Representatives or the Senate propose the bill.

3. The House and the Senate vote to approve the bill.

4. The governor signs the bill. If he or she chooses not to sign the bill, it is called a **veto**.

yes ☐ no ☑

5. If the bill is vetoed, another vote can be taken. If more than 1/2 of the House and the Senate vote to approve it, the bill becomes a law.

Chart Skill

What is the third step in making a law?

A bill-signing ceremony for a law to help Hoosier veterans

Judicial Branch

The judicial branch of government explains our state laws. This branch is made up of judges who work in courts. The judges hear cases and interpret, or explain, the law. One of their important jobs is to make sure state laws do not break the rules of the state constitution.

The highest court in our state is the Indiana Supreme Court. It is located in Indianapolis. The court has five justices, or judges, one of whom is the chief justice. The governor appoints these justices.

The Court of Appeals hears cases in which people believe another court has made an error. Nine judges serve on the Court of Appeals. Indiana cities and towns also have courts to hear cases.

Checks and Balances

Like the national government, our state government has a system of checks and balances that limits the power of each branch of government. It divides power to make sure that no person or group of people can gain too much power. In this system, the powers of one branch of government are balanced by the powers of another. For example, the legislative branch can make a law, but if the judicial branch finds the law does not follow the rules of the state constitution, the law is thrown out.

QUICK CHECK

Summarize **What does the system of checks and balances do?**

The state government pays for the services it provides to the people of Indiana by collecting taxes. To decide how much to spend on each type of service, government leaders create a **budget**. A budget is a plan for using money. The datagraphic on this page shows Indiana's state budget for 2007 through 2009.

Office of Management and Budget

Before becoming governor of Indiana in 2005, Mitch Daniels was appointed by President George W. Bush to be director of the Office of Management and Budget (OMB) in Washington, D.C. The OMB reports on how tax dollars are spent. There, Daniels created a system that showed when tax money was spent wisely.

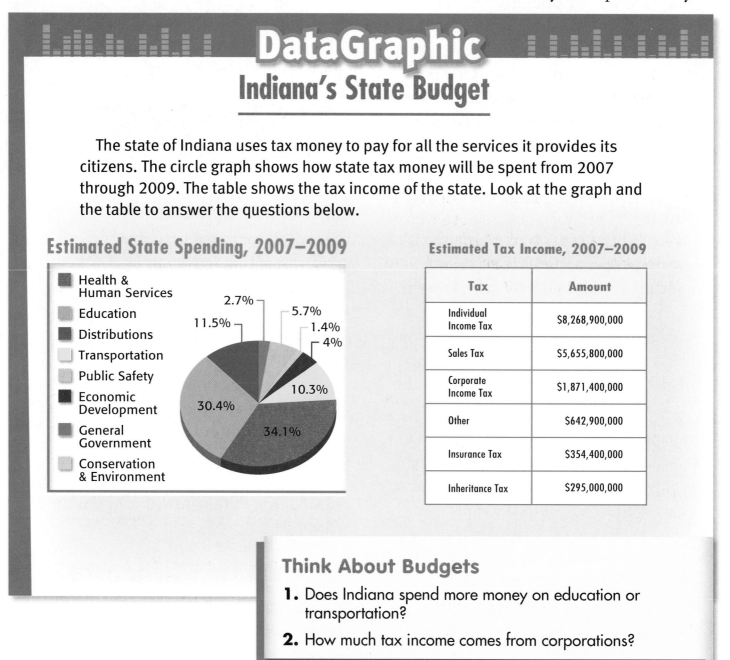

DataGraphic
Indiana's State Budget

The state of Indiana uses tax money to pay for all the services it provides its citizens. The circle graph shows how state tax money will be spent from 2007 through 2009. The table shows the tax income of the state. Look at the graph and the table to answer the questions below.

Estimated State Spending, 2007–2009

- Health & Human Services
- Education
- Distributions
- Transportation
- Public Safety
- Economic Development
- General Government
- Conservation & Environment

2.7%
5.7%
1.4%
4%
11.5%
10.3%
30.4%
34.1%

Estimated Tax Income, 2007–2009

Tax	Amount
Individual Income Tax	$8,268,900,000
Sales Tax	$5,655,800,000
Corporate Income Tax	$1,871,400,000
Other	$642,900,000
Insurance Tax	$354,400,000
Inheritance Tax	$295,000,000

Think About Budgets

1. Does Indiana spend more money on education or transportation?

2. How much tax income comes from corporations?

When Mitch Daniels became governor of Indiana, the Indiana legislature, at the request of Daniels, created the Indiana OMB. Like the OMB in Washington, the Indiana OMB reports on how tax dollars are spent. Before the Indiana OMB, few state agencies reported on how well they were spending tax dollars.

State Government and the Economy

Governor Daniels also helped create the Indiana Economic Development Corporation (IEDC). The IEDC is a government agency that helps businesses locate and grow in Indiana. One part of its plan to grow the state's economy is to encourage motorsports businesses to move to Indiana. Governor Daniels explained:

> **"**Indiana is the racing capital of the world. This is yet another area where we will take advantage of Indiana's assets and its talent base to launch an economic comeback for Hoosiers.**"**

Indiana has hundreds of motorsports events each year, including the Indy 500 and the U.S. Grand Prix. The IEDC has worked to reduce the taxes motorsports businesses pay. It claims the lower taxes will attract businesses to Indiana. It believes this will result in new jobs for Hoosiers and more tax income for the state.

QUICK CHECK

Summarize **What is the job of the OMB?**

Check Understanding

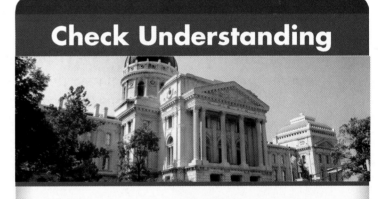

1. **VOCABULARY** Write a paragraph about state government using the terms below.

   appoint   **budget**

2. **READING SKILL** Summarize Use your chart from page 230 to write about how Indiana's state government works.

   Summary

 3. **Write About It** Write an essay about how state government affects people's lives.

Chart and Graph Skills

Read Flow Charts

VOCABULARY

flow chart

In the last lesson, you read a **flow chart** on how a bill becomes a law. A flow chart shows the different steps necessary to complete an activity. It can help you understand and remember the steps in the right order.

Learn It

- Read the title of the flow chart. The flow chart on this page shows how a bill becomes a law.

- Look at the pictures and read the labels. Both the labels and pictures give information.

- The numbers and arrows show the order of the steps. Read the steps in number order and follow the arrows. You can see that if a bill is vetoed, it goes back to the House and Senate.

How a Bill Becomes a Law

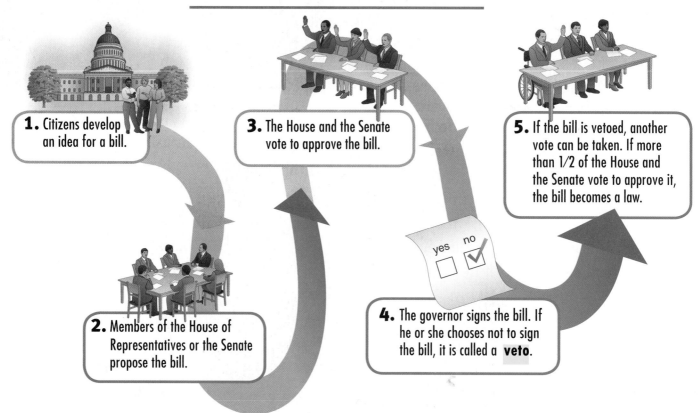

1. Citizens develop an idea for a bill.

2. Members of the House of Representatives or the Senate propose the bill.

3. The House and the Senate vote to approve the bill.

4. The governor signs the bill. If he or she chooses not to sign the bill, it is called a **veto**.

yes   no

5. If the bill is vetoed, another vote can be taken. If more than 1/2 of the House and the Senate vote to approve it, the bill becomes a law.

Try It

Answer the questions by reading the flow chart on page 236.

- Who writes a bill?

- Who can veto a bill?

- What happens when a bill is vetoed?

Apply It

- Make your own flow chart to show the steps in a process that you know well. Draw a picture for each step. Then write a label to go with each picture. Use arrows and numbers to show the order of the steps. Do you know how to bake a cake, catch a fish, or make a sandwich? Show how you do it with a flow chart.

▲ Students urge lawmakers to ban smoking in the Indiana State House.

▲ State Senator Sue Landske votes on the state budget.

▲ A representative of theater owners speaks out against a daylight-savings bill.

Local Government

VOCABULARY

mayor p. 239

jury p. 242

patriotism p. 243

READING SKILL

Summarize

Copy the chart below. Use it to summarize the goods and services of local government.

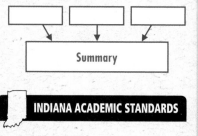

Summary

INDIANA ACADEMIC STANDARDS

4.2.5, 4.2.6, 4.4.9

Fighting fires is an important service of local government.

Visual Preview

How does local government affect people's lives?

A Hoosiers vote for representatives to county, municipal, and township governments.

B Local government provides services such as schools and libraries.

C The citizens of Indiana have rights and responsibilities.

A HOW LOCAL GOVERNMENT WORKS

Do you ever wonder who makes sure that the water you drink is clean, or who chooses the location for a new park in your town? These are just some of the many decisions that the leaders of local government make.

There are three types of local government in Indiana: county, municipal, and township. Each type of government has its own duties and its own members.

County Government

A county is an area or section into which a state is divided. Each of the 92 counties in Indiana has its own county government.

In county government, voters of each county elect a board of county commissioners and a county council. The board carries out the county laws. The council decides how to spend county tax dollars. The members of these groups meet in a town or city called the county seat.

Municipal Government

Municipal is the government for a city or town. Indiana is made up of 569 municipal governments. Hoosiers who live in cities elect a **mayor** and a city council. The mayor is the head of the municipal government.

▲ Hammond City Hall

A city council makes the local laws for cities. A town council makes laws for towns in Indiana.

Townships

Indiana is the only state where every portion of the state is part of a township government. Indiana has 1,008 townships. The head of a township is called a trustee and is elected to a four-year term.

QUICK CHECK

Summarize **How is local government divided?**

Citizenship
Volunteering

Hoosiers all over Indiana volunteer to help their communities. For example, many towns in Indiana have volunteer fire departments. Men and women in these towns work at regular jobs, but they are also ready, at a moment's notice, to fight fires. What are some ways you can volunteer in your community? You can volunteer at a senior citizen center, organize a canned food drive, or work for a political candidate in your community. Many people volunteer to register voters each year.

Write About It Write an essay about ways you can volunteer in your community.

Local government provides public services for all of its citizens. County, municipal, and township governments in Indiana share responsibilities, but each type of government also has specific duties.

Duties of Local Government

County government is in charge of hospitals and health programs, and it maintains highways. It also operates court systems and the county police, and it is responsible for conducting elections.

Municipal governments provide police and fire services. They maintain parks, keep the streets clean, and pick up garbage. City workers do many jobs to help a city run smoothly.

Townships mainly provide help to people in need and figure out how much property is worth. The value of property is used to determine the amount of tax property owners will pay. In rural areas, townships also provide services such as road maintenance and fire protection.

Public services are not the same everywhere. For example, some municipal governments provide public water service. In other places, citizens have to dig their own wells for water. Similarly, some communities have hospitals and libraries, while other smaller communities may not have the money for these things. People in small communities often rely on the county to provide these services.

Departments of Local Government

 Fire Department provides ambulance, fire, and rescue services

 Parks and Recreation Department maintains parks

 Planning Department plans for city projects

 Police Department keeps citizens safe

 Public Health Department helps citizens fight disease

 Building Inspection Department grants permits for new buildings, inspects plans

Environmental Services Department collects garbage and recycling

 Finance Department collects taxes, handles city money

Maintenance Department repairs streets, signs, traffic lights

Chart Skill

Which department would you call if a streetlight was broken?

Special-Purpose Districts

There are two types of special-purpose districts in Indiana: school districts and special districts. Unlike county or municipal governments, special-purpose districts only serve one specific purpose.

School districts are the largest type of special-purpose district in Indiana. They have one important job—to run the public school system. About half of all local government spending goes to education.

County legislatures create a special district to provide a specific good or service. For example, some towns in Indiana do not have water service. A town that wants water service must ask the county legislature to make a law that creates a special district to build and maintain water service. A district board is appointed to oversee the district. The board then appoints a chief executive to run the day-to-day operations of the good or service. The law that creates special districts may give the district the power to raise money through taxes.

Special districts can provide a wide range of goods and services, including schools, fire departments, public libraries, and parks. Once the projects are built, special districts manage and maintain the good or service provided.

QUICK CHECK

Summarize **What are special-purpose districts?**

▼ School districts are a type of special-purpose district.

Hoosiers are citizens of both Indiana and the United States. A citizen is a person who is born in a country or who has earned the right to be a member of that country. All citizens have rights and responsibilities.

Rights and Responsibilities

Citizens have rights that are explained in the U.S. and Indiana constitutions. They include freedom of speech, freedom of religion, and the right to an education.

Voting is another right. However, with the right to vote also comes the responsibility to be informed about the issues that affect your community, state, nation, and the world.

Citizens must also obey laws and pay taxes. Local governments use tax dollars to provide services, such as operating schools and keeping neighborhoods safe.

At times, citizens are called upon to serve on a **jury**. A jury is a group of citizens chosen to hear the facts of a court case and make a decision.

Civic Virtues

Citizens are also expected to show civic virtues. Civic virtues are qualities that contribute to the healthy working of a democracy. Civic virtues include honesty, respect for others, and working for the common good. Other virtues are listed in the chart on page 243.

Throughout Indiana's history, Hoosiers have shown their civic virtues in many ways. For example, in 1887 Ida Husted Harper worked for the common good when she helped organize a woman suffrage society in Terre Haute. Richard Hatcher also worked for the common good when he became mayor of Gary in 1968. He worked to help the poor and to fight rising crime.

Working for Democracy

Democracy cannot be kept alive unless everyone works at it. This means people must be informed about the issues affecting their community, state, and country. They must vote to select their leaders and get involved in their communities. If people do not participate, then democracy cannot survive.

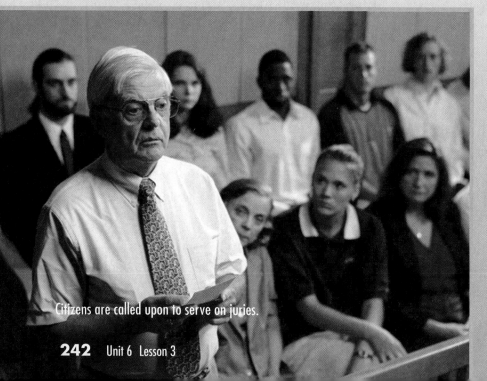

Citizens are called upon to serve on juries.

Civic Virtues

Virtue	What It Means
Individual responsibility	Taking responsibility for your actions
Self-discipline	Correcting yourself for the purpose of improvement
Civility	Being polite
Respect	Having regard for the rights and dignity of all people and the law
Honesty	Being truthful
Courage	Having the strength to overcome difficulty or fear
Compassion	Understanding other people's pain
Patriotism	Being loyal to your country
Fairness	Treating everyone equally
Commitment to the common good	Working for the well-being of all people

Democratic Values

To keep our democracy strong, good citizens support democratic values in both words and deeds. Values are the beliefs that guide the way people live. For example, Hoosiers uphold our democratic values when they speak out against policies that harm the common good.

Working toward the common good is also part of **patriotism**. Patriotism is respect for and loyal support of one's country. You show patriotism when you wave a flag, recite the Pledge of Allegiance, or sing the national anthem. You are also being patriotic when you show civic virtues and support our democracy.

QUICK CHECK

Summarize **What rights do Hoosiers have?**

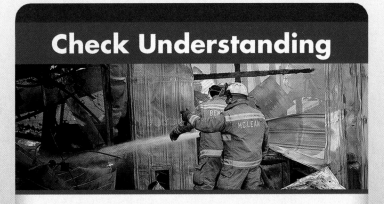

Check Understanding

1. **VOCABULARY** Draw a picture that shows the vocabulary word below.
patriotism

2. **READING SKILL** Summarize
Use your chart from page 238 to write about the goods and services local governments provide.

 3. **Write About It** Write about how local government affects your life.

HOW THE ECONOMY WORKS

Lesson 4

VOCABULARY

scarcity p. 245

supply p. 246

demand p. 246

free enterprise p. 247

profit p. 247

READING SKILL

Summarize

Copy the chart below. Use it to summarize how our economy works.

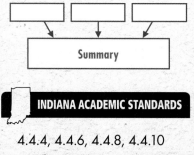

Summary

INDIANA ACADEMIC STANDARDS

4.4.4, 4.4.6, 4.4.8, 4.4.10

Buyers and sellers in a music store

Visual Preview

How does the economy affect people's lives?

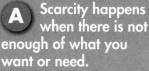

A Scarcity happens when there is not enough of what you want or need.

B Supply and demand determine the prices people pay for goods and services.

A ECONOMIC CHOICES

Hoosiers make economic choices every day. Economics is the study of how we make decisions in a world where resources are limited. Knowing how the economy works will help you make wise economic decisions.

Money is one tool people use to make economic decisions. Over the years, it has been used in many different forms. Native Americans used wampum as a form of money. Wampum is beads or shells strung or woven together. Today, we use metal coins and paper money to pay for the things we need and want.

Needs and Wants

What do you really need to live? Food? A home? How about a skateboard? We call things such as food, clothing, and shelter needs. You can't live without them. Once you have met the most basic needs, everything else is a want.

A want, such as a skateboard, is something you can live without. You don't need an MP3 player or a pair of $100 sneakers to live, do you? You can make your own music and wear an inexpensive pair of sneakers. Wants might make your life easier or more interesting, but you do not need them to live.

▲ Prices give us clues about the scarcity of a product like gas.

Scarcity

Sometime you can't have what you want because of **scarcity**. Scarcity happens when there isn't enough of what you want. The reason for scarcity is that the things we want will always be greater than the things that we can produce. There simply are not enough resources to satisfy everybody's wants. Scarcity means that we all have to make choices.

QUICK CHECK

Summarize **What are some ways you deal with scarcity?**

SUPPLY AND DEMAND

If prices can tell us about the scarcity of a good or service, where does price come from? Prices are usually determined by what economists call **supply** and **demand**. Supply is the amount of a good or service that businesses are willing to sell at various prices. Demand is the amount of a good or service that people are willing and able to buy at various prices.

Prices tell businesses if they should provide more of a good or service. If the price of a good or service is high, businesses will want to produce more of the product. This means that the supply will go up. If the price is low, businesses will want to produce less of the product. This means that the supply of what they provide will go down.

Savings Plan

If you want to buy something, but you feel that the price is too high, you can choose to buy the good or service later. Some people know that they want to buy something in the future, so they make up a savings plan. A savings plan is a way people increase the amount of money they have. One way to save money is to earn more money than you spend. Another way to save money is to spend less of the money you earn.

▲ Many families have savings accounts.

▲ Prices for goods are usually determined by supply and demand.

Free-Enterprise System

Some Hoosiers save their money to start a business. An economic system in which anyone can own and run a business is known as **free enterprise**. Under this system, business owners known as entrepreneurs decide what to sell or make. Customers decide what to buy based on what they want or need, and how much they are willing to pay.

Profit Motive

Entrepreneurs take risks by creating products or offering services they think people will buy. If a business does well, an entrepreneur makes a **profit**. Profit is the money left over after a business pays for all of its expenses.

The profit motive is what drives entrepreneurs and businesses to increase their wealth. The profit motive is largely responsible for growth in a free-enterprise system.

QUICK CHECK

Summarize **What is a free-enterprise system?**

Check Understanding

1. Write a paragraph about what affects the price of goods and services. Use the words below in your paragraph.
   supply　　**demand**

2. **READING SKILL** Summarize
   Use your chart from page 244 to summarize how our economy works.

3. **Write About It** Write a poem about how money affects people's lives.

◀ Entrepreneurs decide what to sell or make.

TRANSPORTATION *and* INDIANA'S ECONOMY

VOCABULARY

import p. 249

export p. 249

interstate highway p. 250

READING SKILL

Summarize

Copy the chart below. Use it to summarize the effects of Indiana's location and transportation system on the economy.

Summary

INDIANA ACADEMIC STANDARDS

4.4.3, 4.4.5

Indiana's transportation system attracts businesses to our state.

Visual Preview

How does Indiana's transportation system help companies grow?

A Companies import and export goods all over the world.

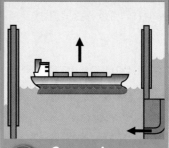

B Companies use Indiana's highways, rails, waterways, and airports to move goods.

Ⓐ THE CROSSROADS OF AMERICA

All economies need a good transportation system. Indiana's excellent transportation system earned our state the motto "The Crossroads of America." This system, along with Indiana's central location, makes our state attractive to businesses.

As you read in Unit 1, Indiana is home to many companies that need good transportation to move their products. Companies such as Eli Lilly, Biomet, Cummins Engine, and Orville Redenbacher's Gourmet Popping Corn all started in Indiana.

Companies use Indiana's transportation system to ship their products from Indiana to other states and to countries around the world. For example, Roche Diagnostics is a Swiss company that makes medical products. Its North American headquarters is in Indianapolis. This company **exports** many of its products to countries around the world. An export is something that is sold or traded to another country.

Indiana's leading exports are manufactured goods. To learn more about Indiana's manufactured exports, look at the circle graph on this page.

Many companies also depend on our state's transportation system to buy materials or parts to make their finished products. For example, Chrysler manufactures automobiles in Indiana. To get the best price for automobile parts, this company **imports** parts made in Asia. An import is a good brought in from one country for sale or use in another country.

QUICK CHECK

Summarize Why do companies choose to do business in Indiana?

Indiana's Manufacturing Exports, 2005

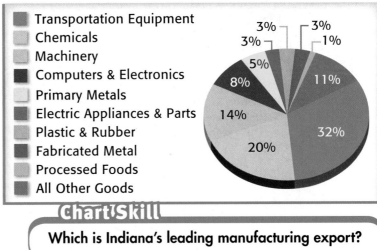

- Transportation Equipment
- Chemicals
- Machinery
- Computers & Electronics
- Primary Metals
- Electric Appliances & Parts
- Plastic & Rubber
- Fabricated Metal
- Processed Foods
- All Other Goods

3% | 3% | 3% | 1% | 5% | 11% | 8% | 14% | 32% | 20%

Chart Skill

Which is Indiana's leading manufacturing export?

Companies in Indiana can use our roads, railways, airports, and waterways to ship their goods. The way they ship their products depends on what they produce and where it is going.

Highways and Rail Lines

Many of the products made in Indiana are first transported by highway. Indiana has 13 **interstate highways**—more than any other state. An interstate highway connects two or more states. Trucks on these roads carry products made in our factories and grown on our farms to other states, or to other transportation sites, such as railroad stations.

Indiana's central location has made transporting products by rail a good choice for many companies.

In 1847 workers built Indiana's first rail line. It connected Indianapolis and Madison. More railroads were built in the 1850s. Today, Indiana is a rail center. Many raw materials are shipped to Indiana by rail. Companies use these raw materials to make their finished products.

Travel by Air

Air travel is another important part of our state's transportation system. The state's busiest airport is the Indianapolis International Airport. International means between two or more nations.

When companies need their products shipped quickly, they use cargo planes. Cargo planes do not carry passengers. They carry products made in Indiana to other parts of the world.

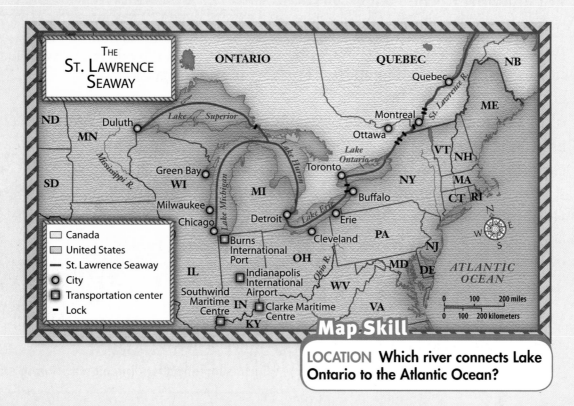

THE ST. LAWRENCE SEAWAY

Legend:
- ☐ Canada
- ☐ United States
- — St. Lawrence Seaway
- ○ City
- ☐ Transportation center
- ‑ Lock

Map Skill

LOCATION Which river connects Lake Ontario to the Atlantic Ocean?

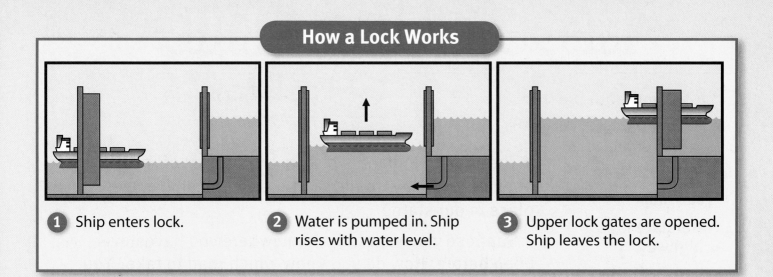

How a Lock Works

1. Ship enters lock.
2. Water is pumped in. Ship rises with water level.
3. Upper lock gates are opened. Ship leaves the lock.

Waterways

Companies in Indiana also use ships to move products across the country and all over the world. Indiana has three international ports. Look at the map on page 250. Two of Indiana's major ports are on the Ohio River. They are the Southwind Maritime Centre and the Clark Maritime Centre. The Burns International Harbor sits on Lake Michigan. Ships carry goods to and from the port on the St. Lawrence Seaway.

For many years, rapids, waterfalls, and uneven water levels kept ships from transporting goods from the Great Lakes to the Atlantic Ocean. To solve the problem of changing water levels, engineers built locks. A lock is a part of a canal where water can be pumped in or out to raise or lower ships. Look at the diagram of how a lock works on this page.

Check Understanding

1. **VOCABULARY** Draw a diagram showing the terms below.

   import   interstate highway
   export

2. **READING SKILL** Summarize
   Use your chart from page 248 to write about the effects of Indiana's location and transportation system on the economy.

3. **Write About It** Write an essay about how transportation systems affect people's lives.

QUICK CHECK

Summarize **How do companies move goods into and out of Indiana?**

Map and Globe Skills

Use Road Maps

VOCABULARY

road map

interstate highway

route

Throughout Indiana's history, thousands of roads have been built. Today, roads can take you to almost every place in our state.

Suppose you want to go somewhere you have never been before. How do you know which road to take? You use a **road map**. Road maps show you where the roads in a certain area go. By reading a road map, you can figure out how to get from one place to another.

Learn It

- Map A has several different kinds of roads. The thick red lines are **interstate highways**. An interstate highway connects two or more states.

- Interstate highways run through states and major cities across the United States. They usually have at least two lanes running in each direction.

- Study the map key on Map A. The orange line identifies a state highway. State highways are those that run within a state.

- The "name" of each interstate and state highway is a number. Notice the different symbols for each of the three kinds of highways. Which highway runs from Jeffersonville to Vincennes?

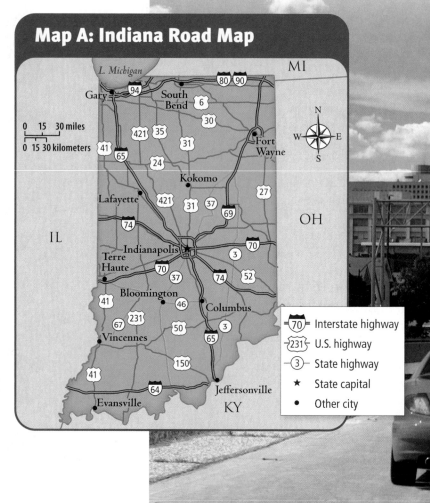

Map A: Indiana Road Map

L. Michigan

MI

Gary · 94 · South Bend · 6 · 80 90

0 15 30 miles
0 15 30 kilometers

421 · 35 · 30

41 · 65 · 31 · Fort Wayne

24 · Kokomo

IL

Lafayette · 421 · 31 · 37 · 69 · 27

74

Indianapolis · 70 · OH

Terre Haute · 70 · 37 · 74 · 52 · 3

Bloomington · 41 · 46 · Columbus

67 · 231 · 50 · 3

Vincennes · 65

41 · 150

41 · 64 · Jeffersonville

Evansville · KY

Key:
- 70 — Interstate highway
- 231 — U.S. highway
- 3 — State highway
- ★ State capital
- ● Other city

Try It

- Look at Map A. How is Interstate Highway 70 different from State Highway 46?

- Which **route** would you take to get from Kokomo to Fort Wayne? A route is the course you take to get somewhere.

Apply It

Road maps can also be useful for smaller areas. Smaller area road maps show how different streets connect.

- Look at Map B. It shows a section of Terre Haute.

- What are two routes you could take to get from Mulberry St. to Ohio Blvd. and N. 6th St.?

- What kinds of roads would you find on a map of the area where you live?

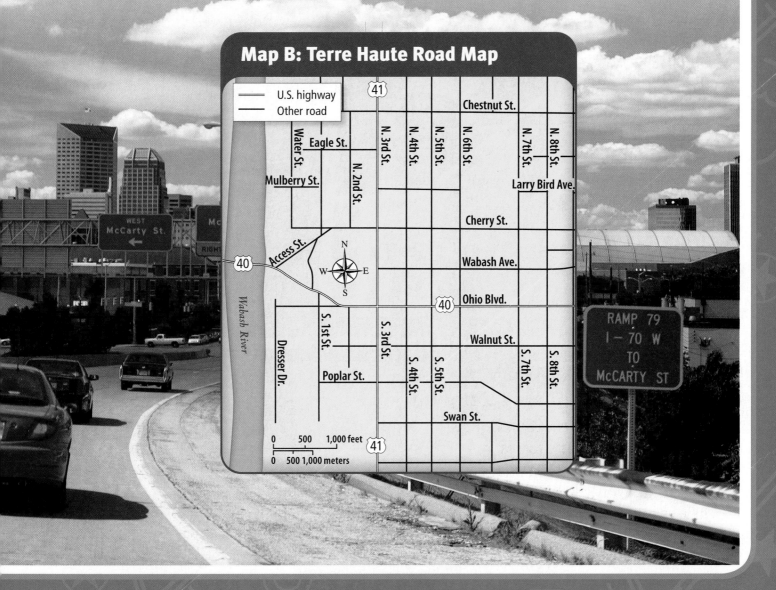

Map B: Terre Haute Road Map

Legend:
- U.S. highway
- Other road

Streets labeled: Chestnut St., Eagle St., Water St., Mulberry St., N. 2nd St., N. 3rd St., N. 4th St., N. 5th St., N. 6th St., N. 7th St., N. 8th St., Larry Bird Ave., Cherry St., Access St., Wabash Ave., Ohio Blvd., Walnut St., S. 1st St., S. 3rd St., S. 4th St., S. 5th St., S. 7th St., S. 8th St., Dresser Dr., Poplar St., Swan St., Wabash River

Highways: 41, 40

Scale: 0 500 1,000 feet / 0 500 1,000 meters

Lesson 6

VOCABULARY

tariff p. 255

North American Free Trade Agreement p. 255

interdependent p. 256

specialization p. 258

globalization p. 258

READING SKILL

Summarize

Copy the chart below. Use it to summarize why Indiana trades with the world.

Summary

INDIANA ACADEMIC STANDARDS

4.4.2, 4.4.3, 4.4.5

Trading with the WORLD

China is one of Indiana's leading trade partners.

Visual Preview

How has world trade affected Indiana's economy?

A NAFTA has increased Indiana's exports to Canada and Mexico.

B Hoosiers enjoy goods from all over the world.

C Globalization has opened up new markets for Indiana's products.

A INDIANA AND WORLD TRADE

The economies of the world are connected. Indiana has connections to countries all over the world. These connections have affected the products we buy, the prices we pay, and the way we live.

When countries want to do business with each other, they often create plans called trade agreements. These agreements set up the rules countries follow when they trade with each other. Some of these agreements set up free trade, or trade without **tariffs**. Tariffs are taxes on goods brought into a country.

One such agreement that has been important to Indiana is NAFTA, or the **North American Free Trade Agreement**. Under NAFTA, the United States, Canada, and Mexico agreed to open up free trade with each other.

Canada is Indiana's leading trade partner. Indiana exports goods such as automobiles and machinery to Canada. The second-largest export country for Indiana is Mexico. Indiana supplies Mexico with goods such as electronics and metals. As part of the Corn Belt, Indiana is also a major producer of crops. Indiana sells corn, soybeans, wheat, and other grains to Canada, Mexico, and the rest of the United States.

Since NAFTA, the United States, Canada, and Mexico have increased the amount of goods they ship to each other. Because of NAFTA, Hoosiers enjoy many more goods from Canada and Mexico. Likewise, people in Canada and Mexico enjoy many more products made in Indiana.

QUICK CHECK

Summarize How did NAFTA change the way its member countries trade with each other?

▲ Some protesters felt NAFTA would create low paying jobs.

GLOBAL PARTNERS

Because of global trade, Hoosiers enjoy goods from all over the world. Global trade has allowed Hoosiers to buy clothing from China, oil from the Middle East, bananas from Honduras, and coffee beans from Colombia and Brazil. Global trade is the same for other countries. Germans buy goods produced in France, Italy, and Japan.

In recent years, trade between countries has become much easier because of improvements in technology and transportation. Countries have also become more **interdependent**, or connected. This means that countries rely on each other to meet the needs and wants of its people. Interdependence has strengthened the world's economy.

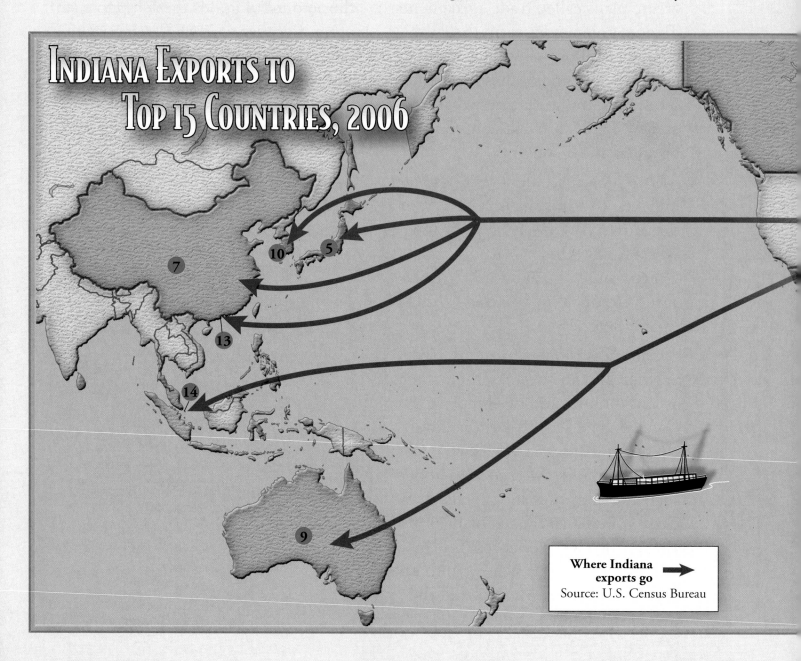

INDIANA EXPORTS TO TOP 15 COUNTRIES, 2006

Where Indiana exports go →
Source: U.S. Census Bureau

Today, Indiana trades with many countries in Western Europe. Great Britain is Indiana's third-largest trading partner, after Canada and Mexico. Other trading partners include France, Germany, and the Netherlands. These nations import many goods made in Indiana, including transportation equipment. Transportation equipment is Indiana's largest manufacturing sector. It includes products that are used to make planes, trains, and automobiles.

The Indiana Economic Development Corporation is working to expand Indiana's global trade. They have representatives working in Australia, China, Germany, Japan, and Taiwan. These representatives help develop business relationships between companies in Indiana and companies overseas.

QUICK CHECK

Summarize Why will Indiana become more interdependent with the world in the future?

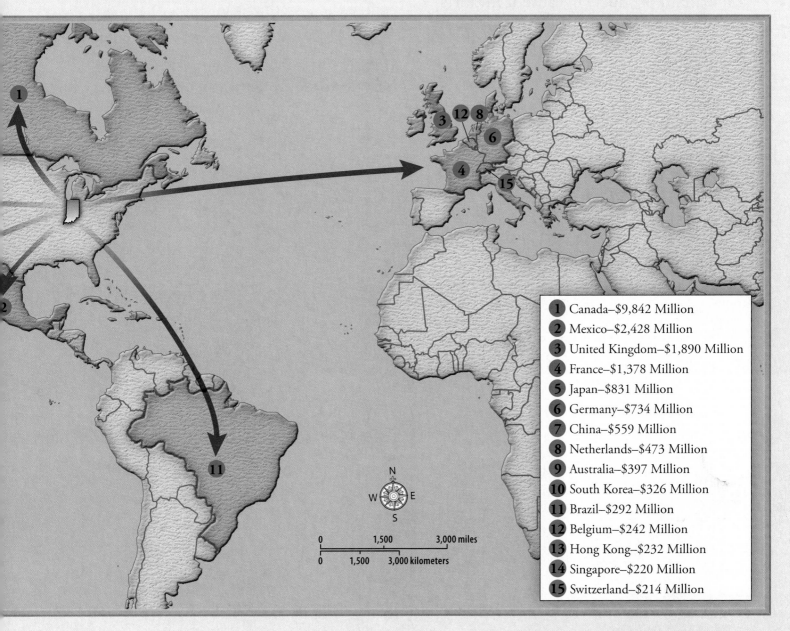

1 Canada–$9,842 Million

2 Mexico–$2,428 Million

3 United Kingdom–$1,890 Million

4 France–$1,378 Million

5 Japan–$831 Million

6 Germany–$734 Million

7 China–$559 Million

8 Netherlands–$473 Million

9 Australia–$397 Million

10 South Korea–$326 Million

11 Brazil–$292 Million

12 Belgium–$242 Million

13 Hong Kong–$232 Million

14 Singapore–$220 Million

15 Switzerland–$214 Million

C SPECIALIZATION AND CHALLENGES

Indiana has always been a leader in industry because of its rich resources. The kinds of resources found in Indiana promote **specialization**. Specialization means producing a few products instead of many different products. Specialization allows Indiana, and the nation as a whole, to put resources to their best use.

Indiana is able to specialize in making a few main products because it imports many other goods it needs from other countries. Indiana then exports the products it makes to meet the needs of other countries. If we did not trade with others for the goods we need, we would have to make everything ourselves. We would also have to do without many things we are unable to make or grow.

Globalization

In today's economy, companies usually do not consider national boundaries when they decide where to buy goods and services. This trend is called **globalization**. Globalization has lowered prices for consumers and opened new overseas markets to Indiana's products.

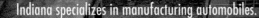
Indiana specializes in manufacturing automobiles.

However, to produce things cheaply, businesses sometimes move to countries that have the resources or technology to manufacture products at a lower cost. This in turn leads to a loss of jobs in some countries.

Global Economic Challenges

Overseas competition and advances in manufacturing technology have made companies productive and profitable. However, it will also mean fewer manufacturing jobs in Indiana. Many of these workers will need to be trained to do jobs in other sectors, or areas, of the economy.

Some economists look at these kinds of changes as good for Indiana's economy. Dave McKinnis, director of Purdue's Technical Assistance Program, says:

66One theory of economics is that change in one sector frees up people to do other things that contribute to society. This certainly has happened in the agriculture sector over the past 100 years, and now it's happening in manufacturing.99

QUICK CHECK

Summarize **Why will there be fewer manufacturing jobs in Indiana in the future?**

Check Understanding

1. **VOCABULARY** Write a paragraph about world trade using the words below.

   interdependent   **specialization**

   tariff   **globalization**

2. **READING SKILL** Summarize
   Use your chart from page 254 to write about why Indiana trades with the world.

   Summary

3. **Write About It** Write an essay about how world trade has affected your life.

EXPLORE The Big Idea

Environmental Challenges

VOCABULARY

fossil fuel p. 261

acid rain p. 261

conservation p. 261

global warming p. 262

READING SKILL

Summarize

Copy the chart below. Use it to summarize the effect that industry and people have had on the environment.

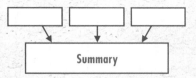

Summary

This factory produces pollution that harms the environment.

Visual Preview

How has pollution affected the environment?

A Pollution from factories and cars has harmed forests and aquatic life.

B Global warming has forced us to look for other ways of producing energy.

A   THE PROBLEM OF POLLUTION

People, animals, and plants all need a clean environment in which to live. If the environment is not taken care of, many of our natural resources can be damaged or destroyed. Protecting these resources has been a challenge throughout history.

People all over the world burn **fossil fuels**—coal, oil, and natural gas. These fuels power our lights, cars, and factories. They also heat our homes. Fossil fuels have helped our economy grow and made our lives more comfortable. However, burning these fuels pollutes the air, endangering all who breathe it.

Acid Rain

Chemicals from factories and cars can also be dangerous. They can dissolve in rainwater to form **acid rain**, or rain containing high amounts of harmful chemicals. Acid rain has harmed forests and aquatic life in lakes in parts of Indiana. For example, the sugar maple tree population in Indiana has been harmed by acid rain.

An important way to reduce pollution is through **conservation**. Conservation is the protection and careful use of natural resources. If we cut down trees, for example, we should plant new ones. Conservation limits the use of fossil fuels and restores our forests.

One way that Hoosiers conserve is by recycling. Recycling is the reuse of materials. Recycling saves natural resources and energy. Today, Indiana businesses and citizens work together to practice conservation.

The IDEM

In 1986 the Indiana Department of Environmental Management (IDEM) was created to protect Indiana's air, land, and water resources. One of its jobs is to make sure Indiana's industries help conserve natural resources and protect the environment.

QUICK CHECK

Summarize **How can people reduce pollution?**

This forest shows the effects of acid rain.

261

B GLOBAL WARMING

Many scientists argue that pollution has created a serious problem: **global warming**. Global warming is an overall rise in the temperature of Earth's atmosphere.

Causes of Global Warming

Global warming is brought about by what scientists call the greenhouse effect. The greenhouse effect is when heat is trapped in Earth's atmosphere and warms the Earth. Many scientists claim that a rise in greenhouse gases has led to global warming. Greenhouse gases include water vapor, carbon dioxide, methane, nitrous oxide, and ozone. As we add greenhouse gases to the air, temperatures rise. Ice caps begin to melt, and ocean waters rise.

EVENT

The environment produces carbon dioxide naturally. However, carbon dioxide production has been increasing steadily since the **Industrial Revolution**. The Industrial Revolution began in the late 1700s in Great Britain. It was a period of time when major changes in agriculture, manufacturing, and transportation changed the way goods were made.

Industrial Revolution

Some scientists believe that the rise in temperatures from global warming can also cause extreme weather conditions, including powerful hurricanes. An increase in global temperatures can cause rising sea levels and changes in the amount and pattern of precipitation. These changes may cause floods, droughts, heat waves, and tornadoes.

The Future

Scientists predict Indiana's climate will grow warmer during this century. By 2030, Indiana's summer climate is expected to feel like that of present-day Tennessee. By 2095, summer may be like the current climate of Louisiana.

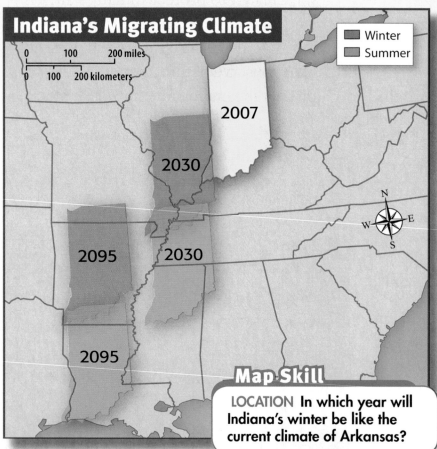

Indiana's Migrating Climate

Winter
Summer

0   100   200 miles
0   100   200 kilometers

2007
2030
2095   2030
2095

Map Skill

LOCATION **In which year will Indiana's winter be like the current climate of Arkansas?**

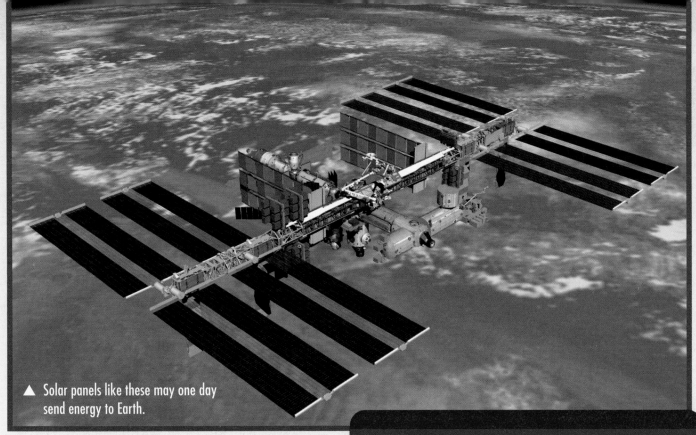

▲ Solar panels like these may one day send energy to Earth.

The growing season for crops could be three to six weeks longer. Scientists also predict droughts will be more common.

Solving Global Warming

Some scientists say that to solve the problem of global warming, we need to change the way we produce energy. One way would be to use more clean and renewable sources of energy. These include the sun's energy, wind energy, and fuels such as ethanol, which is made from corn. Countries such as Denmark produce large amounts of energy with huge windmills. Someday we may even place huge panels in space to collect solar energy, or energy from the sun, and send it back to Earth.

QUICK CHECK

Summarize **How can Hoosiers help solve the problem of global warming?**

Check Understanding

1. **VOCABULARY** Write a paragraph about environmental challenges using the terms below.

   fossil fuel   **conservation**

   acid rain   **global warming**

2. **READING SKILL** Summarize
   Use your chart from page 260 to write about the effect people have had on the environment.

3. **Write About It** Write an essay about ways people can solve the problem of global warming.

Vocabulary

Copy the sentences below. Use the list of vocabulary words to fill in the blanks.

profit   conservation

export   budget

1. A _____ is a plan for using money.

2. _____ is the protection and careful use of natural resources.

3. If a business does well, it makes a _____.

4. Something that is sold or traded to another country is called an _____.

Comprehension and Critical Thinking

5. What is a free-enterprise system?

6. Why did NAFTA expand trade in North America?

7. **Critical Thinking** Explain the right and responsibility of voting.

8. **Reading Skill** What are civic virtues?

Skill

Use Road Maps

Write a complete sentence to answer each question.

9. Which roads would you use to get from Gary to Bloomington?

10. In which direction do odd-numbered highways run?

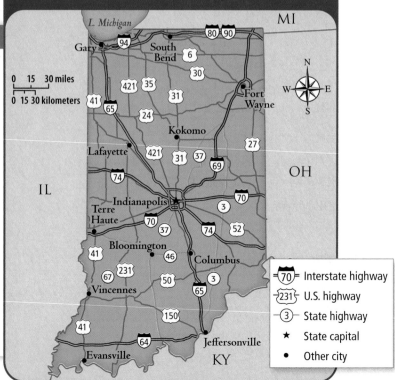

Map A: Indiana Road Map

L. Michigan   MI

Gary   94   South Bend   6

80   90

0   15   30 miles
0   15   30 kilometers

421   35   30

41   65   31   Fort Wayne

24

Kokomo

27

Lafayette   421   31   37   69

IL   74   OH

Indianapolis   70

Terre Haute   3

70   37   74   52

Bloomington   41   46   Columbus

67   231   50   3

Vincennes   65

150

41

64   Jeffersonville

Evansville   KY

Legend:
- 70   Interstate highway
- 231   U.S. highway
- 3   State highway
- ★   State capital
- •   Other city

UNLEADED

NO GAS

Indiana Statewide Test Practice

Read the passage below. Then choose the best answer or write a short response to each of the following questions.

> When Indianapolis was founded as the state capital in 1821, city planners thought it would never grow beyond its original square mile. However, Indianapolis's location made it a transportation and business center. Over the years, Indianapolis's suburbs grew and expanded throughout Marion County.
>
> In 1970 the city of Indianapolis and Marion County joined to form one local government. It was called the unified government, or Unigov. A mayor heads this form of government. A city-county council is the legislative branch of Unigov. Under Unigov, many of the police departments in the cities of Marion County remained separate from the main government. In 2005 the City-County Council changed that. They combined the Indianapolis Police Department and the Marion County Sheriff's Department to create the Indianapolis Metropolitan Police Department.

1 The passage is MAINLY about _____.

Ⓐ the growth of Indianapolis and Marion County

Ⓑ the transportation and business center of Indianapolis

Ⓒ the unified governments of cities in the United States

Ⓓ the unified government of Indianapolis and Marion County

2 Which is the legislative branch of Unigov?

Ⓐ City Council

Ⓑ County Council

Ⓒ City-County Council

Ⓓ Mayor

3 Who heads the executive branch of Unigov?

Write your answer on a separate piece of paper.

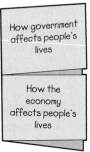

The Big Idea Activities

> How do government and the economy affect people's lives?

Write About the Big Idea

Descriptive Essay
Use the Unit 6 Foldable to help you write a descriptive essay that answers the Big Idea question, *How do government and the economy affect people's lives?* Use the notes you wrote under each tab in the Foldable. You may choose to write about one of the Foldable topics. Begin with an introduction that expresses the main idea of your essay. In the body of your essay, summarize each point of your topic. Be sure to use descriptive words. End with a conclusion about how the economy and/or government affect people's lives.

> How government affects people's lives
>
> How the economy affects people's lives

Create a Newcast

Work with a partner to present a newscast on environmental issues affecting Indiana. You and your partner will be co-anchors of a nightly news program. Follow these steps to produce your newscast.

1. Use Web sites as well as newspapers and television to research and write a story about an environmental issue affecting Indiana.

2. Compare the information you gather with the information your partner gathers.

3. Divide your newscast into two parts. The first part will be facts about the topic. The second part will be an editorial expressing an opinion about the topic.

After you and your partner have rehearsed your newscast, present it to the class.

Reference Section

The Reference Section has many parts, each with a different type of information. Use this section to look up people, places, and events as you study.

Unit 1 • Reading Skills

Main Idea and Details

Unit 1 is about the land, economy, and culture of Indiana. Thinking about the main idea and details will help you understand how and why the state has changed over time.

The main idea is what a paragraph is all about. Often it is the first sentence in a paragraph. The supporting details tell about, or support, the main idea.

Learn It

- Think about what a paragraph is all about.

- Decide whether the first sentence states the main idea.

- Look for details. Think about what these details explain.

- Now read the paragraph below. Look for the main ideas and details.

Main Idea
The first sentence states the main idea.

Supporting Details
These details tell why manufacturing and farming are leaders.

Indiana is a leader in the country in the manufacturing and farming industries. The manufacturing industry grew during and after World War I and World War II, when ammunition and other military products were made. Many settlers came to Indiana to grow crops in the fertile soil. Farming provides jobs for many people in our state.

Try It

Copy the chart below. Then fill in the chart with the main idea and details from the paragraph on page R2.

Main Idea	Details

How did you find the main idea and supporting details?

Apply It

- Review the steps for finding the main idea and details in Learn It.
- Now read the paragraph below. Make a chart to show the main idea and supporting details.

Agriculture is an important part of Indiana's economy. Agriculture is the business of growing crops and raising animals. Some of the most important crops in Indiana are corn, soybeans, and wheat. Farmers also raise cattle, hogs, chickens, and turkeys for food. There are about 60,000 farms in Indiana, covering 15 million acres of land.

Unit 2 • Reading Skills

Compare and Contrast

Unit 2 is about what happened when Native Americans and European settlers met. Each group had their own cultures, traditions, and ways of life. You can compare and contrast these groups as you read. Learning to compare and contrast will help you understand what you read about in social studies.

Learn It

- To compare two or more things, note how they are similar, or alike.
- To contrast two things, note how they are different.
- Read the passage. Think about how hunter-gatherers were similar to and different from farmers.

Similarities
Hunter-gatherers and farmers both lived in Indiana.

Differences
Hunter-gatherers hunted animals and collected fruits and nuts. Farmers grew their own vegetables.

The first people to live in what is now Indiana were hunter-gatherers. They hunted animals and collected fruits, nuts, and other foods to eat. The animal meat was a source of food, animals skins were made into clothing, and animal bones were carved and made into tools.

About 1,500 years ago, most Native Americans chose an area of what is now Indiana to farm. They cut down trees to clear fields, and used the trees to build canoes. They grew corn, squash, beans, and pumpkins. They also fished in nearby rivers.

Try It

Copy and complete the Venn diagram to help you compare and contrast the information. Fill in the chart with details from the paragraphs on page R4.

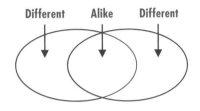

Different   Alike   Different

What information did you look for to compare and contrast?

Apply It

- Review the steps for comparing and contrasting in Learn It.
- Read the passage below. Then create a Venn diagram using the information.

    The British and American armies fought the Revolutionary War in the American Colonies. The British army was one of the best in the world. Its soldiers were well trained. They had more weapons and money than the colonists. They also had uniforms. Most colonists in the American army were farmers, not soldiers. When they began to fight, they did not have uniforms. They learned skills and were given weapons by the French. They used these skills to fight to defend their homes and win freedom from British rule.

Unit 3 • Reading Skills
Cause and Effect

Unit 3 is about the events that led to Indiana's statehood. Thinking about causes and effects will help you understand how and why Indiana became the nineteenth state in the Union.

A cause is an event that makes something happen. An effect is what happens. When one thing causes another thing to happen, they have a cause-and-effect relationship.

Learn It

- As you read, ask yourself what happened. This will help you find an effect.

- Ask yourself why something happened. This will help you find a cause.

- Look for the words *because, therefore, so,* and *as a result.* These clue words point to causes and effects.

Cause
Native Americans were upset because they were forced to give up their land to American settlers.

Effect
Both sides tried to come to an agreement, but they still fought over land rights.

Many Native Americans did not like that treaties had been signed that caused them to give up their lands in the Indiana Territory. In 1810, Governor Harrison agreed to meet with Tecumseh at Vincennes. The two men could not come to an agreement on how to split the land fairly.

After the failed meeting, Tecumseh and his people gained more support for their cause from their people. Before dawn on November 7, 1811, the Battle of Tippecanoe began when Native American warriors launched a surprise attack on Harrison's camp. Many Native Americans died, and the Americans won the battle.

Try It

Copy the chart below. Then fill in the chart with causes and effects from the paragraph on page R6.

Cause	→	Effect
	→	
	→	
	→	

What questions helped you identify cause and effect?

Apply It

- Review the steps for understanding cause and effect in Learn It.

- Read the passage below. Then create a cause and effect chart using the information.

The Harmonists worked hard. They planted corn, fruit trees, and grapes. They sold these crops to other people in the area and became wealthy. Some people in Indiana were jealous of the Harmonists and thought they had become too wealthy. Indiana became a less friendly place for George Rapp and his followers. They moved away in 1825.

Unit 4 • Reading Skills

Fact and Opinion

Unit 4 is about the Civil War and its aftermath. When people write about historical events, they often include both facts and opinions. Facts are statements that can be proven true. Opinions are feelings and beliefs. Opinions cannot be proven true or false. Being able to tell between fact and opinion will help you understand what you read in social studies.

Learn It

- Facts can be checked and proven true.

- Opinions are personal views. They cannot be proven true or false.

- Clues words such as *think*, *felt*, *believe*, and *it seems* often state opinions.

- Now read the passage below. Look for facts and opinions.

Fact
The information in these sentences are facts because they can be proven true.

Opinion
President Lincoln's personal view is an opinion.

When the Civil War was over, bitter feelings still existed between the North and the South. Thousands of soldiers had been killed. Cities and farms across the South were destroyed. Newly freed African Americans dealt with many challenges. The nation faced the task of rebuilding. Before he died, President Lincoln had said he did not believe the South should be punished. He wanted Americans to put away their malice, or desire to harm, with these words: "with malice toward none, with charity for all."

Copy the chart below. Then fill in the chart with facts and opinions from the paragraph on page R8.

Fact	Opinion

How did you determine which statement was a fact and which was an opinion?

- Review the steps for understanding fact and opinion from Learn It.

- Read the paragraph below. Then make a chart that lists two facts and opinions from the paragraph.

Indiana government leaders believed education was important. They wanted children to learn how to be responsible members of their community. In 1851 a new state constitution called for new taxes to pay for public schools. Between 1852 and 1858 more than 2,700 schoolhouses were built in Indiana. Due to discrimination, however, African American children were not allowed to attend. In Indiana's larger cities, African Americans attended their own private schools.

Unit 5 • Reading Skills

Draw Conclusions

Unit 5 is about Indiana's history during the 20th century. Sometimes meanings and connections are not clear. Drawing conclusions is one way to better understand what you read. A conclusion is based on several pieces of information that act as text clues to help explain what those facts mean.

Learn It

- As you read, ask yourself what the topic is about.

- Gather text clues about the topic.

- Make a conclusion or a statement. It connects the text clues, or facts, you have gathered.

- Now read the paragraph below. Draw conclusions as you read.

Topic
Inventions changed the way of life in America in the 1900s.

Text Clues
Inventions in farming, lighting, and technology changed the way people worked.

Between 1900 and 1930, many inventions changed American culture. An invention is a newly created product. Farmers had new machinery that made work easier. Electric lights made it safer for people to work indoors and at night. New inventions in technology improved the telephone, which made it easier for people to talk to doctors, order groceries, and stay in touch with one another. Steel was used to improve railroad tracks, and the automobile and the airplane made traveling easier.

Try It

Copy the chart below. Then fill in the chart with your conclusions from the paragraph on page R10.

Text Clues	Conclusion

What conclusions can you draw about the inventions of the 1900s?

Apply It

- Review the steps for drawing conclusions in Learn It.
- Read the paragraph below. Then draw conclusions using the text clues from the paragraph.
- Name some occasions when drawing conclusions can help you study.

The men and women of Indiana supported the war effort during World War I. More than 130,000 people from the state fought in the war, and more than 3,000 of them died in battle. At home, people made bandages that doctors used to treat the wounded. Factory workers in Indiana made military supplies, weapons, and vehicles. Others helped raise the money needed to carry on the war.

Summarize

Unit 6 is about Indiana's economy and government. Learning how to summarize, or stating the important ideas in a reading passage, will help you remember what you learned. A summary gives the main ideas, but leaves out minor details. Summarizing will help you understand and remember what you read.

Learn It

- Find the main topic in a passage. Restate these important points briefly.

- Find important supporting facts and combine them in your summary.

- Leave out details that are not important.

- Now read the paragraph below and think about how you would summarize it.

Main Topic
This is the main topic of the paragraph.

Supporting Facts
These facts support the main topic.

Companies in Indiana can use our roads, railways, airports, and waterways to ship their goods. Many of the products made in Indiana are first transported by highway. Indiana has 13 interstate highways—more than any other state. Trucks on these roads carry products made in our state to other forms of transportation, such as railroads. When companies need their products shipped quickly, they use cargo planes. Cargo planes carry products to other parts of the world. Ships are also used to move products across the country and all over the world.

Try It

Copy the chart below. Then fill in the chart with your conclusions from the paragraph on page R12.

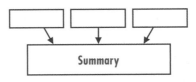

Summary

What did you look for to summarize the paragraph?

Apply It

- Review the steps for summarizing in Learn It.
- Read the paragraphs below. Then summarize the passage by using a summary chart.

Local government provides public services for all of its citizens. County government is in charge of hospitals, health programs, and maintaining highways. Municipal governments provide police and fire services and maintain parks. Townships mainly provide help to people in need and figure out how much property is worth.

However, these public services are not the same everywhere. For example, some municipal governments provide public water service. In other places, citizens have to dig their own wells for water. Similarly, some communities have hospitals and libraries. Other communities are too small or do not have the money for hospitals and libraries.

Geography Handbook

Geography and You

Geography is the study of our Earth and the people who live here. Most people think of geography as learning about cities, states, and countries, but geography is more than that. Geography includes learning about land, such as plains and mountains. Geography also helps us learn how to use land and water wisely.

Did you know that people are part of geography? Geography includes the study of how people adapt to live in a new place. How people move around, how they move goods, and how ideas travel from place to place are also parts of geography.

In fact, geography includes so many things that geographers have divided this information into six elements, or ideas, so you can better understand them.

Six Essential Elements

The World in Spatial Terms: Where is a place located, and what land or water features does this place have?

Places and Regions: What is special about a place, and what makes it different from other places?

Physical Systems: What has shaped the land and climate of a place, and how does this affect the plants, animals, and people there?

Human Systems: How do people, ideas, and goods move from place to place?

Environment and Society: How have people changed the land and water of a place, and how have the land and water affected the people of a place?

Uses of Geography: How does geography influence events in the past, present, and the future?

Five Themes of Geography

You have read about the six elements of geography. The five themes of geography are another way of dividing the ideas of geography. The themes, or topics, are **location**, **place**, **region**, **movement**, and **human interaction**. Using these five themes is another way to understand events you read about in this book.

1. Location

The White House

In geography, *location* means an exact spot on the planet. A location is usually a street name and number. You write a location when you address a letter.

2. Place

The Grand Canyon

A *place* is described by its physical features, such as rivers, mountains, or valleys. Human features, such as cities, language, and traditions can also describe a place.

3. Region

Wheat field in the Midwest

A *region* is larger than a place or location. The people in a region are affected by landforms. Their region has typical jobs and customs. For example, the fertile soil of the Mississippi lowlands helps farmers in the region grow crops.

4. Movement

Passenger Train

Throughout history, people have moved to find better land or a better life. Geographers study why these *movements* occurred. They also study how people's movements have changed a region.

5. Human Interaction

Hoover Dam

Geographers study the ways that people adapt to their environment. Geographers also study how people change their environment. The *interaction* between people and their environment explains how land is used.

Dictionary of Geographic Terms

1 BASIN A bowl-shaped landform surrounded by higher land

2 BAY Part of an ocean or lake that extends deeply into the land

3 CANAL A channel built to carry water for irrigation or transportation

4 CANYON A deep, narrow valley with steep sides

5 COAST The land along an ocean

6 DAM A wall built across a river, creating a lake that stores water

7 DELTA Land made of soil left behind as a river drains into a larger body of water

8 DESERT A dry environment with few plants and animals

9 FAULT The border between two of the plates that make up Earth's crust

10 GLACIER A huge sheet of ice that moves slowly across the land

11 GULF Part of an ocean that extends into the land; larger than a bay

12 HARBOR A sheltered place along a coast where boats dock safely

13 HILL A rounded, raised landform; not as high as a mountain

14 ISLAND A body of land completely surrounded by water

15 LAKE A body of water completely surrounded by land

16 MESA A hill with a flat top; smaller than a plateau

17 **MOUNTAIN** A high landform with steep sides; higher than a hill

18 **MOUNTAIN PASS** A narrow gap through a mountain range

19 **MOUTH** The place where a river empties into a larger body of water

20 **OCEAN** A large body of salt water; oceans cover much of Earth's surface

21 **PENINSULA** A body of land nearly surrounded by water

22 **PLAIN** A large area of nearly flat land

23 **PLATEAU** A high, flat area that rises steeply above the surrounding land

24 **PORT** A place where ships load and unload their goods

25 **RESERVOIR** A natural or artificial lake used to store water

26 **RIVER** A large stream that empties into another body of water

27 **SOURCE** The starting point of a river

28 **VALLEY** An area of low land between hills or mountains

29 **VOLCANO** An opening in Earth's surface through which hot rock and ash are forced out

30 **WATERFALL** A flow of water falling vertically

Read a Physical Map

Maps are drawings of places on Earth. Most maps use colors and symbols to show information. Physical maps show and label landforms, such as mountains and deserts, and water features, such as lakes and rivers. Map makers use shading and color to show different physical features, such as blue to show water or dark shading to show mountains.

Map Title Map titles tell you what information is on the map.

Inset Map An inset map is a small map set into the main map. It shows an area that is too large, too small, or too far away to be included on the main map. Inset maps usually use a different scale than the main map.

Map Key The map key, or legend, gives the meaning of the colors and symbols on a map.

Map Scale The map scale is a line that shows the relationship between distances on a map and distances on Earth. Here, the length of the line on the map represents 400 miles on Earth.

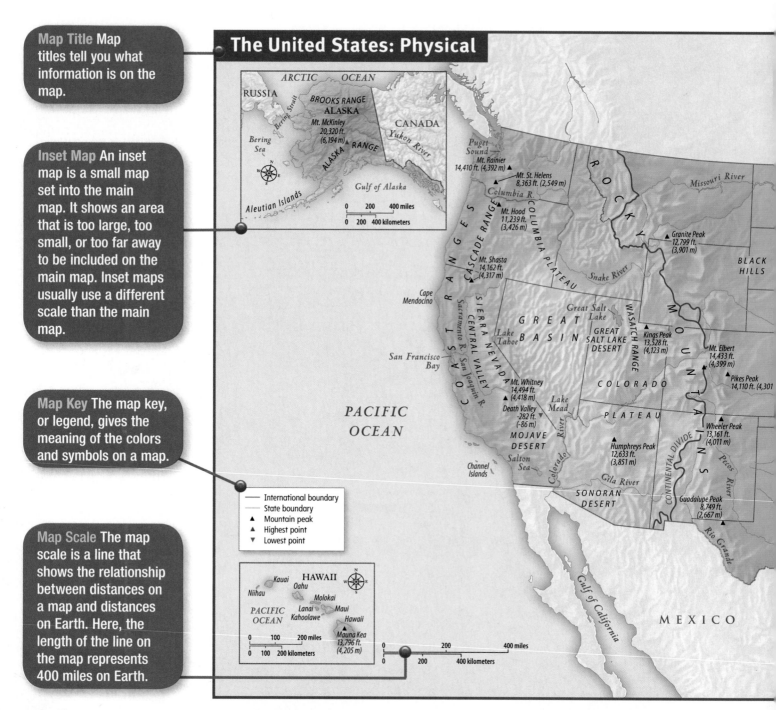

The United States: Physical

ARCTIC OCEAN

RUSSIA

BROOKS RANGE
ALASKA

Mt. McKinley
20,320 ft.
(6,194 m)

CANADA
Yukon River

Bering Strait

Bering Sea

ALASKA RANGE

Gulf of Alaska

Aleutian Islands

0   200   400 miles
0   200   400 kilometers

Puget Sound
Mt. Rainier
14,410 ft. (4,392 m)

Mt. St. Helens
8,363 ft. (2,549 m)

Columbia R.

ROCKY

Missouri River

Mt. Hood
11,239 ft.
(3,426 m)

COLUMBIA PLATEAU

Granite Peak
12,799 ft.
(3,901 m)

BLACK HILLS

Mt. Shasta
14,162 ft.
(4,317 m)

Snake River

CASCADE RANGE

Cape Mendocino

COAST RANGES

Sacramento R.

San Joaquin R.

SIERRA NEVADA

CENTRAL VALLEY

Great Salt Lake

GREAT BASIN

Lake Tahoe

WASATCH RANGE

GREAT SALT LAKE DESERT

Kings Peak
13,528 ft.
(4,123 m)

MOUNTAINS

Mt. Elbert
14,433 ft.
(4,399 m)

Pikes Peak
14,110 ft. (4,301

San Francisco Bay

Mt. Whitney
14,494 ft.
(4,418 m)

Death Valley
-282 ft.
(-86 m)

Lake Mead

COLORADO

PLATEAU

Wheeler Peak
13,161 ft.
(4,011 m)

PACIFIC OCEAN

MOJAVE DESERT

Colorado River

Humphreys Peak
12,633 ft.
(3,851 m)

CONTINENTAL DIVIDE

Pecos River

Salton Sea

Channel Islands

Gila River

SONORAN DESERT

Guadalupe Peak
8,749 ft.
(2,667 m)

Rio Grande

—— International boundary
—— State boundary
▲ Mountain peak
▲ Highest point
▼ Lowest point

HAWAII

Kauai
Oahu
Niihau
Molokai
Lanai   Maui
Kahoolawe   Hawaii

PACIFIC OCEAN

Mauna Kea
13,796 ft.
(4,205 m)

0   100   200 miles
0   100   200 kilometers

Gulf of California

MEXICO

0   200   400 miles
0   200   400 kilometers

Think About It About how far is it from Mt. Hood to Mt. Shasta in the Cascade Range?

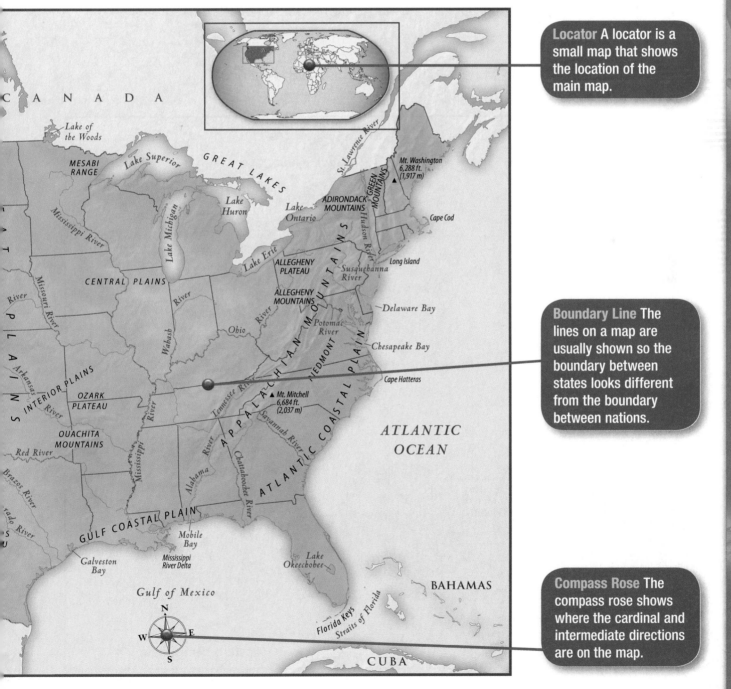

Locator A locator is a small map that shows the location of the main map.

Boundary Line The lines on a map are usually shown so the boundary between states looks different from the boundary between nations.

Compass Rose The compass rose shows where the cardinal and intermediate directions are on the map.

Hemispheres

You can think of Earth as a sphere, like a ball or a globe. A hemisphere is half of a sphere. Geographers have divided Earth into the Northern Hemisphere and the Southern Hemisphere at the equator, an imaginary line that circles Earth halfway between the North Pole and the South Pole. Another important imaginary line is the prime meridian. It divides Earth from east to west. The area west of the prime meridian is called the Western Hemisphere, and the area east of the prime meridian is called the Eastern Hemisphere.

Think About It In which two hemispheres is North America?

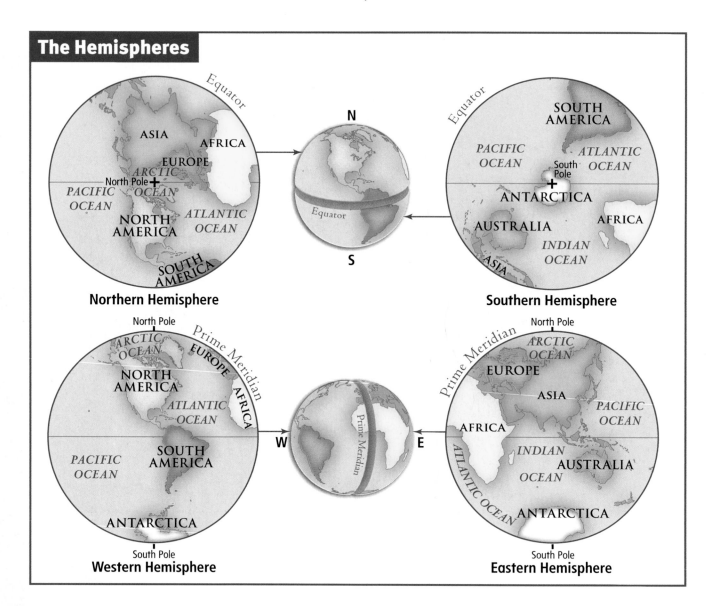

The Hemispheres

Northern Hemisphere

Southern Hemisphere

Western Hemisphere

Eastern Hemisphere

Latitude and Longitude

Earth can be divided into a grid of lines called latitude and longitude. Lines of latitude measure how far north or south a place is from the equator. Lines of longitude measure distance east or west from the prime meridian. Both the equator and the prime meridian represent 0 degrees. The symbol for degrees is °. Latitude lines measure the distance in degrees from the equator, and longitude lines measure the distance in degrees from the prime meridian. Look at the map. You can see that Los Angeles is located very near the longitude line labeled 120°W at the top of the map. That means that Los Angeles is about 120° west of the prime meridian.

Think About It Is Lagos north or south of the equator?

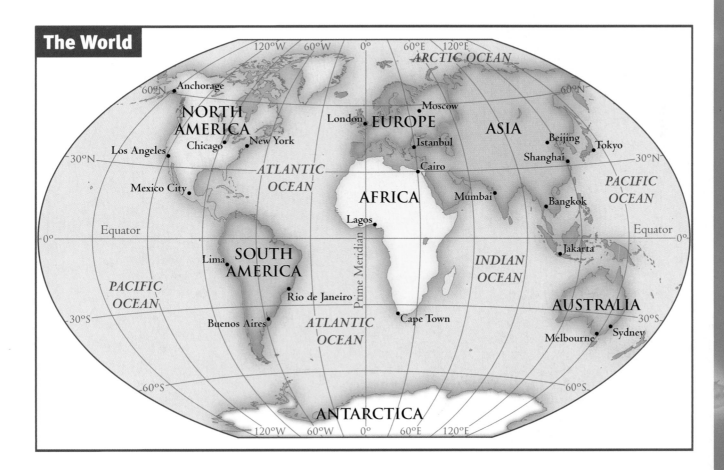

The World

Use Elevation Maps

An elevation map is a physical map that uses colors to show the elevation, or height of land above or below sea level. The height is usually measured in feet or meters. Sea level is measured as 0 feet or meters around the world. Read the key to understand what each color means. The map on this page uses purple to show land below sea level.

Identify the area of your town or city on the map. How high above sea level is your area?

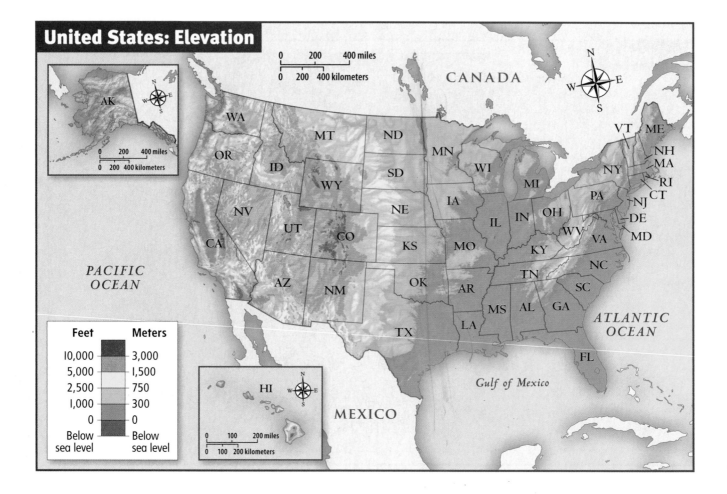

United States: Elevation

Feet		Meters
10,000		3,000
5,000		1,500
2,500		750
1,000		300
0		0
Below sea level		Below sea level

Use Road Maps

Suppose you want to go somewhere you have never been before. How do you know what road to take? You could use a road map. Road maps show where the roads in a certain area go. By reading a road map you can figure out how to get from one place to another.

Look at the road map of Indiana. The map key tells you which kinds of roads are shown on the map. Interstate highways run through two or more states and have two or more lanes in each direction. U.S. highways are usually two lane highways that also connect states. State highways stop at a state's borders. The name of each highway is a number. Notice the different symbols for each of the three kinds of highways.

Which roads would you use to get from South Bend to Terre Haute?

Maps at Different Scales

All maps are smaller than the real area that they show. To figure out the real distance between two places, most maps include a scale. The scale shows the relationship between distances on a map and real distances.

The scales on the maps in this book are drawn with two horizontal lines. The top line shows distances in miles. The bottom line shows distances in kilometers. You can use a ruler or mark a strip of paper under the scale to measure the distance between places on the map.

The maps on this page are drawn at different scales. Map A and Map B both show the Hawaiian Islands, but Map B shows a larger area with less detail. It is a small-scale map. Map A is a large-scale map. It shows a smaller area with more detail. The scales are different, but the distance between the places shown on both maps is the same.

On both maps, what is the distance in miles between Niihau and Molokai?

What details on Map A are not on Map B?

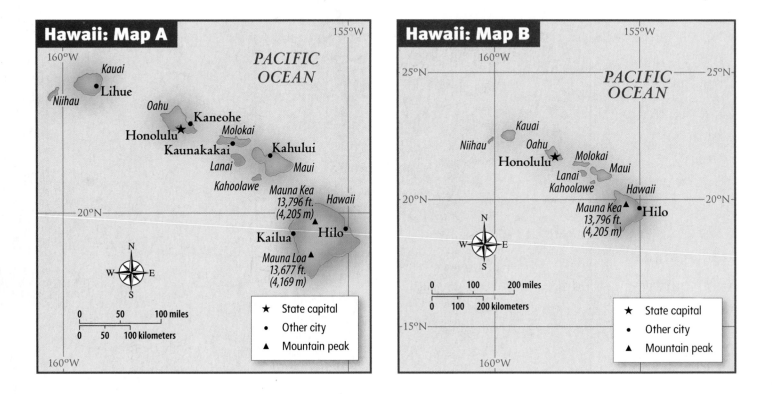

Use Population Maps

When you need to know the number of people who live in a place, or where people live, you can look at a population map. Most population maps show population density—how many people live in a certain area. Another kind of population map shows population distribution—where in an area people live.

Look at the population distribution map of the United States below. Population distribution maps often use different colors to stand for numbers of people per square mile or kilometer. The map key shows the number each color stands for. For example, between 5 and 24 people per square mile live in areas that are shaded yellow.

Which color is used to show the areas with the most people?

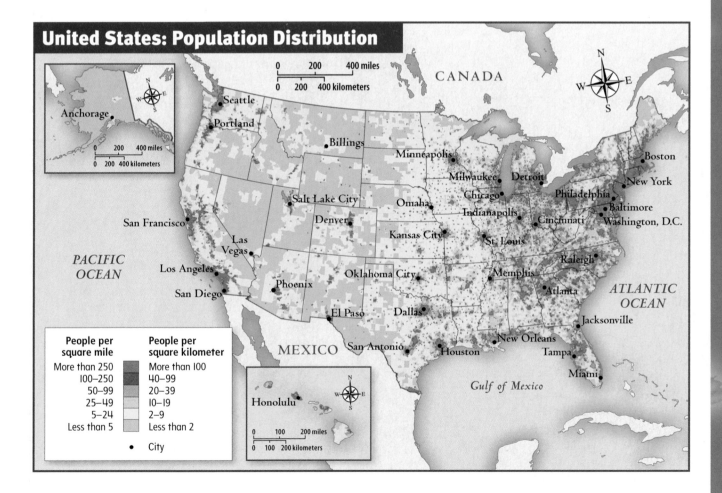

United States: Population Distribution

Lake Michigan

MI

Michigan City

South Bend

St. Joseph River

Elkhart

Hammond

La Porte

Mishawaka

Goshen

Gary

Valparaiso

Merrillville

Kankakee River

Fort Wayne

St. Marys River

IL

Logansport

Wabash River

OH

West Lafayette

Kokomo

Lafayette

Wabash River

White River

Muncie

Anderson

Carmel

Fishers

Richmond

Speedway

Lawrence

★ Indianapolis

N
W   E
S

Terre Haute

Columbus

Bloomington

Monroe Lake

White River

Madison

Vincennes

Ohio River

New Albany

KY

Jeffersonville

Wabash River

Evansville

Ohio River

	State boundary
	County boundary
★	State capital
●	City

0   15   30 miles
0   15   30 kilometers

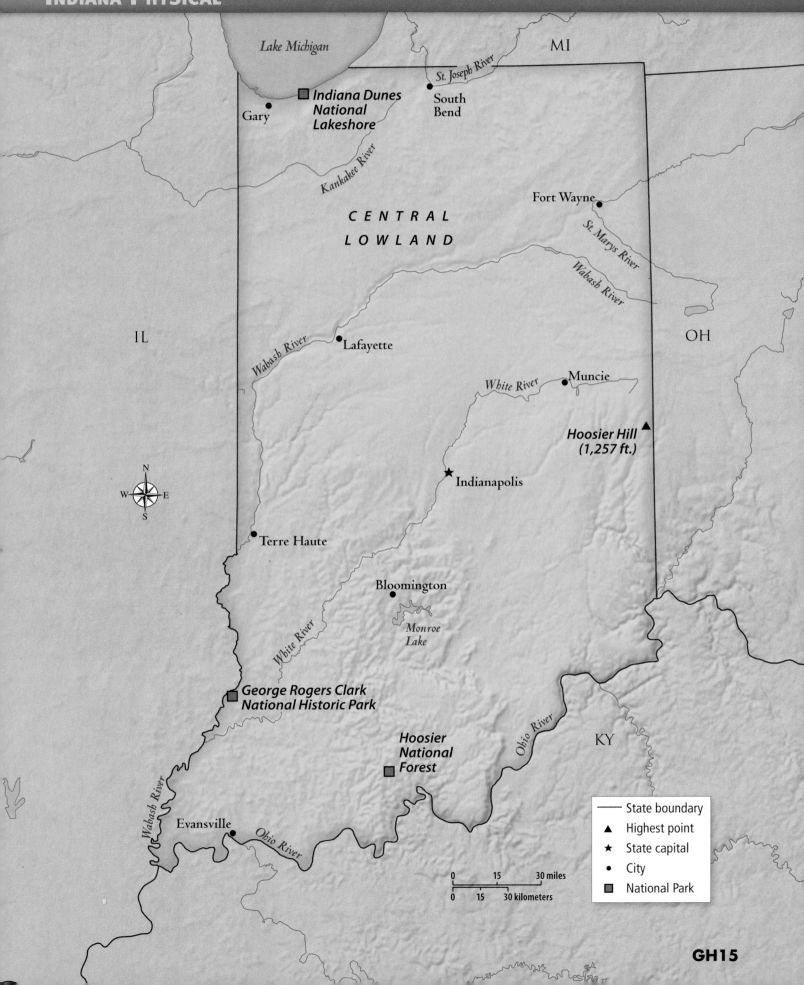

Lake Michigan

MI

St. Joseph River

□ **Indiana Dunes National Lakeshore**

South Bend

Gary

Kankakee River

C E N T R A L
L O W L A N D

Fort Wayne

St. Marys River

Wabash River

IL

Wabash River

• Lafayette

OH

White River

Muncie

Hoosier Hill ▲
(1,257 ft.)

★ Indianapolis

Terre Haute

Bloomington

Monroe Lake

White River

□ **George Rogers Clark National Historic Park**

Ohio River

KY

Hoosier National Forest □

Wabash River

Evansville

Ohio River

——	State boundary
▲	Highest point
★	State capital
●	City
■	National Park

0   15   30 miles

0   15   30 kilometers

ARCTIC OCEAN

180°W 70°N 120°W
RUSSIA
Arctic Circle
CANADA
Nome · Yukon R. · Fairbanks ·
ALASKA
60°N
Anchorage ·
130°W
Juneau ★
0 200 400 miles
0 200 400 kilometers
170°W 160°W 150°W 140°W
40°N
130°W

Seattle · River
Olympia ★ Spokane ·
WASHINGTON
Columbia
Portland ·
Salem ★
Eugene ·
OREGON

Great Falls · Missouri River
Helena ★ MONTANA
Billings ·

IDAHO
Boise ★
Snake River Pocatello ·

WYOMING
Casper ·
Cheyenne ★

Eureka ·
Redding ·

Great Salt Lake
Ogden ·
Salt Lake City ★ Provo ·
UTAH
Colorado River

Denver ★
COLORADO
Colorado Springs ·
Pueblo ·

Reno ·
Sacramento ★ Carson City ·
San Francisco · Oakland · NEVADA
San Jose ·
Fresno ·
CALIFORNIA
Las Vegas ·

Bakersfield ·

PACIFIC OCEAN

30°N

Long Beach · Los Angeles ·
San Diego ·

Santa Fe ·
Albuquerque ·
ARIZONA
Phoenix ★ NEW MEXICO

Tucson ·

El Paso ·
Rio Grande

130°W

160°W 155°W
Kauai HAWAII
Oahu
Niihau Molokai
Honolulu ★
PACIFIC Lanai Maui
OCEAN Kahoolawe
20°N
Hilo ·
Hawaii
0 100 200 miles
0 100 200 kilometers

Gulf of California

MEXICO

Tropic of Cancer

20°N

120°W 110°W

0 200 400 miles
0 200 400 kilometers

— International boundary
— State boundary
⊛ National capital
★ State capital
· Other city

CANADA

NORTH DAKOTA
Grand Forks
Fargo
Bismarck

Lake Superior

Duluth
MINNESOTA

Marquette
MICHIGAN

Lake Huron

NEW HAMPSHIRE
VERMONT
MAINE
Augusta
Montpelier
Portland
Concord

SOUTH DAKOTA
Pierre

St. Paul
Minneapolis

Green Bay
WISCONSIN
Milwaukee
Madison

Lake Michigan

Grand Rapids
Lansing

Lake Ontario

Lake Erie

Albany
NEW YORK
Buffalo

Boston
MASSACHUSETTS
Providence
RHODE ISLAND
CONNECTICUT
Hartford
Newark
New York
Trenton
NEW JERSEY

Sioux Falls

Cedar Rapids
IOWA

Chicago

Detroit
Toledo Cleveland

PENNSYLVANIA
Harrisburg

Philadelphia
Baltimore
Dover
DELAWARE

NEBRASKA
Omaha
Lincoln

Missouri River
Platte River

Des Moines
Davenport
ILLINOIS

Gary
INDIANA

OHIO
Columbus

Pittsburgh

Washington, D.C.
WEST VIRGINIA
Charleston

Annapolis
MARYLAND

Indianapolis
Springfield

Cincinnati

Frankfort

Richmond
Norfolk

Kansas City
Topeka
KANSAS
Kansas City
Wichita

St. Louis
Jefferson City
MISSOURI

Evansville
Ohio River

Louisville
KENTUCKY

VIRGINIA

Nashville
Tennessee River
Knoxville

Raleigh
NORTH CAROLINA
Charlotte

Tulsa
Oklahoma City
OKLAHOMA

Fort Smith
ARKANSAS
Little Rock

Arkansas River
Red River

Memphis

Mississippi River

TENNESSEE

Columbia
SOUTH CAROLINA
Charleston

Fort Worth
Dallas
TEXAS

Shreveport
LOUISIANA

Birmingham
MISSISSIPPI
Jackson

ALABAMA

Atlanta
GEORGIA
Columbus
Montgomery

Savannah

Brazos River
Colorado River

Austin
San Antonio

Baton Rouge
New Orleans
Houston

Mobile
Biloxi

Jacksonville
Tallahassee

ATLANTIC OCEAN

Corpus Christi
Laredo

Gulf of Mexico

Orlando
FLORIDA
Tampa

Lake Okeechobee

Miami

BAHAMAS

N W E S

CUBA

50°N
40°N
70°W
30°N
80°W
90°W
100°W

GH17

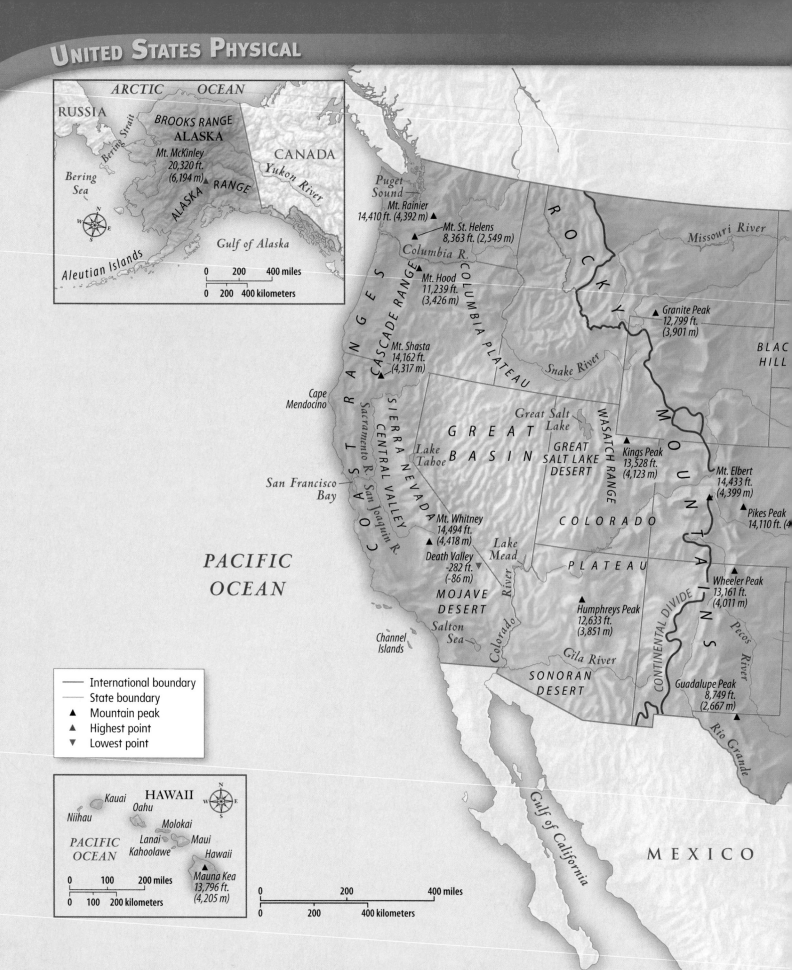

ARCTIC OCEAN

RUSSIA

BROOKS RANGE
ALASKA

Mt. McKinley
20,320 ft.
(6,194 m) ▲

CANADA

Yukon River

Bering Strait

Bering Sea

ALASKA RANGE

Gulf of Alaska

Aleutian Islands

N W E S

| 0 | 200 | 400 miles |
| 0 | 200 | 400 kilometers |

Puget Sound —
Mt. Rainier
14,410 ft. (4,392 m) ▲
→ Mt. St. Helens
8,363 ft. (2,549 m) ▲

Columbia R.

COLUMBIA PLATEAU

R O C K Y

Missouri River

Granite Peak
▲ 12,799 ft.
(3,901 m)

BLACK HILL

Mt. Hood
11,239 ft.
(3,426 m) ▲

Snake River

CASCADE RANGE

Mt. Shasta
14,162 ft.
(4,317 m) ▲

Cape Mendocino

C O A S T   R A N G E S

Sacramento R.

CENTRAL VALLEY

SIERRA NEVADA

Great Salt Lake

WASATCH RANGE

GREAT BASIN

GREAT SALT LAKE DESERT

Kings Peak
▲ 13,528 ft.
(4,123 m)

Lake Tahoe

San Francisco Bay

San Joaquin R.

Mt. Whitney
14,494 ft.
(4,418 m) ▲

Lake Mead

COLORADO

PLATEAU

Mt. Elbert
14,433 ft.
(4,399 m) ▲

Pikes Peak
14,110 ft. (4 ▲

Death Valley
-282 ft. ▽
(-86 m)

Colorado River

M O U N T A I N S

Wheeler Peak
▲ 13,161 ft.
(4,011 m)

PACIFIC OCEAN

MOJAVE DESERT

Salton Sea

Humphreys Peak
▲ 12,633 ft.
(3,851 m)

CONTINENTAL DIVIDE

Pecos River

Channel Islands

Gila River

SONORAN DESERT

Guadalupe Peak
▲ 8,749 ft.
(2,667 m)

Rio Grande

Legend

⎯⎯	International boundary
—	State boundary
▲	Mountain peak
▲	Highest point
▽	Lowest point

Gulf of California

M E X I C O

Kauai

HAWAII

N W E S

Niihau

Oahu

Molokai

Maui

Lanai

PACIFIC OCEAN

Kahoolawe

Hawaii

Mauna Kea
13,796 ft.
(4,205 m) ▲

| 0 | 100 | 200 miles |
| 0 | 100 | 200 kilometers |

| 0 | 200 | 400 miles |
| 0 | 200 | 400 kilometers |

CANADA

Lake of
the Woods

MESABI
RANGE

Lake Superior

GREAT LAKES

St. Lawrence River

Mt. Washington
6,288 ft.
(1,917 m) ▲

GREEN MOUNTAINS

Mississippi River

Lake
Huron

Lake Michigan

Lake
Ontario

ADIRONDACK
MOUNTAINS

Cape Cod

Hudson River

CENTRAL PLAINS

River

Lake Erie

ALLEGHENY
PLATEAU

Susquehanna
River

Long Island

GREAT PLAINS

Missouri River

Wabash

River

ALLEGHENY
MOUNTAINS

Potomac
River

Delaware Bay

Platte

River

Ohio

APPALACHIAN MOUNTAINS

Chesapeake Bay

Arkansas

INTERIOR PLAINS

OZARK
PLATEAU

Mississippi

River

PIEDMONT

Cape Hatteras

River

Tennessee River

▲ Mt. Mitchell
6,684 ft.
(2,037 m)

OUACHITA
MOUNTAINS

Red River

Savannah River

ATLANTIC COASTAL PLAIN

ATLANTIC
OCEAN

Brazos River

River

Alabama

Chattahoochee River

Colorado River

ARDS
TEAU

GULF COASTAL PLAIN

Mobile
Bay

Galveston
Bay

Mississippi
River Delta

Lake
Okeechobee

BAHAMAS

Gulf of Mexico

Florida Keys

Straits of Florida

N
W   E
S

CUBA

160°W   120°W
80°N
ALASKA
(U.S.)
60°N
CANADA
NORTH AMERICA
40°N
UNITED STATES
BERMUDA
(U.K.)
MIDWAY ISLANDS
(United States)
ATLANTIC OCEAN
Tropic of Cancer
See inset below
HAWAII
(United States)
20°N
MEXICO
Caribbean Sea
GUYANA
SURINAM
FRENCH
GUIANA
(France)
VENEZUELA
PACIFIC OCEAN
GALAPAGOS ISLANDS
(Ecuador)
COLOMBIA
0° Equator
ECUADOR
SOUTH AMERICA
PERU
BRAZIL
AMERICAN
SAMOA
(United
States)
COOK
ISLANDS
(New
Zealand)
SAMOA
FRENCH POLYNESIA
(France)
BOLIVIA
TONGA
PARAGUAY
20°S
Tropic of Capricorn
PITCAIRN
ISLAND
(United Kingdom)
CHILE
URUGUAY
ARGENTINA
FALKLAND
ISLANDS
(United K.)
40°S
60°S
Antarctic Circle
80°S
120°W
60°W
160°W
20°N

Central America and West Indies

90°W   80°W   70°W
Gulf of Mexico
FLORIDA
(United States)
0   200   400 miles
0   200   400 kilometers
Tropic of Cancer
BAHAMAS
ATLANTIC
OCEAN
20°N
TURKS &
CAICOS
ISLANDS
(United Kingdom)
20°N
CUBA
VIRGIN IS.
(United Kingdom)
PUERTO RICO
(United States)
ST. KITTS & NEVIS
MEXICO
CAYMAN IS.
(United Kingdom)
HAITI
DOMINICAN
REPUBLIC
ANTIGUA &
BARBUDA
BELIZE
VIRGIN IS. (United States)
GUADELOUPE
(France)
GUATEMALA
JAMAICA
MONTSERRAT (United Kingdom)
HONDURAS
Caribbean Sea
DOMINICA
MARTINIQUE
(France)
EL
SALVADOR
NICARAGUA
N
W   E
S
NETHERLANDS ANTILLES
(Netherlands)
ST. LUCIA
ST. VINCENT &
THE GRENADINES
BARBADOS
ARUBA (Netherlands)
GRENADA
TRINIDAD
& TOBAGO
10°N
60°W
COSTA
RICA
PACIFIC
OCEAN
PANAMA
COLOMBIA
VENEZUELA
GUYANA

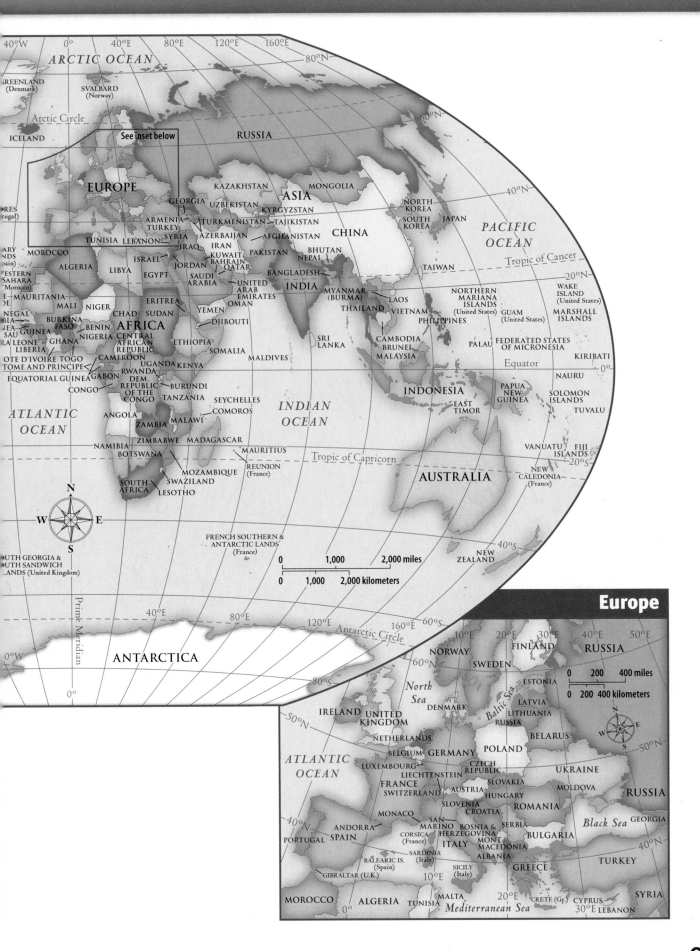

ARCTIC OCEAN

40°W   0°   40°E   80°E   120°E   160°E

80°N

GREENLAND
(Denmark)

SVALBARD
(Norway)

Arctic Circle

ICELAND

60°N

RUSSIA

See inset below

EUROPE

RES
tugal)

GEORGIA

KAZAKHSTAN   MONGOLIA

ASIA

40°N

ARMENIA   UZBEKISTAN   KYRGYZSTAN

TURKEY   TURKMENISTAN   TAJIKISTAN

NORTH
KOREA   JAPAN

SOUTH
KOREA

PACIFIC
OCEAN

TUNISIA   LEBANON   SYRIA   AZERBAIJAN   AFGHANISTAN   CHINA

ARY
NDS
pain)

MOROCCO

IRAQ   IRAN   PAKISTAN

KUWAIT   BHUTAN

Tropic of Cancer

ALGERIA   LIBYA   ISRAEL   JORDAN   BAHRAIN   QATAR   NEPAL   BANGLADESH   TAIWAN

20°N

ESTERN
SAHARA
Morocco)

EGYPT   SAUDI
ARABIA   UNITED
ARAB
EMIRATES   INDIA   MYANMAR
(BURMA)   LAOS

WAKE
ISLAND
(United States)

E   MAURITANIA   MALI   NIGER   CHAD   SUDAN   ERITREA   YEMEN   OMAN   THAILAND   VIETNAM   PHILIPPINES   NORTHERN
MARIANA
ISLANDS
(United States)   GUAM
(United States)   MARSHALL
ISLANDS

NEGAL   BURKINA
FASO   BENIN   NIGERIA   DJIBOUTI

IBIA   CENTRAL
AFRICAN
REPUBLIC   ETHIOPIA   SRI
LANKA   CAMBODIA   PALAU   FEDERATED STATES
OF MICRONESIA

AU   GUINEA   GHANA   AFRICA   SOMALIA   MALDIVES   BRUNEI
MALAYSIA   KIRIBATI

A LEONE
LIBERIA   OTE D'IVOIRE   TOGO   CAMEROON   UGANDA   KENYA   Equator   NAURU

TOME AND PRINCIPE   GABON   RWANDA
DEM.   BURUNDI   0°

EQUATORIAL GUINEA   CONGO   REPUBLIC
OF THE
CONGO   TANZANIA   SEYCHELLES   INDONESIA   PAPUA
NEW
GUINEA   SOLOMON
ISLANDS

ATLANTIC
OCEAN   ANGOLA   INDIAN
OCEAN   EAST
TIMOR   TUVALU

ZAMBIA   MALAWI   COMOROS

NAMIBIA   ZIMBABWE   MADAGASCAR   VANUATU   FIJI
ISLANDS   20°S

BOTSWANA   MAURITIUS   Tropic of Capricorn   NEW
CALEDONIA
(France)

N   MOZAMBIQUE   REUNION
(France)   AUSTRALIA

SOUTH
AFRICA   SWAZILAND

W   E   LESOTHO

S

UTH GEORGIA &
UTH SANDWICH
ANDS (United Kingdom)   FRENCH SOUTHERN &
ANTARCTIC LANDS
(France)   40°S   NEW
ZEALAND

0   1,000   2,000 miles

0   1,000   2,000 kilometers

Prime Meridian   40°E   80°E   120°E   160°E   60°S   Antarctic Circle

0°W   ANTARCTICA   80°S

0°

Europe

FINLAND   RUSSIA

NORWAY   20°E   30°E   40°E   50°E

60°N   SWEDEN   ESTONIA   0   200   400 miles

North
Sea   DENMARK   Baltic Sea   LATVIA   0   200   400 kilometers

50°N   LITHUANIA   N

IRELAND   UNITED
KINGDOM   RUSSIA   W   E

NETHERLANDS   BELARUS   S

BELGIUM   GERMANY   POLAND   50°N

ATLANTIC
OCEAN   LUXEMBOURG   CZECH
REPUBLIC   UKRAINE

LIECHTENSTEIN

FRANCE   SLOVAKIA   MOLDOVA

SWITZERLAND   AUSTRIA   HUNGARY   ROMANIA   RUSSIA

SLOVENIA   Black Sea   GEORGIA

MONACO   CROATIA

40°N   ANDORRA   SAN
MARINO   BOSNIA &
HERZEGOVINA   SERBIA   BULGARIA

PORTUGAL   SPAIN   CORSICA
(France)   MONT.   TURKEY   40°N

ITALY   MACEDONIA

BALEARIC IS.   SARDINIA   ALBANIA

(Spain)   (Italy)   GREECE

GIBRALTAR (U.K.)   10°E   SICILY
(Italy)   SYRIA

MOROCCO   ALGERIA   TUNISIA   MALTA   20°E   CRETE (Gr.)   CYPRUS   LEBANON

0°   Mediterranean Sea   30°E

GH21

ARCTIC OCEAN

80°N

160°W   120°W   80°W   40°W

GREENLAND

Mackenzie River

Arctic Circle

60°N

ALASKA RANGE

Mt. McKinley
20,320 ft.
(6,194 m)

NORTH
AMERICA

ROCKY MOUNTAINS

CANADIAN SHIELD

40°N

Mississippi River

APPALACHIAN MTS.

PACIFIC OCEAN

Rio Grande

Tropic of Cancer

Gulf of
Mexico

ATLANTIC
OCEAN

20°N

Caribbean Sea

Equator

Amazon River

SOUTH
AMERICA

20°S

Tropic of Capricorn

ANDES

MOUNTAINS

Mt. Aconcagua
22,834 ft.
(6,960 m)

ATLANTIC
OCEAN

40°S

PACIFIC OCEAN

Cape Horn

60°S

Antarctic Circle

80°W

Weddell
Sea

120°W

40°W

160°W

Vinson Massif
16,067 ft.
(4,897 m)

ARCTIC OCEAN

40°E 80°E 120°E 160°E

80°N

Lena River

Yenisey River

Ob River

60°N

Sea of Okhotsk

URAL MTS.

Volga River

EUROPE

Caspian Sea

ASIA

GOBI

40°N

Blanc
1 ft.
7 m)

Black Sea ▲ Mt. Elbrus
18,510 ft.
(5,642 m)

HINDU KUSH

Mediterranean Sea

SYRIAN
DESERT

HIMALAYA

Yangtze River

Tropic of Cancer

A H A R A

River

Red Sea

Ganges
River

DECCAN
PLATEAU

Mt. Everest
29,035 ft.
(8,850 m)

20°N

Nile

Arabian
Sea

South
China
Sea

Philippine
Sea

PACIFIC OCEAN

AFRICA

Mt. Kilimanjaro
19,340 ft.
(5,895 m)

Equator 0°

River

Congo

▲

INDIAN
OCEAN

Coral
Sea

NAMIB DESERT

KALAHARI
DESERT

Tropic of Capricorn

GREAT
SANDY
DESERT

20°S

ape of
Hope

AUSTRALIA

Darling River

Mt. Kosciuszko
7,310 ft.
(2,228 m)

▲

N

W   E

S

0   1,000   2,000 miles

0   1,000   2,000 kilometers

40°S

40°E 80°E 120°E 160°E

60°S

Antarctic Circle

80°S

ANTARCTICA

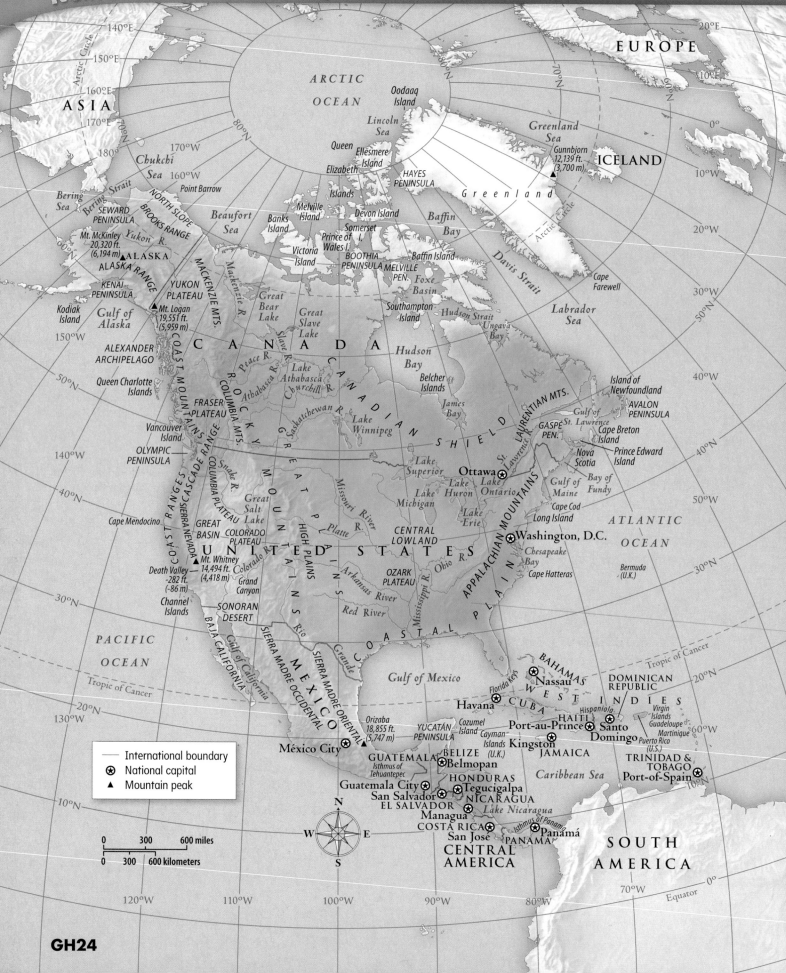

EUROPE

ASIA

ARCTIC OCEAN

Chukchi Sea

Bering Strait

Bering Sea

SEWARD PENINSULA

BROOKS RANGE

NORTH SLOPE

Point Barrow

Mt. McKinley 20,320 ft. (6,194 m) ▲

ALASKA

ALASKA RANGE

KENAI PENINSULA

Yukon R.

YUKON PLATEAU

Kodiak Island

Gulf of Alaska

Mt. Logan 19,551 ft. (5,959 m) ▲

ALEXANDER ARCHIPELAGO

MACKENZIE MTS.

Mackenzie R.

Queen Charlotte Islands

COAST MOUNTAINS

FRASER PLATEAU

Vancouver Island

OLYMPIC PENINSULA

Peace R.

Athabasca R.

ROCKY MOUNTAINS

COLUMBIA MTS.

COLUMBIA PLATEAU

Snake R.

CASCADE RANGE

Cape Mendocino

COAST RANGES

SIERRA NEVADA

Great Salt Lake

GREAT BASIN

COLORADO PLATEAU

Mt. Whitney 14,494 ft. (4,418 m) ▲

Death Valley -282 ft. (-86 m)

Grand Canyon

Channel Islands

SONORAN DESERT

BAJA CALIFORNIA

Gulf of California

SIERRA MADRE OCCIDENTAL

SIERRA MADRE ORIENTAL

MÉXICO

México City ⊛

Orizaba 18,855 ft. (5,747 m) ▲

C A N A D A

Great Bear Lake

Great Slave Lake

Slave R.

Lake Athabasca

Churchill R.

Saskatchewan R.

GREAT PLAINS

Lake Winnipeg

CANADIAN SHIELD

Hudson Bay

James Bay

Belcher Islands

Banks Island

Melville Island

Victoria Island

Somerset Island

Prince of Wales I.

BOOTHIA PENINSULA

MELVILLE PEN.

Foxe Basin

Southampton Island

Baffin Island

Baffin Bay

Devon Island

Ellesmere Island

Queen Elizabeth Islands

Oodaaq Island

Lincoln Sea

HAYES PENINSULA

Greenland

Gunnbjorn 12,139 ft. (3,700 m) ▲

ICELAND

Greenland Sea

Arctic Circle

Davis Strait

Cape Farewell

Labrador Sea

Hudson Strait

Ungava Bay

Island of Newfoundland

AVALON PENINSULA

Cape Breton Island

Prince Edward Island

Nova Scotia

GASPÉ PEN.

LAURENTIAN MTS.

St. Lawrence R.

Gulf of St. Lawrence

Bay of Fundy

Gulf of Maine

Cape Cod

Long Island

Ottawa ⊛

Lake Superior

Lake Michigan

Lake Huron

Lake Ontario

Lake Erie

U N I T E D   S T A T E S

Missouri River

Platte R.

HIGH PLAINS

CENTRAL LOWLAND

OZARK PLATEAU

Arkansas River

Red River

Colorado R.

Rio Grande

Mississippi R.

Ohio R.

APPALACHIAN MOUNTAINS

COASTAL PLAIN

Washington, D.C. ⊛

Chesapeake Bay

Cape Hatteras

Bermuda (U.K.)

ATLANTIC OCEAN

PACIFIC OCEAN

Tropic of Cancer

Gulf of Mexico

Florida Keys

Cozumel Island

YUCATÁN PENINSULA

Isthmus of Tehuantepec

GUATEMALA

Guatemala City ⊛

San Salvador ⊛
EL SALVADOR

BELIZE

Belmopan ⊛

HONDURAS

Tegucigalpa ⊛

NICARAGUA

Managua ⊛

Lake Nicaragua

COSTA RICA

San Jose ⊛

PANAMA

Panamá ⊛

Isthmus of Panama

CENTRAL AMERICA

SOUTH AMERICA

BAHAMAS

Nassau ⊛

CUBA

Havana ⊛

Cayman Islands (U.K.)

Kingston ⊛

JAMAICA

HAITI

Port-au-Prince ⊛

Hispaniola

DOMINICAN REPUBLIC

Santo Domingo ⊛

Puerto Rico (U.S.)

Virgin Islands

Guadeloupe

Martinique

WEST INDIES

Caribbean Sea

TRINIDAD & TOBAGO

Port-of-Spain ⊛

Equator

Tropic of Cancer

Legend

— International boundary
⊛ National capital
▲ Mountain peak

N
W E
S

| 0 | 300 | 600 miles |
| 0 | 300 | 600 kilometers |

Glossary

This Glossary will help you to pronounce and understand the meanings of the vocabulary terms in this book. The page number at the end of the definition tells where the term first appears.

Pronunciation Key

a	at	ē	me	ō	old	ū	use	ng	song
ā	ape	i	int	ô	fork	ü	rule	th	thin
ä	far	ī	ice	oi	oil	ù	pull	<u>th</u>	this
âr	care	î	pierce	ou	out	ûr	turn	zh	measure
e	end	o	hot	u	up	hw	white	ə	about, taken, pencil, lemon, circus

abolition (ab ə lish'ən) an end to slavery (p. 137)

acid rain (asid rān) precipitation containing harmful chemical pollution that can destroy trees and wildlife and poison water (p. 261)

agriculture (ag'ri kul chər) the business of growing crops and raising animals (p. 25)

alliance (ə lī'əns) an agreement between two or more people or groups to work together in doing something (p. 55)

Allied Powers (a'līd pou'ərz) Countries that fought in World War I on the side led by Britain, France, Russia, Italy, and the United States (p. 186)

amendment (ə mend'mənt) an addition to the United States Constitution (p. 85)

appoint (ə point') to select someone for an office or position (p. 232)

archaeology (är kē ol'ə jē) the study of people who lived long ago (p. 46)

arms race (ärmz rās) the build up of arms between two or more competing countries (p. 211)

artifact (är' ti fakt) remains of objects made or used by people who lived in the past (p. 46)

assembly line (ə sem'blē līn) a line of workers and machines that put together products in steps (p. 182)

Axis Powers (ak'sis pou'ərz) countries that fought in World War II on the side led by Germany, Italy, and Japan. (p. 198)

B

bar graph (bär graf) a graph that can be used to show changes over time or changes among different types of information (p. 140)

Battle of Fallen Timbers (bat'əl uv fô'lən tim'bərz) a battle between United States troops led by General Anthony Wayne and a force of Native Americans commanded by Blue Jacket (p. 94)

Battle of the Thames (ba' təl uv the temz) a battle between United States soldiers, Tecumseh, and the British Army along the Thames River in Canada (p. 107)

Battle of Tippecanoe (ba' təl uv tip'ə kə nü) a battle that occurred on November 7, 1811 between the United States and Native Americans (p. 106)

Bill of Rights (bil uv rits) a formal statement of rights guaranteed to citizens (p. 85)

biotechnology (bī ō tech nol'ə gē) the science of using natural materials like plants and improving them to make products (p. 28)

budget (buj'it) a plan for using an amount of money for specific purposes (p. 234)

C

canal (kə nal') a human-made waterway (p. 126)

census (sen'səs) a count of the population (p. 103)

checks and balances (cheks and bal'ən səz) the system that balances power among the branches of government (p. 229)

chronology (krə' nä lə jē) the order in which things happened (p. 96)

circle graph (sər' kəl graf) a visual representation that shows how parts of something fit into the whole (p. 23)

civilization (si və lə zā' shən) a group of people who have highly developed trade, agriculture, government, art, and science (p. 49)

civil rights (siv'əl rits) the individual rights of all citizens to be treated equally under the law (p. 206)

civil war (siv'əl wôr) a war fought between people in one nation; used to refer to the war in the United States between the Union states of the North and the Confederate states of the South, 1861–1865 (p. 143)

climate (klī' mit) the pattern of weather in a certain place over many years (p. 13)

Cold War (kōld wär) the global struggle between the United States and the Soviet Union for power (p. 211)

colony (kol'ə nē) a country or region that is ruled by another country (p. 66)

Columbian Exchange (kə lum'bē ən eks chānj') the movement of foods, animals, and diseases between the Eastern and Western hemispheres (p. 66)

communication (kə myü nə kā' shən) the exchange of information between people (p. 179)

communism (kom'yə niz əm) a system in which business, property, and goods are owned by the government (p. 211)

Confederacy (kən fed'ər ə sē) the Confederate States of America, formed by 11 Southern states that seceded from the United States (p. 143)

conservation (kon sər vā'shən) the careful use of a natural resource (p. 261)

constitution (kon sti tü'shən) a plan for a government (p. 85)

continent (kon'tə nent) one of Earth's seven great bodies of land—Africa, Antarctica, Asia, Australia, Europe, North America, and South America (p. 5)

coureur de bois (kü rər' də bwä') a person who trapped animals for the fur trade without a license (p. 71)

culture (kul'chər) the way of life shared by a group of people, including their language, beliefs, music, foods, and holidays (p. 31)

cutaway diagram (kut'ə wā dīə gram) a drawing that shows the inside and the outside of an object at the same time (p. 62)

D

decade (de kād') a 10-year period (p. 185)

degree (di grē') a unit for measuring distance (p. 10)

delegate (del'i git) a person chosen to speak for a group (p. 113)

demand (di mand') what consumers are willing and able to buy at various prices (p. 246)

democratic republic (dem kra'tik ri pub'lik) a government in which citizens elect representatives to run the government (p. 227)

Department of Homeland Security a federal agency developed to protect the United States against acts of terrorism (p. 218)

depression (di presh' ən) a time when people have little money and there are not enough jobs (p. 153)

dictator (dik' tā tər) a person who rules a country without sharing power or consulting anyone else (p. 198)

discrimination (di skrim ə nā shən) unfair difference in the treatment of people (p. 152)

drought (drout) a long period of little or no rainfall (p. 196)

dugout (dug'out) a canoe made by hollowing out a large log (p. 57)

E

economy (i kon'ə mē) the way a place uses and produces natural resources, goods, and services (p. 25)

elevation (el'ə vā'shən) the height of land above sea level (p. 68)

entrepreneur (än trə prə nûr') a person who starts a new business (p. 180)

environment (en vī'rən mənt) the surroundings in which people, plants, or animals live on Earth (p. 19)

equator (i kwā' tər) an imaginary line encircling Earth halfway between the North Pole and the South Pole, designated as 0° latitude; see **latitude** (p. 10)

ethnic group (eth' nik grüp) a group of people whose ancestors are from the same country or area (p. 31)

executive branch (eg zek' yə tiv branch) the branch of government that carries out laws and is run by the President (p. 228)

explore (ek splôr') to travel to unfamiliar places in order to find out and learn about them (p. 66)

export (ek spôrt') something sold or traded to another country (p. 249)

F

ferry (fer'ē) a boat used to carry people and goods across a body of water (p. 117)

flatboat (flat'bōt) a large, flat-bottomed, wooden boat with square ends that could only travel downstream (p. 126)

flow chart (flō chärt) pictures that show the steps necessary to complete an activity (p. 236)

fossil fuel (fä-səl fyü' əl) a fuel, such as oil, natural gas, and coal, that is formed from the remains of plants and animals that lived millions of years ago (p. 261)

free enterprise (frē en'tər prīz) the economic system that allows people to own and run their own businesses (p. 247)

Freedmen's Bureau (frēd'mənz byür'ō) a government agency created in 1865 that provided food, schools, and medical care for newly freed African Americans and others in the South (p. 152)

frontier (frun tîr') the edge of a settled area (p. 82)

G

geography (jē og'rə fē) the study of Earth and the way people live on it (p. 5)

glacier (glā' shər) a large sheet of moving ice (p. 7)

global grid (glō'bəl grid) lines that cross each other on a globe or map (p. 10)

globalization (glō bə lə zā' shən) a trend where companies don't usually consider national boundaries when they decide where to buy goods and services (p. 258)

global warming (glō' bəl wûr' ming) the overall rise in the temperature of Earth's atmosphere (p. 262)

Grange (grānj) a group founded in 1867 to help farmers (p. 157)

graph (graf) a drawing that compares information by showing relationships between things (p. 23)

Great Depression (grāt di presh'ən) period of widespread economic hardship in the 1930s (p. 195)

Great Migration (grāt mī grā'shən) the time in history when many African Americans moved north to find jobs (p. 33)

H

Harmonist (här'mə nist) a follower of George Rapp who lived in Harmonie, Indiana (p. 121)

heritage (her'ə tij) the history that a group of people share (p. 31)

historian (hi stōr'ē ən) a person who studies the past (p. 52)

historical map (his tər'i-kəl map) a map that shows where events from the past took place (p. 202)

hunter-gatherer (hun'tər gath'ər ər) one who hunted animals and collected fruits, nuts, and other foods to eat (p. 45)

I

immigrant (im'i grənt) a person who moves to a new country to live (p. 32)

import (im pôrt') something brought in from another country for sale or use (p. 249)

Indian Removal Act (in'dē ən ri mü'vəl akt) a law passed by Congress that forced most Native Americans to move to lands west of the Mississippi River in 1829 (p. 109)

industry (in' də strē) all the businesses that make one kind of good or provide one kind of service (p. 160)

integration (in tə grā' shən) the act of making something open to people of all ethnic groups (p. 205)

interdependent (in tər di pen' dənt) relying on one another to meet needs and wants (p. 256)

interstate highway (in'tər stāt hī'wā) a road with at least two lanes of traffic in each direction that connects two or more states (pp. 250, 252)

invention (in ven' shən) a newly created product (p. 179)

J

judicial branch (jü dish' əl branch) the branch of government that interprets, or explains, laws and makes sure that laws are followed (p. 229)

jury (jür'ē) a group of citizens in a court of law who decide if someone accused of a crime is innocent or guilty (p. 242)

L

labor union (ūn′yən) a group of workers organized to get better working conditions (p. 170)

lacrosse (lə krôs′) a ball game first played by Native Americans in which a curved wooden stick is used to throw a ball to the goal (p. 60)

lake effect (l āk i fekt′) the change in the weather near large bodies of water; the water eventually falls from the sky as snow (p. 14)

Land Ordinance of 1785 (land′ or′də nəns) a law that set up rules for land sales in the Northwest Territory (p. 99)

landform (land′form) any of the natural features that make up Earth's surface (p. 6)

large-scale map (lärj skāl map) a map that shows many details in a small area (p. 110)

latitude (lat′i tüd) lines running east and west and measuring distance north or south of the equator; *See* **parallel**. (p. 10)

lean-to (lēn′ tü) a simple shelter that had three walls made of tree branches and twigs (p. 118)

legislative branch (lej′ is lā tiv branch) the branch of government that makes laws (p. 228)

limestone (līm stōn) a soft rock that is crushed and used to make roadways and buildings (p. 21)

line graph (līn graf) a graph that shows patterns and amounts of change over time (p. 192)

log cabin (lôg kab′in) a home made of logs from big trees (p. 118)

longitude (lon′ji tüd) lines running north and south and measuring the distance east or west of the prime meridian; *See* **meridian**. (p. 10)

M

mass production (mas prə dək′shən) manufacturing of many products at one time (p. 182)

manufacturing (man yə fak′ chər ing) making goods by machinery (p. 25)

map scale (map skāl) the measurement a map uses to indicate the real size of a place on Earth (p. 110)

mayor (mā′ ər) the elected head of the city government (p. 239)

meridian (mə rid′ē ən) another name for a line of longitude; *See* **longitude**. (p. 10)

migrate (mī grāt) to move from one place to another (p. 45)

mineral (min′ər əl) a natural substance found on Earth that does not come from plants or animals (p. 21)

missionary (mish′ə ner ē) a person who teaches others about his or her religion (p. 72)

moraine (mə'rān) a line of low hills formed by rocks pushed by glaciers (p. 7)

mound (mound) a hill or ridge of earth, stone, or other material (p. 49)

N

navigable (na' vi gə bəl) when waterways are wide and deep enough for boats to use without getting stuck (p. 126)

New Deal (nü dēl) a plan to use federal tax money to create jobs (p. 197)

nonrenewable resource (non ri nü' əbəl rē' sôrs) a natural substance that cannot be replaced (p. 21)

North American Free Trade Agreement (NAFTA) (north e mer'i ken frē trad e gre'ment) a treaty signed by Canada, Mexico, and the United States that removed import tariffs (p. 255)

Northwest Ordinance (nōrth'west' or'də nəns) a law passed in 1787 organizing the Northwest Territory for settlement and eventual statehood (p. 99)

O

Owenite (ō'wen īt) a follower of Robert Owen who settled in New Harmony (p. 122)

P

parallel (par'ə lel) another name for a line of latitude; *See* **latitude**. (p. 10)

patriotism (pā' trē ə ti zəm) the respect and loyal support of one's government (p. 243)

pharmaceutical (fär mə sü' ti kəl) medicine sold in a drugstore (p. 28)

pioneer (pī' ə nēr) a member of a group of people who are the first to settle in a new region (p. 93)

plantation (plan tā' shən) a large farm that often grows one crop (p. 137)

Pontiac's Rebellion (pän tē aks' ri bel' yən) an armed fight between Native Americans and the British which began in 1763 to drive the British from lands west of the Appalachian Mountains (p. 76)

population (pop yə lā' shēn) the total number of people living in a particular area or place (p. 103)

population map (pop yə lā' shən map) a map that shows the number of people that live in a certain area (p. 164)

preacher (prēch ûr) a person who speaks about a religious subject (p. 121)

precipitation (pri sip i tā shən) the amount of rain, snow, sleet, or hail that falls in a certain area (p. 16)

prime meridian (prīm mə rid'ē ən) the starting place for measuring distances east and west on a map or globe that is designated as 0° longitude. See **longitude** (p. 10)

Proclamation of 1763 (prok lə mā'shən) gave all the land east of the Appalachian Mountains to the colonists and all the land west of the mountains to the Native Americans (p. 77)

productivity (prə duk'tiv ə'tē) the amount of goods or services made in a period of time (p. 26)

profit (prof' it) the money a business earns after it pays for tools, salaries, and other costs (p. 247)

protest (prō' test) to have an objection or complaint against something (p. 206)

public service (pə' blik sər' vəs) an act, such as firefighting or garbage collecting, that helps people (p. 162)

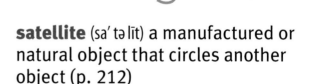

rationing (ra' shən ing) to give things out in limited portions (p. 187)

reaper (rē' pər) a horse-drawn machine that cuts and bundles grain (p. 155)

Reconstruction (rē kən strək' shən) the period following the Civil War in which the United States Congress passed laws that would help rebuild the country (p. 151)

region (rē' jən) an area with one or more common features (p. 8)

religion (ri lij'ən) the way people worship (p. 50)

renewable resource (ri nü'ə bəl rē'sôrs) a natural substance that can be replaced for later use, such as energy from the sun (p. 19)

resident (re' zə dənt) a person who lives in a specific place (p. 113)

resource (rē'sôrs) material used by people (p. 19)

road map (rōd map) a map that shows roads (p. 252)

Roaring Twenties (rôr ing twen' tēz) the decade of the 1920s which got its nickname because of the time's prosperity and excitement (p. 190)

route (rout) the course you take to get somewhere (p. 253)

satellite (sa' tə līt) a manufactured or natural object that circles another object (p. 212)

scarcity (skâr' sə tē) when there isn't enough of what you need or want (p. 245)

sea level (sē lev'əl) the level of the surface of the sea, an elevation of zero (p. 68)

secede (si sēd') to withdraw or formally leave an organization such as a government (p. 143)

segregation (se gri gā' shən) the practice of keeping ethnic groups separate (p. 205)

self-sufficient (self sə fi' shənt) when you provide for almost all your own needs (p. 155)

sharecropping (sher' kräp ing) when a worker farms the land and pays for rent and farming supplies with part of the crop (p. 153)

slavery (slā'və rē) the practice of treating people as property and forcing them to work (p. 99)

small-scale map (smôl skāl map) a map that shows a large area but not much detail (p. 110)

specialization (spesh'ə liz ā' shən) producing only a few kinds of products instead of many different kinds of products (p. 258)

states' rights (stāts rīts) the belief that each state should be allowed to make its own decisions about issues affecting it (p. 143)

steamboat (stēm' bōt) boat powered by steam that made traveling upstream easier (p. 126)

stock (stok) a certificate that shows part ownership in a company (p. 195)

strike (strīk) refusal by a group to work until its demands are met (p. 170)

suffrage (suf' rij) the right to vote (p. 188)

supply (sə plī') what producers are willing and able to sell at various prices (p. 246)

T

tax (taks) money people pay to the government (p. 79)

tariff (ter' əf) a tax on goods brought into a country (p. 255)

technology (tek nol' ə jē) the use of skills, ideas, and tools to meet people's needs (p. 145)

temperature (tem' pər chuər) the measure of how hot or cold the air is in a certain place (p. 13)

territory (ter' i tôr ē) an area of land owned by a country either within or outside the country's borders (p. 93)

terrorism (ter' ər izm) using violence or threats to achieve a goal (p. 217)

time line (tīm' līn) a list that shows the order of important events (p. 96)

tornado (tor nā' dō) a dangerous wind that forms a funnel shape and moves over the ground very quickly (p. 17)

trade (trād) to buy or sell goods, or to exchange goods with other people to get things you want but do not have (p. 47)

transportation (trans pər tā′ shən) the moving of goods and people (p. 125)

treason (trē′ zən) not being loyal to one's country (p. 79)

Treaty of Greenville (trē′ tē uv grēn′ vil) an agreement confining Native Americans in Ohio to the northwest part of the state, 1795 (p. 94)

Treaty of Paris of 1763 (trē′tē uv par′is) an agreement by Great Britain and France that brought an end to the French and Indian War (p. 75)

truce (trüs) an agreement to stop fighting (p. 213)

Underground Railroad (un dər ground′ rāl′ rōd) the system of secret routes used by people in the North and South to help enslaved African Americans escape to freedom (p. 138)

Union (yün′ yən) the group of Northern states that did not want to secede from the United States (p. 143)

urban (ûr′bən) a city and its surrounding communities (p. 33)

voyageur (vwä yä zhûr′) a hunter and French trapper in New France (p. 71)

War of 1812 (wor uv ā tēn′ twelv) when the United States declared war on Great Britain because they were fighting over land and waterways in what is now Canada (p. 107)

Index

This index lists many topics that appear in the book, along with the pages on which they are found. Page numbers after a *c* refer you to a chart or diagram, after a *g*, to a graph, after an *m*, to a map, after a *p*, to a photograph or picture, and after a *q*, to a quotation.

Sissle, Noble, 191

Skillman, Becky, 235

Slavery, 136–39
  and Emancipation
    Proclamation, 148, *q*148
  and Indiana constitution,
    114
  and Liberia Colonization
    Movement, 138–39
  and Northwest
    Ordinance, 99, 114
  and plantations, 137,
    *p*137
  and population trends,
    *g*140–41
  and Thirteenth
    Amendment, 151
  and Underground
    Railroad, *p*134, 138.
    See also African
    Americans

Smallpox, 76

Smith, Hamilton, *c*181

Snow, 15, *p*15, 16

Society of Friends
  (Quakers), 138, 139

Soil resources, 19, 22

South Bend, Indiana
  automobile factories in,
    185
  climate of, 14
  growth of, 159
  and industry, 161
  and La Salle, *p*42, 67

South Korea, 213, *m*213

South Vietnam, 214

Southern Flying Squirrels,
  *p*19

Southern Lowlands region
  of Indiana, *m*8, 9, *p*9

Southern states, 143

Southwind Maritime
  Centre, 251

Soviet Union, 198, 211, 214

Soybeans, 26

Space program, 212

Spain, 84

Specialization, 258

Special-purpose districts,
  241

Speech, freedom of, 85,
  227

Spencer, Indiana, 114

Sports, 35

Spring Fest, *p*169

St. Lawrence Seaway, 251

State government, 230–35
  branches of, 232–33
  and budgets, 234, *g*234
  and state constitution,
    231

Statehood for Indiana,
  112–15

States' rights, 143

Steam engines, 128, 129,
  *p*129

Steamboats, 126

Steel
  and economy, 185
  and immigrants, 33
  and manufacturing
    industries, 21
  and railroads, 179
  steel mills, *p*185
  U.S. Steel Corporation,
    *p*3, 28, 185

Stocks, 195

Stowe, Harriet Beecher,
  137

Streams, *p*19

Streight, Lovina, 147

Strikes, 170–71

Strip mining, 29, *p*29

Studebaker, Clement, 161

Studebaker, Henry, 161

Studebaker Company,
  *c*181, 182

Sugar maple tree, 261

Supply and demand, 246

Supreme Court, U.S., 109

Swing (dance), 191

T

Taíno, 65

Tariffs, 255

Tarkington, Booth, 36

Taxes
  and local government,
    240
  and public education, 167
  and Revolutionary War, 79

Team, 138

Technologies
  and agriculture, 26, 155,
    *p*155, 179, 180
  and child labor, 167
  and Civil War, 145
  and manufacturing, 28
  and the Roaring Twenties,
    190

Tecumseh, *q*58, 105, *p*105,
  106, 107

Telegraph, 145

Temperatures
  definition of, 13
  and global warming, 262
  in Indiana, 14, *m*14
  and lake effect, 15, *p*15

Ten Mile March for
  Freedom, *p*205

Tenskwatawa "the
  Prophet," 105, 106

Terre Haute, Indiana
  latitude and longitude of,
    *m*11
  location of, *g*128
  and natural resources, 161
  and voting rights, *p*224,
    242

Terrorism, 216–19
  and the Middle East, 218
  September 11, 2001
    (terrorist attacks), 217

Territory, 93

Tharp, Twyla, 36

Thirteenth Amendment,
  151

38° Parallel, 212, 213,
  *m*213

Three Sisters, 58

Till areas, 7, *p*8

Time lines, *c*96

Tippecanoe River, 105

Tools, 46, *p*46

Tornadoes, 17

Townships, 99, 117, 239,
  240

Traces, 125

Trade, 254–59
  and globalization,
    256–57, 258–59
  in Indiana, 249, 255–59
  of Native Americans, 47,
    50, 52, 55, 57, 71

and specialization, 258

Trains, 128, 129. *See also*
  railroads

Transportation
  air travel, 250
  definition of, 125
  and economy, 248–51
  and roads, 125, 250
  steam engines, 128
  and trade, 256
  trains, 250
  waterway travel, 20,
    126–27, 251

Treason, 79

Treaty of Greenville, 94, 99

Treaty of Paris, 75

Trees, 19

Truce, 213

Trustees, 239

Turkey, 186

28th Regiment of the
  United States Colored
  Troops, 135, *p*135, 148

U

Uncle Tom's Cabin (Stowe),
  137

Underground Railroad,
  134, 138

Union, the, 143, *m*144

Unions, labor, 170–71,
  *p*170, *p*171

United Mine Workers
  Union, 171

United States Steel
  Corporation, 185

Universities, 168–69,
  *p*168–69

University of Notre Dame,
  35, 169

Urban centers, 33

U.S. Route 40, 125

U.S. Route 421, 125

U.S. Steel Corporation, *p*3,
  28, 185

V

Valparaiso, Indiana, 27,
  *p*224

Values, 243

Victory gardens, 200

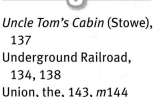

Index

Credits